The SHAKESPEARES *and*
"THE OLD FAITH"

THE SHAKESPEARES AND "THE OLD FAITH"

JOHN HENRY de GROOT

Essay Index Reprint Series

BOOKS FOR LIBRARIES PRESS
FREEPORT, NEW YORK

LIBRARY OF CONGRESS CATALOG CARD NUMBER:

68-57315

PRINTED IN THE UNITED STATES OF AMERICA

This book is for
ETHEL

ACKNOWLEDGMENTS

I AM deeply indebted to Professor Oscar James Campbell of Columbia University for the suggestion which started me upon the program of study leading to the writing of this book. Throughout that program he supplied invaluable guidance and offered friendly encouragement. He read the manuscript, chapter by chapter, and made many wise suggestions for improvement. His cordiality was unfailing. A mere acknowledgment in words seems painfully inadequate.

To Professor Marjorie Nicholson and Professor William Haller, both of Columbia University, I am sincerely thankful for their patient reading of the manuscript and for their scholarly criticism.

To her for whom this book is inscribed, my wife, my debt is deepest of all. She shared the early uncertainties, the later toil, the denials, the discouragements, the trials and the triumphs that go with a venture such as this. Always she understood, always she sympathized, always she supported. None could be more loyal.

For the privilege of quoting published material, my hearty thanks are due to the following publishers and copyright holders:

The Bibliographical Society for material from H. Anders' "The Elizabethan ABC with the Catechism" and H. G. Pfander's *"Dives et Pauper"* printed in *The Library;* Burns, Oates & Washbourne, Ltd., for material from H. S. Bowden's *The Religion of Shakespeare* and from Herbert Thurston's "A Controverted Shakespeare Document" in the *Dublin Review;* The Catholic University of America Press for material from Gerard M. Greenewald's *Shakespeare's Attitude Towards the Catholic Church in "King John";* Columbia University Press for material from William Haller's *The Rise of Puritanism* and A. M. Stowe's *English Grammar Schools in the Reign of Elizabeth;* The Dugdale Society for material from Savage and Fripp's *Minutes and Accounts of the Corporation of Stratford-upon-Avon and Other Records;* Ginn and Company for material from Edward P.

Cheyney's *A Short History of England;* Harper & Brothers for material from W. J. Rolfe's *Shakespeare the Boy;* Houghton Mifflin Company for material from Joseph Q. Adams' *A Life of William Shakespeare;* Longmans, Green & Co., Inc., for material from Thomas Spencer Baynes' *Shakespeare Studies* and from James O. Halliwell-Phillipps' *Outlines of the Life of Shakespeare;* The Macmillan Company for material from Walter Raleigh's *Shakespeare,* H. Maynard Smith's *Pre-Reformation England,* Foster Watson's *English Grammar Schools to 1660,* and J. Dover Wilson's *The Manuscript of Shakespeare's Hamlet,* the last two titles being publications of the Cambridge University Press, England; Oliphants, Ltd., for material from T. Carter's *Shakespeare: Puritan and Recusant;* Oxford University Press for material from A. R. Bayley's "Shakespeare's Schoolmasters" in *Notes and Queries,* from Sir Edmund K. Chambers' *William Shakespeare,* from E. I. Fripp's *Master Richard Quyny, Shakespeare Studies,* and *Shakespeare: Man and Artist,* and from L. F. Salzman's *English Life in the Middle Ages;* G. P. Putnam's Sons for material from F. A. Gasquet's *The Eve of the Reformation;* Charles Scribner's Sons for material from C. L. de Chambrun's *Shakespeare Rediscovered;* Simpkin Marshall, Ltd., for material from Oliver Baker's *In Shakespeare's Warwickshire and the Unknown Years;* Smith, Elder & Co. for material from Sir Sidney Lee's *A Life of William Shakespeare;* The Society for Promoting Christian Knowledge for material from Richmond Noble's *Shakespeare's Biblical Knowledge;* and Stanford University Press for material from B. Roland Lewis's *The Shakespeare Documents.*

Unless otherwise indicated, quotations from Shakespeare's writings and from the Bible are from the Oxford Shakespeare, edited by W. J. Craig, and the King James Version, respectively.

TABLE OF CONTENTS

INTRODUCTION

*T*HE religion of John Shakespeare has been a subject of investigation for many years, but investigators have reached no agreement in the matter. Some have reasoned that John Shakespeare was a conforming Protestant; others, that he was a Puritan; and still others, that he was a Catholic. In their discussions, most critics have not taken fully into account the Spiritual Last Will and Testament, signed by one "John Shakspear," found during the eighteenth century in the attic of the Henley Street house which had been the home of the poet's father in Stratford. They have rejected the document as spurious. All other evidence with respect to John Shakespeare's religion is of the sort which precludes final judgment. Consequently, the issue has remained unsettled.

Recently, new facts bearing upon the authenticity of the Spiritual Last Will and Testament have come to light. These facts prove that the document is a formula of devotion drawn up originally by Charles Borromeo, Cardinal of Milan. They tend to show that such formulae were circulated in England during the latter part of John Shakespeare's life by the Jesuits and seminary priests of the English Mission of 1580 and later. Though these facts do not meet all critical questions, they do give stronger reason for accepting the Spiritual Last Will and Testament as authentic and for admitting it as determinative evidence that John Shakespeare was Roman Catholic in his religious faith.

If John Shakespeare was a Catholic, the religious training which William Shakespeare received at home would have been in the spirit of the Old Faith. What that Catholic training would have consisted of, how it might have contributed to the development of the young artist, and how it might have revealed itself in the writings of the mature dramatist, become, therefore, interesting questions for study. The plan of this book is to carry out that study.

My purpose in Part I is to review the various arguments presented by critics to prove that John Shakespeare was Puritan, Protestant, or Catholic and to show how these arguments counterbalance one another to leave the issue in a state of doubt.

Part II discusses the Spiritual Last Will and Testament by reviewing the accounts of the discovery of the document, tracing the history of its reception among critics, presenting the facts which have newly come to light, and relating those facts to the authenticity and the evidential value of the document.

Part III is devoted to an examination of the influences likely to have contributed to the religious training of William Shakespeare during his youth in Stratford. The treatment begins with the assumption that William's home environment was Catholic. It proceeds to describe the way in which Catholic and Protestant influences alternated during his years spent at the Grammar School. It concludes with a brief account of the influence of the parish church. I do not seek to establish definite results of this three-fold religious training upon the mind and art of the poet. I merely venture to suggest that from the interplay of conflicting religious influences there developed in William Shakespeare a lingering esteem for the traditional faith of his parents and, more important for his art, a spirit of tolerance toward all organized religion.

Part IV seeks to show how this lingering esteem manifested itself in the writings of the dramatist. The material gathered is not exhaustive, but typical. It is presented not to prove that Shakespeare was himself a Catholic, but only to show that in his adult years he retained a retrospective tenderness for certain aspects of the Old Faith and that this tenderness came to expression in his creative efforts.

This investigation will have achieved its most important end if it enables a reader to attach a new meaning here and there to the lines of Shakespeare's poetry and to receive a new thrill of appreciation of precisely what Shakespeare wished the members of his Elizabethan audience to understand and feel in many important situations in his dramas.

PART ONE

THE RELIGION OF JOHN SHAKESPEARE

1. A Moot Question

THE religious views and affiliations of John Shakespeare, father of the poet, have been for almost two hundred years the subject of much academic contention. Scholars have long understood that an evaluation of the religious forces which helped shape the personality of William Shakespeare and, to some extent, guided him in his creative efforts entails a knowledge of the religion of his parents. The religious training given the dramatist during his formative years in the family household must have meant something in terms of artistic predispositions when the boy grew to manhood. An understanding of the character of that religious training, therefore, must deepen any appreciation of the poet's work. It is for that reason that men have studied John Shakespeare's religion.

This study has been long and arduous, and there has been no stable agreement among investigators. Some, like the Rev. Thomas Carter,[1] Edgar Innes Fripp,[2] and Cumberland Clark,[3] maintain that John Shakespeare early held Protestant views, later adopted ardent Puritan views, and clung to these Puritan views so steadfastly to the end of his life that he was persecuted and reported a recusant on account of them. Others, like Henry S. Bowden,[4] Herbert Thurston, S. J.,[5] John Pym Yeatman,[6] and Clara Longworth de Chambrun,[7] maintain with equal ardor that John Shakespeare was always a staunch Roman Catholic, persevering in his faith under public pressure and permitting himself to be classed as a recusant for the sake of his Catholic, not Puritan, convictions. Also leaning to the Catholic side, though not nearly so elaborate in their argument or extensive in their claims, are J. O. Halliwell-Phillipps,[8] G. B. Harrison,[9] J. Semple Smart,[10] and Sir Edmund K. Chambers,[11] who hint varying degrees of Catholicism as the inner religion of John Shakespeare, whatever the outward manifestations may have been. Steering a middle course and holding that John Shakespeare was a neutral, conforming member of the Church of England are James Walter,[12] H. C. Beeching,[13] Karl Elze,[14]

Mrs. Charlotte C. Stopes,[15] George Brandes,[16] Joseph Quincy Adams,[17] and Sir Sidney Lee.[18]

The foregoing alignment of scholars and their viewpoints is not complete, nor is it intended to be. But it shows that investigators have come to no agreement and that all possible positions are worthily represented. The advantage in the debate seems to pass back and forth from one side to another. The problem seems to be held in equilibrium.

The purpose of the first part of this book is to exhibit the argument in its balanced state and to prepare for the introduction of documentary evidence which throws the scales one way.

A difficulty besetting any investigator of the problem before us is the scarcity and unreliability of criteria by which to determine the religious faith of any ordinary person living in the Reformation decades of the sixteenth century. Even in the case of extraordinary people of that time it is not always easy to be sure about peculiarities of religious faith.

It is hard, for example, to tell just when and to what degree a man changed from a Catholic to a Protestant. He might be thought to have taken the first step when he agreed with the actions of the government in repudiating the temporal and spiritual supremacy of Rome. Such agreement, however, might mean very little change in outward conduct or in habits of worship. But if the convert discarded the missal and began to use the Edwardian Prayer Book, he could be thought to have taken a step toward distinctive Protestantism. If he regularly attended a parish church which had obeyed the injunctions of the government and had carried out such Protestantizing steps as the discarding of certain clerical vestments, the removal of images, the defacement of paintings, and the substitution of a communion table for an altar, he could be expected to feel himself somewhat estranged from the traditions of Catholicism. His views of the sacraments would eventually change, for instead of hearing about and sharing in seven sacraments, he would now hear about only two, and one of these, the Eucharist, would seem modified in some respects. When his awareness of the intercessory powers of the Virgin Mary began to dim and his pious reverence for her diminish, he would have gone still farther toward the New Faith. If he came under the preaching of one of the more advanced reformers, he would begin to stand out among those who bore the name of Protestant. If he was so much influenced by that preaching as to take up the diligent reading and exposition of the Bible, especially of the Pauline Epistles, and if he was strongly given to the singing of metrical Psalms, he might be called a Puritan. If, in the end, the man affiliated himself with some separatist group and remained away from the services of the Established Church, he would, no doubt, be singled out as an extremist among Puritans.

But even the Puritan is not easy to recognize. He is more venerable than we suppose. Professor William Haller points out that

> There were Puritans before the name was invented, and there probably will continue to be Puritans long after it has ceased to be a common epithet. Chaucer met one on the road to Canterbury and drew his portrait. No better and no very different picture . . . was ever drawn by any of the numerous pens which attempted the task two centuries later.[19]

And he calls attention to the fact ". . . that Puritanism, so called, was nothing new or totally unrelated to the past but something old, deep-seated, and English, with roots reaching far back into medieval life."[20]

If the remoter end of Puritanism reaches back into the obscurity of the Middle Ages, making it hard for us to be categorical in calling anyone a Puritan, so the nearer end, separatism, has its uncertainties. It is true that in some of its branches Puritanism developed into separatism and that some separatists may be called Puritans, but separatism did not ripen as a movement until late in the sixteenth century. Those to whom the term Puritan was first applied in the 1560's were not separatists, but merely nonconformists who, though they found fault with the form of church government, wanted to remain within the Church of England. On the other hand, though separatism did not ripen until late in the sixteenth century, ". . . a tendency towards separatism made its appearance in England about 1550,"[21] so that it is possible for scholars to call a Puritan one who showed a sympathy for separatism as early as the middle of the sixteenth century, before the term Puritan itself was invented. In short, it is hard to classify as a Puritan anyone living during the last half of the sixteenth century unless he revealed his opinions in records remaining to us today.

Then, too, it must always be remembered that most church members in any era are likely to be uninformed and somewhat apathetic about all matters of religion except the most fundamental and universal. They probably were so in John Shakespeare's time. A lay contemporary of John Shakespeare would scarcely be aware of his own gradual change from medieval Catholicism to Tudor Protestantism. From year to year he would be carried along in the process of change, but he would have no clear conception of the rate or goal of that change. After many years the difference in him might be appreciable, but it would not be especially obvious to him, for, since he had only his neighbors as standards of comparison and since they most likely had kept pace with him in the change, he could have no great sense of difference. If he could have analyzed himself critically, he most probably would have found in himself much that was traditionally Catholic, much that was coming to be thought of as Protestant, and even something that was recognizably Puritan.

But though the difficulties of religious classification are many, and though in most respects John Shakespeare belongs to that vast throng of people who lived and died undistinguished and who remain scarcely distinguishable, students of the problem of his religion have deigned to label John Shakespeare variously as Catholic, Protestant, or Puritan. We shall undertake to discuss the problem largely in the terms given us by these students, trusting that in each specific detail of the discussion the religious label will be taken for what it seems to mean to the particular scholar using it.

2. *The Argument from Environment*

The first and broadest basis upon which the religion of John Shakespeare is argued is that of environment. From either the Protestant or the Catholic point of view, it is maintained that Warwickshire, the English Midland county in which John Shakespeare spent his life, was a stronghold of Protestantism or of Catholicism, whichever the case requires. The argument is refined to show that Stratford-upon-Avon was a Protestant, Puritan, or Catholic community, as the viewpoint demands, and that John Shakespeare, as a person of some prominence, could not be comfortable or successful in Stratford unless his religion was in harmony with the religious atmosphere of that town.

Thus Edgar I. Fripp, in his essay "Alderman Shakespeare's Religion," maintains that John Shakespeare was first a Protestant because he was born and bred in Snitterfield, "an early home of the Reformation," and because he lived in Stratford, which community under Edward VI, along with the rest of Warwickshire as part of the diocese of Bishop John Hooper, was Protestant. Fripp points out that Bishop Hooper was the third to suffer martyrdom under Catholic Queen Mary, being burned at the stake on February 9, 1555, before his own cathedral at Gloucester. The two martyrs who preceded him, John Rogers and Laurence Saunders, were Warwickshire men. To prove the strong Protestant sympathies of Stratford itself, Fripp points to the difficulties that Roger Edgeworth, the Catholic steward of the Borough, had in managing the affairs of the community, giving as evidence a series of enactments of penalties for offenses occasioned by the tension of the times.*

---

* *Shakespeare Studies*, pp. 82–83. In October, 1553, a fine of 3s. 4d. was imposed for reviling a queen's officer; in April, 1554, this fine was raised to 10s. with three days' imprisonment; also in April, 1554, a fine of £5 was imposed upon anyone refusing or forsaking an office; at Michaelmas, 1557, a Book of Orders was drawn up full of vindictive penalties; and on the 1st of October, 1557, the carrying of arms by single men within the borough limits was prohibited.

With equal assurance, proponents[22] of the Catholic side of the debate affirm that Warwickshire and Stratford-upon-Avon were Catholic strongholds and that John Shakespeare must therefore have found it more convenient, if not necessary, to be a Roman Catholic among his fellows. How did matters stand in Warwickshire and Stratford-upon-Avon, particularly in relation to John Shakespeare?

A. Snitterfield before 1552

That John Shakespeare, the poet's father, was the son of Richard Shakespeare of Snitterfield is educed from the wording of a bond and of a memorandum of the grant of administration upon which the bond is executed, both preserved today in the Worcester Probate Registry. The bond, dated February 10, 1561, names "Johannem Shakespere de Snytterfyld in comitatu Warwici agricolam"[23] as "administrator of the goodes catals and debtes of Richard Shakespere deceased late whiles he lyved of the parishe of Snytterfyld," and the memorandum of the grant of administration, dated February 10, 1600/1, certifies that the administration of the goods "Ricardi Shackespere defuncti nuper dum vixit parochie de Snytterfyld" had been committed to "Johanni Shakespere filio suo."[24] That the John Shakespeare mentioned is the future alderman of Stratford is attested by documents* which link the poet's father with Henry Shakespeare, another (and probably older) son of Richard Shakespeare.

Whether John Shakespeare was born in Snitterfield is not known, but it seems that he was. His father had settled there before 1529, if the Richard Shakespeare appearing as a suitor in the 1528 to 1529 court rolls of a Snitterfield manor owned by the College of St. Mary at Warwick was the father of Henry and John.[25] If these entries do not refer to John's father, more probably a later record, a view of frank pledge in the Court Leet of Snitterfield, dated October 1, 1535, fining Richard Shakespeare " 'xij^d' . . . for overloading the common pasture with his cattle,"[26] does.

It is not known just when John Shakespeare was born. The Snitterfield parish records begin too late to be of service. Fripp assumes the date to be "about 1528,"[27] presumably on the strength of the 1528–29 entries of the Warwick College court rolls mentioned above as showing Richard Shakespeare to have been a resident of Snitterfield at that time. Lewis, not quite so certain of these early entries and assuming that John Shakespeare was twenty-one when he married Mary Arden in 1556–57, prefers the later date of 1535–36.[28] In any event, it seems certain that John

---

* See particularly a Stratford-upon-Avon Court of Record entry, dated February 1, 1588, in which John Shakespeare is sued by Nicholas Lane for the collection of a debt incurred by "Henricus Shaxpere frater dicti Johannis." Lewis, *op. cit.*, I, 24.

Shakespeare spent the years of his childhood and youth in the household of Richard Shakespeare of Snitterfield.

Fripp is of the opinion that the atmosphere of that household was essentially Puritan.* To show that the seeds of the doctrinal Reformation took root in Warwickshire early and that, therefore, the parish of Snitterfield was one of the first to bear the fruit of the new teaching, Fripp points out that

> Ralph Collingwood, the friend of Colet and Erasmus, was Warden of Stratford College from 1503 to 1507, and Dean of Warwick College from 1507 to 1512, when he was promoted to the deanery of Lichfield. Both Tyndale and Latimer were in the neighborhood. Tyndale began his *New Testament* at Little Sodbury in Gloucestershire in 1523. One of his supporters was William Tracy of Toddington. Latimer was rector of West Kington, six miles south-east of Little Sodbury, from 1531 to 1535. Report of his heresies reached Offchurch near Warwick, where talk in an alehouse led to an inquiry at Warwick by the Abbot of Kenilworth, and representations to the Privy Council. Cranmer stood by him, and helped to obtain for him the bishopric of Worcester in 1535. His indefatigable visitation and homely eloquence made him a power in the diocese. Among his friends was William Tracy's son, Richard, of Stanway, who married Barbara Lucy, sister of William Lucy of Charlecote. Latimer was as eager for the reformation and dissolution of monastic houses as Cranmer, though he lived to regret their spoliation. The visitors included John Greville of Milcote, Roger Wigston of Wolston, and Robert Burgoyne of Wroxall. A sermon at Hampton Lucy brought Latimer to Stratford in the autumn of 1537— a discourse by the rector of Hampton, Edward Large, an advocate of the 'New Learning,' on the occasion of a wedding between a maid of his parish and a man 'of good substance' of Stratford. A number of Stratford people being present, he unburdened himself, in a two hours' delivery in the afternoon of Easter Monday, 2 April . . . on doctrines for which he had an evil reputation in Stratford. In the congregation

---

* The term "Puritan" is, of course, an anachronism here. As Principal J. Oswald Dykes points out in his "Prefatory Note" to Carter's *Shakespeare: Puritan and Recusant* (pp. 3–4) ". . . the earliest instance of its employment occurs in the very year of the poet's birth (1564). At that date, the friends of a more drastic reform, reinforced by the return from abroad of the Marian exiles, were on the point of advancing from the question of ceremonies and vestments, which in Henry's reign had been chiefly debated, to some deeper matters of Church discipline and polity which for a century to come were to divide English Churchmen into two camps." The Rev. Ronald Bayne says it was to the members of private congregations using the Genevan form of worship "that the word Puritan was first applied, about the year 1567, probably in derision." *Shakespeare's England* (Oxford; 1916), I, 56–57.

were John Combe of Stratford and Mistress Lucy of Charlecote. William Lucy himself was not present, being sick, else his rector 'never preached but he heard him.' A Stratford man, Cotton, interrupted the preacher, and doing his best, as Squire Lucy heard, 'to set the people by the ears,' exposed himself to the grave charge in those days of 'making a riot.' Stratford was full of the matter for weeks and months later. William Clopton of Clopton took up the cudgels for Cotton energetically. Squire Lucy defended his rector, who was indicted at the Warwick Quarter Sessions for his alleged statements. Lucy appealed to Cromwell; a commission was appointed, there was further litigation, and Lucy, with a letter from Latimer, had a personal interview with the Privy Seal.

. . . From Warwick he [Latimer] wrote on 14 October thanking Cromwell for restoring the vicar of Hampton to his living.

. . . On the passing and enforcement of the 'Six Articles,' Latimer retired from his bishopric, in 1539, to private life. He resided in Warwickshire. . . .

At Coventry lived William Glover, brother of Robert and John, and other prominent Reformers—Thomas Saunders, John Hales, Humphrey Randall. . . .

In Edward's reign Hooper, more Puritan than Latimer, was Bishop of Worcester, from 1551 to 1553.[29]

All this is more than enough to indicate that there was doctrinal ferment in Warwickshire, but it does not prove that Snitterfield, or Richard Shakespeare, was Puritan. To establish this latter view, Fripp makes much of the fact that the Snitterfield manor belonged to the John Hales of Coventry mentioned above as a Puritan and that John's brother, Bartholomew, lived in Snitterfield. But if that argument is valid, equally valid is the argument that Richard Shakespeare was a tenant farmer of Robert Arden of Wilmcote, a Catholic. The connection between Robert Arden and Richard Shakespeare, established by documentary evidence,* is much closer than any connection established between Richard Shakespeare and John Hales.

In the absence of indisputable evidence with regard to the religious environment of Snitterfield and the religion of Richard Shakespeare, there are these considerations upon which to base an assumption. Richard himself was born and reared in pre-Reformation days, so that his religious

* A deed of conveyance of property by Robert Arden, dated July 17, 1550, the original of which is among the "Miscellaneous Documents" in the Birthplace Museum and a transcript of which appears in Lewis, *op. cit.*, I, 83–86.

experience must have been gained within the Roman Catholic Church.*
When his son John was born, the Act of Supremacy of 1535 either had
not yet been passed or had just been passed. The changes in the English
Church introduced by this act were not doctrinal, but governmental.
Any change would take place slowly in Snitterfield, a rural Midland parish. Even though there were leaders of doctrinal reform in the neighborhood of Snitterfield, those leaders were in the minority and their influence
would be slow in affecting the small farmers.

It seems, therefore, quite plausible that the religious atmosphere of
Snitterfield and of the household of Richard Shakespeare was Catholic
and that John Shakespeare was reared in the Old Faith. As a Catholic
youth he left his father's house in Snitterfield sometime before 1552, when
we find him in Stratford-upon-Avon.

B. Stratford-upon-Avon, 1552 and later

The earliest documentary evidence we have of John Shakespeare,
father of the poet, proves him to be living in Stratford-upon-Avon in
1552. The document is a "view of frank pledge" by the Court Leet of
Stratford-upon-Avon. Dated the 29th day of April in the sixth year of
the reign of Edward VI (1552), the record shows that "Johannes Shakyspere" was fined "xij.*d.*" for having made a "sterquinarium," or refuse
pile, in the neighborhood called "Hendley Strete" against the ordinance
of the Court.[30]

It is generally thought that John Shakespeare went to Stratford-upon-
Avon to be apprenticed to a tradesman. There is some ground for thinking the tradesman was Thomas Dickson, *alias* Waterman, glover and
whittawer of Bridge Street. That John Shakespeare became a glover we
know from his identification as a glover in a Court of Record entry for
June 17, 1556, in connection with a suit by Thomas Siche of Arscote
against "John Shakyspere de Stretford in Com. Warwic glouer"[31] for the
recovery of a debt of £8. Thomas Dickson was married to Joan Townsend, the daughter of John Townsend of Snitterfield, and the elder

---

* There remains, of course, the possibility that Richard Shakespeare had come under
the influence of Lollardy. The probability may be estimated on the strength of what
H. Maynard Smith writes: "Lollards were chiefly concentrated in London and the
eastern counties, but they appear sporadically elsewhere. . . . Writing in 1533, Sir
Thomas More tells Saint German that if he omits the dioceses of London and Lincoln
he will not find four persons punished for heresy in five years, and in most dioceses not
five in fifteen, and not one handed over to the secular arm in twenty years." Smith goes
on to say that, though "there seems to have been very little persecuting of Lollards on
the eve of the Reformation. . . . that [fact] . . . does not help us to know how many
Lollards there were, or how much sympathy they excited." He believes it an error "to
suppose that the sect was all but extinct." *Pre-Reformation England* (London, 1938),
pp. 288–91.

Townsend may have known Richard Shakespeare and helped him get his son apprenticed to Dickson. If this assumption is true, then by 1552 the young man had already worked out his seven-year apprenticeship and had set himself up in business in the house in Henley Street before which he made a dunghill to incur the aforementioned fine. It cannot be ascertained whether this house in Henley Street was the house which John Shakespeare later bought in 1556 and which became part of the Birthplace, but it is reasonable to assume that it was.

The religious surroundings in which the young bachelor glover found himself in Stratford-upon-Avon are taken to prove his Protestantism, Puritanism, or Catholicism, whichever the case requires. What was the religious environment of Stratford likely to be in 1552 and in the next decades during which John Shakespeare married, reared a family, and rose to civic prominence?

Bowden, in opposition to Fripp, is quite certain that Stratford was a Catholic community. In *The Religion of Shakespeare* he reviews the history of the Guild of the Holy Cross, the earliest extant records of which date back to the reign of Henry III (1216–72) and which at the time of its dissolution provided Stratford with the only government the town had. He concludes: "The history of this Guild shows Stratford both in its civil and religious life to have been essentially a Catholic stronghold down to the middle of the sixteenth century. . . ."[32]

The Guild was dissolved by the Chantries Act of 1547. Six years of civic disorganization followed. Then the local government was taken over by the Stratford-upon-Avon Corporation, chartered by Edward VI in 1553. Under the terms of the charter, the borough was to be governed by fourteen aldermen and fourteen chief burgesses. The membership of the original Corporation must have been representative of Stratford in 1553 and for some years afterwards, so that an examination of the religious sympathies of the first and original aldermen, as Lewis[33] lists them, is interesting:

Protestant	*Catholic*	*Not classified*
Thomas Gilbert, Bailiff	Richard Lord	Hugo Reynolds
William Smith	John Jeffreys	Thomas Phillips
Adrian Quiney		Thomas Winfield
		Thomas Dickson
		George Whateley
		Henry Biddle
		William Whateley
		Robert Moore [Morse?]
		Robert Bratt

Perhaps the only conclusion that can be drawn from this classification is that most of the members of the new Corporation were non-committal. The fact that only two out of fourteen aldermen are called Catholics does not impel one to conclude that the Corporation and the community it represented were Catholic. But one must admit that some of the aldermen not classified likely were of the Catholic faith, for several of them had been Masters of the Guild or had held other responsible offices in that Catholic organization. On the other hand, neither does the listing of only three Protestant aldermen make a strong case for the Protestantism of Stratford. But again, the listing does not necessarily limit the number of Protestant members to three. When it is recalled that the charter of the Corporation was issued by the Protestant government of Edward VI and that the Guild had been a civil, as well as a religious, organization, it becomes evident that some of the unclassified aldermen could well have been of Protestant leaning.

If anything can be concluded about the religious environment of John Shakespeare in Stratford-upon-Avon and in surrounding Warwickshire, it is that town and countryside were in a state of divisive unrest and that the air was charged with tension. That tension had been heightened soon after John Shakespeare established himself in Henley Street by an unforeseen change of monarchs. No sooner were the Protestant policies of the Protectorate getting well under way with such steps as the adoption of the first Prayer Book in 1549, of the second Prayer Book in 1552, and of the Forty-two Articles (later to become the Thirty-nine Articles) in 1553, than Edward VI became desperately ill. His death seemed inevitable. According to the will of Henry VIII, if Edward died childless, his successor was to be his elder sister Mary. But Mary was a Catholic. Her accession to the throne would mean a complete reversal of the religious situation and the overthrow of the Duke of Northumberland, the actual ruler after the fall of Somerset. To forestall this conceivable turn of affairs, the Duke of Northumberland had arranged the marriage of his son to Lady Jane Grey, a seventeen-year-old cousin of Edward, and had induced Edward to draw up a paper setting aside his father's will and appointing Lady Jane to the throne. The king abetted the scheme so far as to induce a large number of those in authority to sign the document and to pledge their support of Lady Jane.

Therefore, when Edward VI died in 1553, the lords of the Council hailed Lady Jane as queen. She was proclaimed queen in London and treated with royal honors. The Duke of Northumberland carried on the government in her name.

But Mary's claim to the throne was a better one than Lady Jane's, and Mary knew it. She declared herself to be the rightful queen. Nobles gathered to her support. The troops of Northumberland who were sent to imprison her disobeyed orders. In a few days the position of usurper and rightful claimant was reversed: Mary was queen and Lady Jane was a prisoner in the Tower.

The significance of this swift turn of events for a discussion of John Shakespeare's religious environment in Warwickshire is that the Duke of Northumberland so suddenly bereft of power was John Dudley, Earl of Warwick, and that Lady Jane Grey, as the wife of Guildford Dudley, was the sister-in-law both of Robert Dudley, later the Earl of Leicester, and of Ambrose Dudley, later the Earl of Warwick. The struggle for the crown thus directly involved the religious partisanship of Warwickshire. The Dudleys had furthered Protestantism in Warwickshire, and their loss of power was a blow to Protestant forces in that county. A keener, if not heavier, blow was dealt Warwickshire Protestantism when John Dudley, mounting the scaffold to be executed, recanted his Protestantism and declared himself a Catholic.[34] Thus was confusion confounded, tension intensified.

The accession of Mary, a Catholic, to the throne of England in 1553 and her subsequent marriage to Philip II of Spain introduced serious complications in the religious situation. Ardent Protestants were martyred; Protestant clergymen were deposed and replaced by Catholic priests; the progress of the English Reformation was halted.

What happened in Stratford can be learned from Fripp's statement, already quoted, of the difficulties of Roger Edgeworth, the Catholic steward of the Borough of Stratford, and of the measures that were taken to cope with the tense times. Fripp's elaboration of that statement in another place is informative. In the *Minutes and Accounts of the Corporation of Stratford-upon-Avon and Other Records* he writes:

The Book of Orders drawn up at Michaelmas, 1557, is full of vindictive penalties. Aldermen were to be fined 20s. and Principal Burgesses 10s. for absence on Election Day. Refusal to act as Bailiff or High Alderman was to be visited with forfeiture respectively of £15 and £12. Those who declined to be Constable or Taster were to be fined £5 or 40s. Non-attendance at an ordinary Hall would involve a payment of 6s. 8d., and failure to wear a gown or join in procession a fine of 12d. For disclosing the 'words or deeds' of the Chamber the punishment would be for the first offence a fine of £5, for the second a fine of £10, and for the third expulsion for ever. Members were not to revile one another within or without the Chamber. They were to be 'brotherlike' in Council, and to 'depart in brotherly love,' under pain of 6s. 8d. And to say, do, or write anything prejudicial or derogatory to the Charter meant a fine of one hundred marks, £66 13s. 4d.[35]

Since the atmosphere of Stratford in the first decade of John Shakespeare's residence there evidently was one of tension and division, John Shakespeare would not have had to be a strong Protestant, as some think, or a Catholic, as others think, in order to find himself at home in the borough and to make his way to success there. The young man's chances of getting ahead would be equally good whether he were a Protestant or a Catholic. In fact, the less ardent he showed himself in his religious views, the more likely he would commend himself to those who had it in their power to set him on the road to success. The argument from environment is, therefore, inconclusive.

3. The Argument from Marriage

Though the religious tempest in Stratford was strong, it was not too strong for love. John Shakespeare found time to woo and win Mary Arden, youngest daughter of his father's landlord, Robert Arden of Wilmcote. The earliest documentary evidence relative to the marriage is an entry in 1558 in the Stratford Parish Register, recording the baptism on September 15 of "Jone Shakspere daughter to John Shakspere."[36]

Just when the marriage took place we cannot say. There may have been a child earlier than "Jone." The Parish Register begins with an entry dated March 25, 1558, so that the christening record of an earlier child cannot be expected to appear in it. Rowe's statement that there were ten Shakespeare children,[37] though entries for the baptism of only eight can be found in the Parish Register, lends support to the hypothesis that there was a previous child. But if the Shakespeares were married early enough to have a child before Jone, they could not have been married before November 24, 1556, for that is the date of Robert Arden's will, according to which Mary Arden was still single.

The marriage of John Shakespeare to Mary Arden is cited as evidence to support the position that John was Roman Catholic. There seems little reason to doubt that the Arden family was Catholic. But that there were Protestants among the Ardens is pointed out by proponents of the Puritan side of the debate like Fripp, who mentions Simon Arden of Longcroft, Yoxall, as a Protestant.[38] The Catholicism of Mary's father is plain from the wording of his will, in which he bequeathed his soul "to Allmyghtye God and to our bleside Laydye Sent Marye and to all the holye companye of heven."[39] That Mary Arden stood in the good graces of her father is suggested by the fact that he made her, with her sister Alice, a co-executor of his will and that he bequeathed to her "all my lande in Willmecote, cawlide Asbyes and the crop apone the grounde sowne and tyllide as hitt is and vj.$^{li.}$ xiij.$^{s.}$ iiij$^{d.}$ of monye to be payde orr ere my goodes be devydide."[40] But that John Shakespeare must necessarily have been a Catholic in order to marry Mary Arden does not follow, for Mary's own sister, Margaret, married Alexander Webbe, a Protestant.[41]

4. The Argument from John Shakespeare's Early Civic Career

It was also in the tense times of Queen Mary's reign, when bonds of friendship were strained and the distinction between Protestant and Catholic was becoming sharper, that John Shakespeare was given his first official position in the Corporation of Stratford-upon-Avon. In September, 1556, the Court Leet chose him to be an aletaster.[42]

The office was a minor one, but it was not without its responsibilities. An aletaster supervised the sale of foodstuffs. Bread and ale were the staples of life, and adulteration of them was a serious thing. The taster was required to be a person of discretion.

John Shakespeare's election to public office took place during the period of Catholic supremacy, but this coincidence does not prove, as some maintain,[43] that he was an ardent Catholic. Of course, the times were not auspicious for the elevation of ardent Protestants, but a man's religious views would not be likely to win for him or keep from him the office of aletaster. That John Shakespeare came to the fore in public life at this time suggests that he was better known to his fellow citizens for his personal integrity than for the distinctiveness of his religious views.

Thereafter, his rise in local officialdom was steady. At Michaelmas (September 29), 1557, he was chosen a chief burgess. As a burgess he would sit in the halls of the Corporation and vote upon all matters of borough import. Fortunately for the peace of Stratford, but unfortunately for those who would like to know how John Shakespeare thought and felt in those days, the deliberations of the Corporation were kept strictly secret. The sober minutes of those meetings in no way reveal the heated arguments that must have been carried on among the aldermen and burgesses. John Shakespeare took part in them and survived them to go on to further civic distinction.

On September 30, 1558, while Queen Mary was still on the throne, the Court Leet appointed him one of the four constables of the town.[44] Though the constables were required to take an oath of office, that oath had nothing to do with religion. Its contents can be reconstructed from Dogberry's speech in *Much Ado about Nothing* (III, iii, 1–100). Nothing can be inferred from the appointment to the constableship with regard to John Shakespeare's religion. The times were troublesome and required men of good judgment. John Shakespeare, presumably, had impressed his fellows as being a man of common sense. In keeping the peace, he would not let either Protestant or Catholic prejudices influence him. The twelve jurors of the Court Leet who appointed him to office must have had among them both Protestants and Catholics.

When Mary died in 1558 and Elizabeth succeeded her, the pendulum of religion swung the other way, but John Shakespeare continued to hold public office. This fact is thought by participants in the debate to prove something with respect to John Shakespeare's religion.

The Rev. T. Carter advances the argument that John Shakespeare must have been a Protestant because he was a member of "the Protestant majority in Stratford Corporation at the beginning of Elizabeth's reign."[45] The argument begs the question. It is not easy to establish the fact of a Protestant majority in the Stratford Corporation in view of the secrecy of its proceedings. Carter also overlooks the fact that John Shakespeare, as a chief burgess, had already been a member of the Stratford Corporation during the reign of Queen Mary. Bowden stresses this latter point and turns the argument to his own account:

> This tenure of municipal office by him (John Shakespeare) in 1557–59, when the laws against heretics were rigidly enforced, is our first direct evidence of his Catholicism. Mr. Carter, in fact, says, speaking of Robert Perrot, then High Bailiff of Stratford, that none but 'an ardent and pronounced Roman Catholic' could have accepted so high an office in times of bitter persecution under a most bigoted king and queen. He, however, entirely overlooks the fact that the same reasoning must apply proportionately to the other members of the corporation at this date, among whom we find, besides John Shakespeare, John Wheeler, his constant associate in his various vicissitudes.[46]

But in view of the fact that it is no easier to determine the religious complexion of the Corporation in 1557, when Mary ruled, than in the early years of Elizabeth's reign, Bowden's argument proves as little as Carter's.

Not only did John Shakespeare continue to hold office in the days of Protestant Elizabeth; he rose in office as well. He received an appointment as affeeror, his fourth official position, on October 1, 1559.[47] (He was appointed to the same office again in May, 1561.) A requisite of an affeeror was that he be a man of sound judgment, for it was his duty to fix the fine or punishment in cases of guilt concerning which the statute books had nothing to say. Such a duty demanded impartiality and level-headedness. There were no religious qualifications.

John Shakespeare's fifth official position was that of chamberlain. To this position he was chosen on October 3, 1561.[48] Chamberlains of the

Corporation were required to take an oath of office, but that oath, if the one employed at Leicester is typical, in no way involved the religious conscience. At Leicester (and most probably at Stratford) the chamberlains swore:

> We shall be faithful and true officers unto our master the bailiff, diligent of attendance, at all times lawful, obedient to his commandments and ready to do his precepts. We shall improve the livelihood belonging to the commonalty of this town to the most behoof of the same, and the tenements thereof we shall well and sufficiently repair during our office. And we shall well and truly charge and discharge ourself of all lands' rents belonging to this town and of all other money as shall come to our hands belonging unto the commonalty of this town, and thereof a true account shall yield up unto the auditors assigned in the end of our year, and all other things lawful that belongeth or pertaineth to our offices well and truly to our powers we shall do. So keep us God, the Holy Evangel and the contents of this Book.[49]

It is now apparent that John Shakespeare succeeded in his quest of public office both during the reign of Mary and during the early years of the reign of Elizabeth and that no conclusions with respect to his religion can be safely drawn from that success.

5. *The Argument from John Shakespeare's Protestantizing Activities*

The oath of the chamberlain quoted above suggests that the chamberlains were to act as business managers of the town, making certain that its revenues were duly received and that its affairs, including the improvement of property, were well taken care of. John Shakespeare fulfilled the duties of chamberlain for two years (1561–63). He must have been efficient in the discharge of his duties, for upon the expiration of his second term he was made acting-chamberlain, along with his old colleague John Taylor, to serve for two more years (1563–65) under the chamberlains William Tyler and William Smith. Lewis points out that "this is unparalleled in the minutes and accounts of the Corporation."[50]

Fripp and others who hold that John Shakespeare was eventually a Puritan make much of the fact that during the chamberlaincy and acting-chamberlaincy of John Shakespeare the Stratford Guild Chapel was Protestantized. The chamberlains' accounts rendered to the Corporation on the 10th day of January, 1563/4, show that "ijs" had been "payd for defasyng ymages in ye chappell."[51] Items reported during John Shakespeare's later incumbency, on March 21, 1565, and February 15, 1566, show activity in connection with the remodelling and improvement of the Chapel.[52] The Protestantizing process amounted to disfiguring images, frescoes, and statues, substituting a communion table for the altar, taking down the rood loft, making seats for worshippers, and erecting a partition between the nave and the chancel.

On the basis of another entry in the previously mentioned report of January 10, 1563/4, to the effect that "iijs" were "payd to shakspeyr for a pece tymbur,"[53] Carter suggests that John Shakespeare actually sold the Corporation some of the lumber needed to Protestantize the Chapel[54] and so, besides supervising the process, made a profit out of it as well. It is plausible to assume, as Carter does, that the "shakspeyr" named is John himself, since a first name or other identification is most likely to be omitted when a man is referring to himself. But to be certain that the "tymbur" was used for the Chapel when there could have been many other uses for lumber in the repair of the tenements of the Corporation is not so plausible.

Equally doubtful is the argument that, since on January 26, 1563/64, ". . . the Chambur ys found in arrerage & ys in det vnto John Shakspeyr xxv^s viij^d,"[55] the money advanced by John Shakespeare to the Corporation must have been used for Protestantizing purposes and must show the strong Protestant sympathies of the lender.[56] Such a conclusion is not tenable, for there were too many other purposes for which the money might have been used.

But if John Shakespeare did not help pay for the Protestantizing of the Guild Chapel, did he supervise the process, and does that supervision prove anything about his religion? Fripp and others who posit John Shakespeare's Puritanism say that he did supervise the Protestantizing of the Chapel and that that action proves him to have been at heart a Puritan. Against the argument, in the first place, are the facts that the Chapel was being Protestanized merely to comply with government regulations and that, since the precedents demanding this change dated back to the Protectorate of the Duke of Somerset (1547–49)[57] and since Elizabeth in 1563 had been on the throne for five years, the Protestantizing was taking place rather tardily. The process had already been carried out in various parts of England simply as a matter of precautionary conformity. In the second place, if any pressure was applied by local leadership to hasten the Protestantizing in Stratford, might it not have been applied by the Protestant high bailiff, Adrian Quiney, whose "faithful and true officer" the chamberlain had pledged himself to be? Most probably the process was carried out by order of the Corporation and not at all upon the initiative of John Shakespeare. Moreover, the poet's father was only one of two *acting*-chamberlains, serving under two regular

chamberlains. To say that any one of the four officers was alone responsible for the process is to make a bold assumption. John Shakespeare
personally may not have approved of the whole procedure.

A second activity of John Shakespeare during these years in Stratford
alleged to prove his growing Protestant sympathies is his cooperation
with John Bretchgirdle, M. A., the vicar who succeeded the Catholic
priest Roger Dyos in 1560.[58] John Shakespeare seems to have cooperated
with the vicar. He contributed "xij^d" to a fund raised by the aldermen
and burgesses of the Corporation on the 30th of August, 1564, "towardes
the releffe of the poore."[59] Since the plague was raging at that time in the
borough, presumably the money was used for the sufferers of the plague,
and the fund may have been started in response to an appeal by the vicar.
But twenty-four other members of the Corporation also contributed,
thirteen of them in larger amounts than John Shakespeare. In another
instance John Shakespeare showed a cooperative spirit when he presumably supervised the repair of the vicar's house, a program which included the rebuilding of the chimney, the restoring of the timbering, the
tiling of the roof, and the claying and sanding of the kitchen floor. Again,
the transformation of the upper story of the Guild Hall into a schoolroom and the repair of the schoolmaster's house during the chamberlaincy
of John Shakespeare are taken to be the fruits of a cooperative spirit,
since the new schoolmaster, John Brownsword, was a pupil and friend of
Bretchgirdle. Corporation funds were expended to help bring Brownsword
and his wife over from Warwick. Finally, there are entries in the accounts
covering the year 1564 to show that money was expended to pay for
clerical assistance to the vicar during the period from July to December
when the plague was at its worst.

But does all this prove anything about John Shakespeare's religion?
What if the vicar were Roman Catholic in his sympathies? Bowden
maintains that he may have been. He points out:

First, John Bretchgirdle, the vicar appointed on February 27, 1560,
in succession to Roger Dios, the Marian priest, was both unmarried
and had no license to preach; the Bishop of Worcester apparently
being unsatisfied as to his orthodoxy. Both these facts point to the
probability of his having been one of the numerous conforming priests.[60]

Fripp, however, argues that Bretchgirdle was a Protestant of the more
extreme sort. He gives this brief account of the vicar's ministry:

Early in the year 1561 John Bretchgirdle arrived in Stratford. His
presentation to the vicarage of Stratford is dated 28 January 1561.
On 27 February he was officially admitted to his charge in virtue of a

commission to Master Richard Cheyney, rector of Hampton Lucy. Behind these proceedings were more than Alderman Smith and the Corporation. They had the approval, beyond question, of Thomas Lucy and the expectant House of Dudley, and, of course, the new Protestant Bishop of Worcester, Edwin Sandys.

From February 1561, then, at the latest, until his untimely death in the summer of 1565, John Bretchgirdle was head of the parish of Stratford, helping to shape the life of the town in the difficult, divided, contentious days of transition from Roman Catholicism to Protestantism. The Prayer Book was introduced, stained glass was removed from the church and chapel, frescoes were whitewashed, and carvings hacked.[61]

Even though it seems as if the Protestants have the better side of the argument on this point, the value of the argument is considerably lessened by the fact that all the activity of John Shakespeare in cooperating with the vicar is to be coupled with the performance of a sworn duty. As one of two chamberlains in 1561–63, and as one of two acting-chamberlains in 1563–65, John Shakespeare was serving under the direction of the Corporation. Even though John Shakespeare was alone responsible for the financial report made on February 13, 1566, a fact indicating that he may have played a greater part in administering the affairs of the acting-chamberlain's office than his colleague John Taylor, that fact does not prove religious zeal. He did nothing during his terms of office that any civic leader with a sense of duty and a concern for public improvement would not have done. Such acts as the repair of the vicar's house, the remodelling of the school, and the hospitable reception of the new schoolmaster involved no religious partisanship.

The activities which an examination of financial reports leads us to assume John Shakespeare engaged in during his chamberlaincy, though some of these activities suggest a Protestant bias in the Corporation, establish nothing with respect to John Shakespeare's religious predispositions.

6. The Argument from the Baptism of the Shakespeare Children

Three entries in the Stratford Parish Register show that John Shakespeare, in turn, received some benefit from the vicar. An entry dated December 2, 1562, records the baptism of "Margareta filia Johannis Shakspere,"[62] and a second entry, dated April 30, 1563, records the burial of little Margaret.[63] The third entry is the most momentous. Dated April 26, 1564, it records the baptism of "Gulielmus filius Johannes Shakspere."[64] By the time Gilbert, the next child of John and Mary Shakespeare, was presented for baptism on October 13, 1566,[65] the Rev. John Bretchgirdle had died.

That John Shakespeare took his children to Bretchgirdle to be baptized proves nothing with respect to the former's religion. In earlier days he had taken his daughter Joan to Roger Dyos to be baptized, and Dyos was of Catholic sympathies. There was no place to go but to the parish church to have one's children baptized. If both John Shakespeare and Bretchgirdle were of Protestant leanings, or both of Catholic leanings, the father could have no scruples. If John Shakespeare was a Catholic and the vicar a Protestant, or vice versa, the father would have to make the best of an awkward situation, realizing that, in any event, the purposes of the sacrament of baptism would be met.

> Catholic parents knew that if the matter and form were duly applied, that sacrament [baptism] was valid, by whomsoever administered, lay or cleric, heretic or Catholic. The law enforced the baptism of all children by the minister in the Parish Church. . . .[66]

7. *The Argument from the Oath of Supremacy*

Before the expiration of his term as acting-chamberlain, and after serving eight years as a burgess, on July 4, 1565, John Shakespeare was elected to the office of alderman of the Corporation.[67] He took the alderman's oath on September 12, 1565.[68] Three years later, on September 4, 1568, he was elected high bailiff,[69] the highest office within the grant of the Corporation. As high bailiff, John Shakespeare became justice of the peace, the Queen's chief officer, and judge of the Court of Record. He took his oath of office as bailiff on October 1, 1568.[70] The oath reads as follows:

> Yow shalle swere that as a Justice of the peace & baylyffe of thys borowghe of St[ratford] & liberties thereof for thys yere to Come, ye shalle to the vttermost of your Cuninge wytt & power may[n]tene & defende the liberties of the same borowghe, and shalle do egall right aswell to the pore as to the riche after your knowledge wytt & power & after the lawes & Customes of this Realme & statutes therof made, And yow shalle not be of Counsell withe any person in any quarrell or sute that shalle Come before yow, nor shall lett for any gyfte or other Cause but well & truly shall do your office in that behaffe, And yow shall not directe or cause to be directed any warrant by yow to be made to the parties to the accon, but ye shalle directe them to the officers & ministers of the seyd borowghe or to some other indifferent person or persons to do execution thereof so helpe yow god, &c.[71]

Advocates of the Protestantism or later Puritanism of John Shake-speare make much of the fact that in order to be an alderman or bailiff of Stratford, he must also have taken the Oath of Supremacy required by the Act of Supremacy in 1559. Cumberland Clark flatly states that John Shakespeare's entrance into the office of bailiff in 1568 "is incontrovertible evidence that John Shakespeare was then a loyal member of the Church of England."[72]

James Walter also believes the swearing of the aldermanic oath clinches the matter of John Shakespeare's Protestantism. In his *Shakespeare's True Life* he writes:

> We have no intention to convey any convictions that either Shake-speare's father or mother were other than honestly members of the reformed faith; we believe with Knight, that both were, at the time of his birth, of the religion established by law. John Shakespeare may appear to have been slow in taking the oath requisite for the attainment of aldermanic honours, easily enough understood, as seeming to reflect on his own and his wife's parents. By holding this high office, after the accession of Queen Elizabeth, he had solemnly declared his adherence to the great principle of the Reformation—the acknowledgment of the civil sovereign as head of the Church. From that day forward there was no hesitation or drawback. Any speculative opinions he may previously have held were loyally abandoned, all would be made to shape to the creed which he must publicly have professed in his capacity of magistrate.[73]

So, too, Halliwell-Phillipps puts emphasis upon the taking of the oath of office, although he believes John Shakespeare made mental reservations. In his *Outlines* he says:

> Under the circumstances there can be little if any doubt that, at the time of his [John Shakespeare's] accession to an office that legally involved the responsibility of taking the oath of supremacy, he had outwardly conformed to the Protestant rule, and there is certainly as little that he was one of the many of those holding a similar position in the Catholic stronghold of Warwickshire who were secretly attached to the old religion.[74]

If John Shakespeare had actually sworn the Oath of Supremacy, these statements would have great weight. The oath required by the Act of Supremacy, passed in January, 1559, (1 Elizabeth, c. 1) was as follows:

> I, *A. B.*, do utterly testify and declare in my conscience, that the queen's highness is the only supreme governor of this realm, and of all other her highness's dominions and countries, as well in all spiritual or

ecclesiastical things or causes, as temporal, and that no foreign prince, person, prelate, state or potentate, has, or ought to have, any jurisdiction, power, superiority, pre-eminence, or authority ecclesiastical or spiritual, within this realm; and therefore I do utterly renounce and forsake all foreign jurisdictions, powers, superiorities, and authorities, and do promise that from henceforth I shall bear faith and true allegiance to the queen's highness, her heirs and lawful successors, and to my power shall assist and defend all jurisdictions, pre-eminences, privileges, and authorities granted or belonging to the queen's highness, her heirs and successors, or united and annexed to the imperial crown of this realm. So help me God, and the contents of this book.[75]

No sincere Catholic could swear that oath without squirming. But in favor of the Catholic side of the debate there is a strong presumption that John Shakespeare did not take that oath in 1568. Bowden argues that

. . . it is one thing to pass a new enactment, another to carry it out. At first the lay peers were exempt from taking the oath, which was aimed specially at the bishops and clergy, and it was not till 1579 that it was required of the justices; and in Warwickshire, out of thirty magistrates, Sir John Throckmorton, Simon Arden, and eight others refused to be thus sworn. Up to 1579, then, one third of the magistrates of Warwickshire were Catholics. There is no proof whatever that John Shakespeare ever had the oath of supremacy tendered to him as a qualification for his municipal office. On the contrary, it is in the highest degree improbable that the Sheriff of the County (1568–69), Robert Middlemore, himself a recusant, should have administered to him an oath which he refused to take himself. As regards the oath of supremacy, then, there is no valid argument for John Shakespeare's Protestantism during these years.[76]

8. *The Argument from Anti-Catholic Political Activities*

Carter and Fripp plead a special side of the argument that in order to be bailiff John Shakespeare must have been at least a Protestant, if not a Puritan. Carter says that John Shakespeare "as chief magistrate was especially active in the suppression of a Roman Catholic rising and the persecution of Robert Perrot. . . ."[77] Fripp points out that the year of John Shakespeare's service as bailiff (1568–69) was a perilous one, when Mary, Queen of Scots, was in the Midlands and when Stratford was "intolerant of 'papists'." As evidence of that intolerance Fripp cites the departure from Stratford of the vicar, William Butcher, "*in animo Catholicus*," of his curate, Hilman, "*fugitivus*, or a runaway priest," and of the schoolmaster.[78] The schoolmaster who departed was John Acton.[79] Fripp does not say whether he was a Catholic. Fripp's point is weakened, however, by the fact that, on Fripp's own reckoning, the vicar and schoolmaster left late in 1569 and the curate in February, 1570,—all when Robert Salisbury, and not John Shakespeare, was bailiff of the town.[80] It is interesting to note how late in Stratford religious history the parish vicar was "Catholic in spirit."

Just how one can prove an extraordinary zeal on the part of John Shakespeare in the suppression of the Catholic rising in the North is not easy to see. It is true that during his term as bailiff "he presided at every recorded meeting of the Corporation and as Judge in each of the thirteen meetings of the Court of Record."[81] But such faithfulness proves little. If John Shakespeare had not been so faithful in attendance, he would have been liable to a costly fine.

That he had not been chosen bailiff with the political and religious crisis in mind is apparent from the fact that the first choice of the Corporation for the office, both in 1567 and in 1568, was Robert Perrott. In 1567, after Perrott's election on September 3 by sixteen votes to three for John Shakespeare and none for Raf Cawdrey,[82] and after Perrott's refusal to serve, though such refusal meant a fine of "x[li]," it was Cawdrey[83] and not John Shakespeare who entered into office. In 1568, Perrott again declined to serve, and John Shakespeare was elected as a second choice.[84] On September 9, 1569, almost at the end of John Shakespeare's term of office as bailiff, Perrott forfeited the fine of "xx[li]" for twice refusing to serve. The entry reads: "At thys Hall the sayd M[r] Robert Perret wylfully made default and forfectyd the sayd payne of xx[li]."[85]

It is in connection with the imposition of this double fine that John Shakespeare is supposed to have been especially active in the persecution of Robert Perrott. From Carter's standpoint the argument might have some weight if Perrott was a Roman Catholic. But it is not certain that Robert Perrott was a Catholic. Carter[86] thinks he was. Lewis disagrees with himself, for in one place he calls Perrott "a devoted Catholic"[87] and in another he speaks of him as "the wealthy Puritan brewer."[88] Fripp makes Robert Perrott an advanced Protestant. To a discussion of the "rather close connexion between Puritanism and the 'trade' [of taverns, inns, and alehouses]" during "the reigns of Edward and Mary and the first half of the reign of Elizabeth," Fripp appends this footnote:

In Stratford *Robert Perrott* and Robert Salisbury, brewers, were advanced Protestants, and John Sadler, owner of the Bear, seems to have been of their party.[89]

In another place Fripp calls Perrott "a well-to-do Puritan"[90] and refers to the preamble of his will, 8 March 1588/9, "which is not only Protestant but Puritan in language and fervour."[91] Fripp thus turns Carter's argument completely around, and instead of seeing John Shakespeare persecute Perrott for being a Roman Catholic, he sees the bailiff persecute his fellow Puritan "for shirking his responsibilities in a critical hour."[92]

Exactly why the Corporation chose to make an example of Robert Perrott is conjectural. It appears that after the trouble quieted down, Perrott was slow in paying the fines imposed upon him and that the Corporation appealed to higher authorities to settle the case. A commission consisting of Sir Fulke Greville, Sir Thomas Lucy, Master Clement Throgmorton of Haseley, and Master Henry Goodere of Polesworth was formed, and at a meeting, without Sir Fulke Greville, in Stratford on January 3, 1571, it issued an order that

> 'in consideration of an oath which Robert Perrott hath made never to be of the Corporation, wherewith he may not be persuaded to dispense with himself in conscience, although he be very sorry for the same, the said Robert Perrott shall from this day forward be exempt from bearing any office, all appearance at the Common Hall and all other charges, in consideration whereof he shall pay £13 6s. 8d. upon the first of May next, and of his own mere and free goodwill and the love he beareth to the Town and Corporation give £40'—at Michaelmas, 1571, £20, and at Michaelmas, 1572, £20—to be employed during his lifetime as he will, and be assured to the Corporation for ever.[93]

The Corporation received its £40 on October 29, 1603,[94] after both Robert Perrott and John Shakespeare were dead. It is pertinent to remark, in connection with what is supposed to be John Shakespeare's strong Puritan interest in this matter, that the "persecution" of Perrott was continued during the terms of Robert Salisbury and John Sadler, successors of John Shakespeare in the office of bailiff.

In the light of the foregoing, it cannot be demonstrated that during his term as high bailiff John Shakespeare was animated by religious zeal or that his political actions were in anyway motivated by religious convictions, Protestant, Puritan, or Catholic.

9. The Argument from John Shakespeare's Attitude toward Players

Another bit of documentary evidence introduced to solve the problem of John Shakespeare's religion has to do with visiting players. The first notation in the records of the Stratford Corporation to attest the payment of funds to a company of players is in the accounts of Robert Salisbury and John Sadler, chamberlains of the Corporation, submitted on January 27, 1569/70, for the year John Shakespeare served as high bailiff. There are two entries.

Item payd to the Quenes Players   ix^s

....

Item to the Erle of Worcesters Pleers xij^d [95]

The next mention of payment to players occurs in the account submitted in 1573.[96] Thereafter the items are fairly numerous until 1587, when no fewer than six entries appear. After that date, items mentioning players become scarcer and scarcer.[97]

Those who oppose the theory of John Shakespeare's Puritanism consider the friendly attitude of the new bailiff toward players as significant. Thus Sidney Lee, in his *Life of Shakespeare*, says, "John Shakespeare's encouragement of actors is conclusive proof that he was no puritan."[98] On the other hand, advocates of John Shakespeare's Catholicism might think that a friendly attitude toward players supports their view. Such friendliness might be in keeping with a Catholic love of the drama. Thus, in discussing William Shakespeare's choice of the actor's profession, Bowden says:

> For a young man in trouble the stage presented perhaps the only opportunity of a livelihood, and to Catholics it offered special attractions. They were trained by their religion to delight in the dramatic representations employed by the Church in her services. . . .[99]

And a third possible position is taken by Fripp, who, concerned with demonstrating that John Shakespeare was a Puritan, emphasizes the alliance made between early Puritanism and the drama.

> Protestant nobles and gentlemen patronized companies of players who supported their opinions, the Earls of Leicester and Warwick and Sir Thomas Lucy among others. Until the building of the London theatres in 1576 there was no antagonism between players and preachers. On the contrary, they were in friendly cooperation, rivals in anti-Catholic propaganda, in the supply of moral edification, and in the provision, it might be said (they were both so run after), of popular entertainment. No towns outside London were more Puritan than Norwich, Coventry, Leicester, and Bristol, and no towns at this period more enthusiastically patronized the drama.[100]

And in his *Master Richard Quyny*, Fripp writes:

> . . . so long as the dread of the Pope and Spain weighed upon the English mind there was little or no hostility between Puritanism and

the drama. Plays were for the most part didactic and anti-Catholic. From the days of the Protestant martyrs there had been, as Foxe tells us, something of an alliance among preachers, printers, and players. Master Robert Willis speaks of the 'harmless' plays and 'morals' of his boyhood (he was born the same year as Shakespeare), welcomed by the corporations of Gloucester and other towns, 'far unlike' the dramas of his old age, which might be termed 'schoolmasters of vice and provocations of corruption'. The change in the drama even more than in the audience explains why Stratford and other boroughs encouraged players in 1569, under Master John Shakespeare's bailiwick, and for a generation afterwards, and then refused to allow them to perform and even paid them to go away.[101]

Thus it is that all three possible positions: Protestantism, Catholicism, Puritanism, take comfort in John Shakespeare's friendliness toward players. In the light of these varying opinions it is hard to conclude anything about John Shakespeare's religion on the basis of the two entries in the chamberlains' accounts reporting payments to players during his year as bailiff.

10. The Argument from John Shakespeare's Association with Adrian Quiney in the Sale of the Chapel Vestments and Other Corporation Business

The principal significance of John Shakespeare's election to his eighth official position in the chain of honors, that of chief alderman, on September 5, 1571, is that he thus became deputy bailiff to Adrian Quiney.[102] Two events which have bearing on this discussion took place while John Shakespeare served as chief alderman.

The first is the sale "to the use of the Chamber" of the Catholic vestments remaining in the Guild Chapel. The authorization of the sale is dated October 10, 1571.[103] John Shakespeare's part in this act is taken to prove his strong anti-Catholicism, if not his Puritanism.

The Catholic rebuttal is again stated by Bowden, in these words:

. . . Mr. Carter quotes the sale of church vestments by the Corporation as an additional proof of John Shakespeare's Puritanism. Now, the time and manner in which the Queen's injunctions on this subject were carried out in any place, offer a fair indication of the state of religious feeling then prevalent. In London, for instance, where the Puritan feeling was strong, at St. Bartholomew's Fair, August 24, 1559, or within a few months of the issue of this injunction, there were blazing in St. Paul's Churchyard two great bonfires for three whole days, of church furniture and vestments. Again, at St. Mary's, Woolnote, in the same year (1559), the copes, vestments, and ornaments were sold with consent. Again, at St. Martin's, Leicester, in 1561, the vestments were sold for 42s. 6d. In contrast with this prompt action, we find that the vestments at Stratford were not sold till September, 1571, and their sale then coincides with the concession of a preaching license to Heycroft, and was probably due to his newly kindled zeal. Thus, as far as this sale proves anything, its late date points to the predominance of a Catholic rather than of a Puritan element in Stratford up to 1570. In that year a new penal statute against Catholics, Elizabeth's answer to the excommunication, was passed.[104]

Presenting a milder view than Carter's and endeavoring to show only that John Shakespeare was a conforming Protestant, H. C. Beeching also points to the delay in disposing of the Romanist vestments and suggests that there must have been special circumstances occasioning disagreement among town leaders. He asks if the Council had been divided and so unable to come to a decision until 1571. He also points out that the Queen's Injunction of 1559 prescribed that an inventory be given of the vestments. The Corporation would have to wait for a commission to be appointed before it could dispose of the vestments. When Nicholas Bullingham, Bishop of Lincoln, was transferred to Worcester in January, 1570/71, he probably was commissioned to dispose of the vestments, so that it is reasonable to expect the sale soon afterwards. To take most of the force out of Carter's argument, Beeching says that, anyway, the transaction need have nothing to do with John Shakespeare's personal views in the matter. If it had, John Shakespeare would more likely have disposed of the vestments three years earlier when he was high bailiff.[105]

It should be remembered that it was Adrian Quiney, a Protestant and perhaps a Puritan, who was high bailiff at the time and who had the power of initiative which that office implies. In fact it was he who was specifically directed by the Corporation to make the sale. Moreover, the chamberlains would have most to do with the actual care and disposal of Corporation property. They were Thomas Barber and Nicholas Barneshurst, the latter of whom Fripp believes to have been a Puritan,[106] and the former of whom Fripp implies to have been a Puritan when he speaks of Joan, his Catholic wife.[107]

The second significant event of the year 1571–72 was the deputation of John Shakespeare and Adrian Quiney to go to London to act as representatives of the borough at the Hilary term of Parliament and to "deale in the affayres concerninge the commonwealthe of the borroughe aforseid accordinge to their discrecions."[108] Because the Parliament of 1572 was fiercely Protestant, the deputation of a Catholic to attend it is supposed by Carter[109] to be unlikely and the deputation of a Puritan most likely, so that therefore John Shakespeare must have been a Puritan. But does this necessarily follow? Adrian Quiney is generally accepted as having been a Puritan. If two men were to be sent by the Corporation to protect and further its interests at a meeting of Parliament and one of the two was a Puritan, thus representing one faction in the Corporation, would not the other man most probably be either a conforming Protestant or a Catholic so as to represent another faction? But from a common sense point of view, it seems quite likely that John Shakespeare and Adrian Quiney were sent to London first of all because of their knowledge of community affairs and because of their long experience in the government of the borough, and not because of their religious sympathies, one way or the other.

11. The Argument from John Shakespeare's Withdrawal from Public Life

Up to this point there seems to be no conclusive evidence to establish either the Catholicism or Puritanism of John Shakespeare. It seems just as reasonable to assume that he took the middle course of conforming Protestantism as to assume that he clung to the Old Faith or pursued the New.

But not long after this a marked change came about in the life of the poet's father. For almost four more years after his delegation to attend Parliament John Shakespeare was an alderman of the Corporation and faithful in attendance, though his name is not once mentioned in connection with any special responsibilities. However, after January 23, 1576/7, Alderman Shakespeare consistently remained away from Corporation meetings. In various records, entries of a financial and legal nature mentioning John Shakespeare do appear; some of them suggest that his business affairs were not as they should be. The evidence hints that the man who had risen from a glover's apprentice to the highest civic position in the community had withdrawn from public life. The climax seems to have come ten years later when he was dropped from the roll of the Corporation. The minutes of a meeting held September 6, 1586, contain this entry:

At thys halle William Smythe & Richard Courte are Chosen to be Aldermen in the places of John Wheler & John Shaxpere for that m[r] wheler dothe desyre to be put out of the Companye & m[r] Shaxspere dothe not Come to the halles when they be warned nor hathe not done of Long tyme.[110]

There are two interesting points to be noted about this entry and the action it records. In the first place, the name of John Shakespeare is closely linked with that of John Wheeler. This linkage is taken as an argument in favor of the Puritanism of John Shakespeare, because John Wheeler is generally believed to have been a Puritan. But it should be observed that a distinction is made between the reasons for which the two Johns were dropped from the Corporation roll. In the case of John Wheeler there is a positive desire to be put out of the Company; in the case of John Shakespeare there is an apparent indifference. It would be more plausible to assume conscientious objection on the part of John Wheeler than on the part of John Shakespeare. If both men were hostile to the policies of the Corporation, or were involved in similar religious difficulties, why should not the same reason account for the dismissal of both from the Corporation?

In the second place it must be noted that John Shakespeare's dismissal came after a long period of lenient treatment. Though the venerable ex-bailiff had made an almost perfect record of attendance for thirteen years *before* January 23, 1577 (he had been absent only once, on September 27, 1565), *after* January 23, 1577, he remained consistently absent for nearly ten years. The one break in the record of absence excites scholarly comment. It seems certain that John Shakespeare was present on September 5, 1582, when, according to record, he voted for John Sadler, and therefore against Adrian Quiney, for bailiff.[111] Fripp thinks that John Shakespeare broke his long record of absences solely "to honour" Sadler, his old colleague.[112] If so, his purpose was frustrated, for Sadler made excuse, and Adrian Quiney was chosen for the office.[113] John Shakespeare's vote at that one meeting cannot mean anything as to his religious convictions. Since Sadler and Quiney were both Protestants, perhaps Puritans, John Shakespeare must have voted for personal, or at least non-religious, reasons.

But to go back to the matter of lenient treatment. Though John Shakespeare attended only one meeting in ten years, he was still kept on the Corporation rolls without penalty of fines. This certainly looks like preferred treatment. Whatever else John Shakespeare may have been, he obviously was a man held in esteem by his Stratford colleagues. But is it necessary to conclude with Carter and Fripp that this esteem and friendly consideration were based on John Shakespeare's Puritan convictions? If the reasons for John Shakespeare's withholding himself from the performance of his aldermanic duties were purely religious, does it not seem probable that he would have been less kindly dealt with? And if his sympathies were so strongly Puritan, why did he not throw himself into the fight which Puritanism was waging? It was the mark of a Puritan to be aggressive in religious life. Retirement from the scene of conflict would have been a most un-Puritan course for John Shakespeare to pursue. It was exactly on the score of apathy that John Shakespeare, according to Fripp, so relentlessly pursued his Puritan colleague Robert Perrott in 1569.

The change which came over John Shakespeare's life in the 1570's and which culminated in his sudden and complete retirement from the Corporation and the magistrate's bench needs to be explained somehow.

A. The Poverty Theory

Many investigators ascribe the change to poverty. Beeching,[114] Elze,[115] Bowden,[116] and Brandes,[117] along with many others, accept John Shakespeare's poverty as a fact. This theory of poverty may seem irrelevant to the problem of John Shakespeare's religion, but it is not, for if the theory could be proved beyond shadow of doubt, then John Shakespeare's retirement from public life could not be used as evidence to argue certain conclusions with respect to his religion. Some scholars use John's retirement exactly to that purpose, and therefore a close study of the poverty theory must be made. The theory is based upon evidence such as the following:

(1) John Shakespeare was involved in many lawsuits, principally to collect money or to avoid the payment of it. These lawsuits are supposed to indicate waning prosperity and increasing financial stringency. But the value of this general body of evidence is limited by such considerations as are noted by Lewis.[118] John Shakespeare participated in fewer lawsuits than is sometimes supposed. Though Carter,[119] for example, finds sixty-seven entries of cases,* these entries apply to only some twenty-five lawsuits. This is no more than the number of suits engaged in by other prominent Stratfordians. It must be remembered that the local court served as a sort of agency for collecting debt and for making business settlements. In the twenty-five cases, John Shakespeare was the defendant in only nine. As a matter of fact, ". . . being the 'plaintiff' or being the 'defendant' in such a legal action cannot, in itself, be taken as conclusive evidence that a given business man was either prosperous or not prosperous."[120] Neither does the outcome of a suit determine solvency or insolvency. The outcome of many of John Shakespeare's

---

* In justice to Carter it should be noted that Carter's exact words are "67 entries of cases" and that he cites the litigious nature of John Shakespeare's career not to prove poverty but to show how exceptional were the years 1591 to 1593 in being free from litigation. It ought to be noted, too, that court cases after 19 Elizabeth could scarcely account for John Shakespeare's withdrawal from public life in 1577, though they might strengthen the assumption of his straitened business circumstances.

lawsuits is not known; some of them must have been settled out of court, or discontinued. Sums involved are sometimes small, sometimes not mentioned. Finally, the court records for the period in question, 1570–84, seem less complete than those for other periods in John Shakespeare's life. Lewis himself concludes that "John Shakespeare's business career was only typical; there was little or nothing unusual about it."[121]

(2) Certain cases, even though they occurred after 1577 when the retirement of John Shakespeare began, are thought to be especially good evidence of the alderman's poverty. Most famous of these is the suit of John Browne, begun on October 27, 1585, to collect a debt from John Shakespeare. A judgment was rendered against John Shakespeare, and the Court of Record issued a "writ of distringas" to enforce the judgment, but on January 13, 1586, the writ was returned with the report that "Joh[ann]es Shackspere nihil habet unde distr[ingi] potest levari."[122] Since this report was made early in the very same year in which John Shakespeare's name was stricken from the Corporation rolls, it is thought to be especially convincing evidence in support of the poverty theory.

But not everyone thinks so. Fripp says, "The commonly accepted evidence of John Shakespeare's poverty in after life, that nothing was found in his house to distrain upon, is quite worthless,"[123] and in a footnote he quotes Halliwell-Phillipps' statement (*Outlines*, II, 238) to the effect that the words of the writ of *distringas* "are not to be taken literally, and that they merely belong to a formula that was in use when a writ of distringas failed in enforcing an appearance." Mrs. Charlotte C. Stopes, who also does not believe in the poverty of the poet's father, thinks that the John Shakespeare involved was the corviser who lived in Stratford at the time. She makes the interesting comment that "the prefix Mr. is not used in the entries,"[124] and infers that therefore Alderman Shakespeare, who should be referred to as "Magister," cannot be meant. Lewis remarks:

(a) The legal phrase "nihil habet unde distringi" was wholly conventional and was often used as reporting that the defendant had not been found or that, for some reason, the writ had not been executed. (b) In several other entries relating to suits against John Shakespeare, at times when he certainly had resources, the same sort of legal writ was ordered by the Court and the same sort of report was made thereon; often for him in his suits against others, this identical legal action was taken and the same report, "nihil habet,"[16] was made. (c) In and of itself the phrase "nihil habet unde distringi" did not prove that the defendant had not goods of any sort to attack—"goods" only (not land) being legally subject to such a writ. (d) Similar writs by the hundreds were issued by the Court against others in Stratford—persons, too, who did not have any sort of "goods" left on which to distrain. It is obvious, then, that from this "nihil habet," in the absence of other confirming documentary evidence, one cannot logically conclude that in 1585–86 John Shakespeare had been reduced to pinching poverty. Certainly his having been released from the Council in 1586 was not the result of poverty on his part: twice in 1586 he sat on a jury, showing that he had not lost caste.[125]

(3) Of course, those who believe in the poverty of John Shakespeare point to what they feel is "other confirming documentary evidence," such as the following:

Interesting entries in the books of the Corporation show John Shakespeare to have been made an exception in the assessment of levies for community purposes. Thus on January 29, 1577/8 (a full year after John Shakespeare had ceased to attend the Corporation meetings),

. . . yt ys agreed that euery alderman, except suche vnder wrytten excepted, shall paye towardes the furniture of thre pikemen ij billmen & one archer vj^s viij^d, & euery burgese except suche vnder wrytten excepted shall pay iij^s iiij^d

m^r plumley	v^s ⎫ Aldermen	
m^r shaxpeare	iij^s iiij^d ⎭	
John walker		ii^s vj^d
Robert bratt	nothinge in this place	
Thomas brogden		ij^s vj^d
William brace		ij^s
Anthony Tanner		ij^s vj^d
	Summa	vj^{li} xiiij^d [126]

The meaning of this entry is that John Shakespeare's assessment was cut from 6s. 8d. to 3s. 4d.; that is, just one half of the full amount.[127] He was shown greater favor than his fellow alderman Mr. Plumley, who got a reduction of only 1s. 8d., but he was not shown as much consideration as Burgess Robert Bratt, who was not assessed at all. Just why seven members of the Corporation out of twenty-eight should have been assessed more lightly than their fellows is difficult to say. The straitened circumstances of all seven of them may be the answer, but if one recalls that John Shakespeare had not attended a meeting for a full year, an assessment of approximately seven dollars for the equipment of soldiers does not seem like a favor to a poverty-stricken man. It is true that on March 11, 1578/9, he was presented for non-payment of a levy amounting to the same sum, perhaps, as Fripp believes, the same levy.[128] But

John Shakespeare was not alone in this delinquency, for nine others were listed with him. Fripp identifies some of these as being persons of property, so that they must have been delinquent for reasons other than poverty.[129] Interestingly enough, Fripp, who points to John Shakespeare's presence on the list as proof of his Puritan obstinacy, likewise singles out two Roman Catholics on the list: "Thomas Reynolds of Old Stratford, gentleman, a Roman Catholic and a Recusant,"[130] and "George Badger, who . . . was a Roman Catholic and obstinate. Hence probably his unwillingness to pay his 12*d.* towards the Pikemen."[131]

A second bit of confirmatory evidence presented by believers in John Shakespeare's poverty is that alderman's exception from an assessment for the poor fund. On November 19, 1578, the Corporation assessed each alderman the sum of 4*d.* a week for the relief of the poor, "savinge mr John Shaxpeare and m^r Rob't bratt who shall not be taxed to paye any thinge."[132] Two other aldermen, Mr. Lewes and Mr. Plumley, were let off for 3*d.* a piece weekly. The burgesses were assessed 2*d.* each. Fripp interprets the exemption of John Shakespeare from the poor levy as the result of the alderman's objection to paying the rate.[133] He suggests that since "the fines by recusants went in part to the poor," John Shakespeare, recusant, felt he was already paying enough to that cause. But we have no record of his objection, or of his paying fines as a recusant. Certainly his excellent attendance record before retirement had saved him from fines for non-attendance. What other fines he would be liable to pay before January 23, 1577, it is hard to guess. As an absentee from Corporation meetings from January 23, 1577, to November 19, 1578, he would be liable to an amercement for each absence, but since "there is no evidence that he paid a single amercement inflicted by the Borough,"[134] it is plausible to assume that he did not pay these fines either and that he could have no reason to object to paying the poor rate *directly* on the grounds that he had been paying it *indirectly*.

Just why the inactive alderman John Shakespeare should have been accorded special treatment by the Corporation in these two instances is a matter of sheer guess. The amounts involved were relatively small, and exemption from payment seems hardly due to poverty. Lewis says that "such exemptions are not uncommon with respect to men who had long served the Corporation,"[135] and if that was the case, John Shakespeare would certainly have been eligible for exemption.

Another instance of financial exemption cited as confirmatory evidence in support of the poverty theory is recorded in the minutes of the meeting of the Corporation on an election day, September 3, 1578. A fine of 20*s.* is marked against the name of John Wheeler, alderman, and of 10*s.* against the name of William Smith, burgess, both of whom were absent.

John Shakespeare also was absent, but no fine is marked against his name. This omission is taken to be a sign of deference toward John's poverty. But to weaken that conclusion is the fact that Burgess "Thomas brogden," also absent from the same meeting, has no fine marked against his name.[136] The minutes of other election-day meetings do not indicate fines or exemptions for anyone.

(4) A fourth type of evidence submitted to support the poverty theory has to do with John Shakespeare's handling of real estate. Four transactions are especially pertinent. Documents relating to these transactions will be quoted at some length not only to provide the basis of a discussion of this phase of the poverty theory, but to lay the groundwork for a discussion of the theory which holds that these transactions bear directly upon John Shakespeare's religion.

The first transaction to be considered occurred on November 14, 1578, when

. . . the Shakespeares mortgaged a house and land, the inheritance of Mary, at Wilmcote in Aston Cantlów, to Edmund Lambert of Barton, a brother-in-law of Mary, as security for a loan of £40 to be repaid by Michaelmas 1580.[137]

The existence of this mortgage is certified by a review of its terms in a Bill of Complaint,[138] dated Michaelmas term, 1588, by John and Mary Shakespeare and their son William against John Lambert, for "trespass" and "damages" amounting to £30. The terms stipulated that Edmund Lambert, his heirs and assigns forever, were "to have and to hold" the property, which consisted of "one messuage or tenement, one virgate of land, and four acres of arable land with the appurtenances in Wilmcote,"

. . . provided always that if the said John Shakespeare, his heirs, executors, administrators or assigns either paid or caused to be paid to the aforesaid Edmund forty pounds of legal English money on the day of the feast of Saint Michael the Archangel, which would then be in the year of our lord one thousand five hundred and eighty, that then the aforesaid indenture and all things contained therein would be void. . . .[139]

This mortgage is taken to mean that John Shakespeare was so badly in need of money in 1578 that he jeopardized his wife's inheritance, Asbies.* But the force of the argument is nullified by the fact that in a second

* When Robert Arden willed this property to his daughter Mary, he called it "Asbyes" (Asbies), but the name was not used as a legal designation. The retention of the name by Shakespeareans as if it designated an identical piece of real estate throughout the lifetime of John Shakespeare has led to some confusion.

Bill of Complaint by John and Mary Shakespeare against John Lambert, filed November 24, 1597, dealing with the same case, it is deposed that the

> . . . said Edmounde [Lambert] did enter into the premisses and did occupie the same for the space of three or fower yeares, and thissues and profyttes thereof did receyve and take; after which your saide oratours did tender unto the saide Edmounde the sayde somme of fowerty poundes, and desired that they mighte have agayne the sayde premisses accordinge to theire agreement; which money he the sayde Edmounde then refused to receyve, sayinge that he woulde not receyve the same, nor suffer your sayde oratours to have the saide premisses agayne, unless they woulde paye unto him certayne other money which they did owe unto him for other matters. . . .[140]

It seems, then, that three or four years after 1578, that is, in 1581 or 1582, John Shakespeare had £40 in cash with which to pay off the mortgage. Indeed, he was late in making the payment, so that the terms of forfeiture were operative and Edmund Lambert had the legal right to retain possession. A temporary shortage of cash at Michaelmas, 1580, when the payment was due, may have induced the Shakespeares to rely on Lambert's good will. But it seems that John Shakespeare put too much faith in his wife's brother-in-law, for Edmund Lambert kept the property.

An aspect of the transaction more complimentary to the Lamberts is suggested by a foot of fine dated in the Easter term, 21 Elizabeth, 1579, whereby John and Mary Shakespeare conveyed "two messuages two gardens fifty acres of land two acres of pasture four acres of pasture and common of pasture for all sorts of beasts with the appurtenances in Aston Cantlow"[141] to Edmund Lambert for "forty pounds sterling." Although Sir Edmund K. Chambers considers this foot of fine to be only a confirmation of the mortgage negotiated on November 14, 1578,[142] the document is a quitclaim instrument effecting an actual change of possession. If the two properties were the same (they are not described identically in the legal instruments), the Lamberts would have had an unassailable legal right to the property. John Lambert appeals to that right in his answer to a second Bill of Complaint filed by John and Mary Shakespeare against him. In their complaint, dated November 24, 1597, the Shakespeares deposed that they had offered the £40 of mortgage money to Edmund Lambert and had been repulsed. In his answer, made the very same day, John Lambert deposed that

> the saide complainante John Shakspeere, by his Deede Pole and Liverie theruppon made, did infeoffe the said Edmunde Lamberte of the saide premisses, to have and to holde unto him the said Edmunde Lamberte

and his heires for ever; after all which, in the terme of Ester, in the one and twenteth yeare of the Queenes Majesties raigne that nowe ys, the said complainantes in due forme of lawe did levye a fyne of the said messuage and yearde lande, and other the premisses, before the Queenes Majesties justices of the comon plees att Westminster, unto the saide Edmunde Lamberte, and his heires, sur conuzance de droyt, as that which the saide Edmunde had of the gifte of the said John Shakspeere, as by the said pole deede, and the chirographe of the said fine, where-unto this defendante for his better certentie referreth himselfe, yt doth and maye appeare; and this defendante further sayeth that the said complainante did not tender or paye the said summe of fortie powndes unto the said Edmunde Lamberte, this defendantes father, uppon the saide feaste daye, which was in the yeare of our Lorde God one thow-sande fyve hundred and eightie, accordinge to the said provisoe in the said indenture expressed.[143]

In a replication to John Lambert's answer, endorsed in the Michaelmas term, 1598/9, though not dated, John Shakespeare reaffirmed his going to the house of Edmund Lambert and offering the forty pounds. The offer is now stated definitely as being made "uppon the feaste daie of St. Michaell tharcheangell, which was in the yeare of our Lorde God one thousand fyve hundred and eightie."[144] But John Shakespeare makes no reference to the foot of fine of the Easter term of 1579. If that foot of fine did not apply to the property in question, surely the astute ex-alderman would have denied the allegation of John Lambert that it did. It does seem, therefore, as if John Shakespeare first mortgaged the property and then sold it outright. But this complicated series of transactions does not necessarily establish the penury of John Shakespeare at the time.

A second real estate transaction in which John Shakespeare engaged also took place in 1578. It had to do with the leasing of some Shakespeare property in Wilmcote. We learn about it from a foot of fine,[145] dated in the Hilary term of 1579 in the Court of Westminster, which confirms a final agreement reached on "the morrow of St. Martin," 20 Elizabeth (November 11, 1578). The original document of this first agreement has not come to light.

The whole transaction is not perfectly clear. It appears to consist of two steps: the leasing of some Shakespeare property in Wilmcote to one Thomas Webbe and Humphrey Hooper and the immediate subleasing of the same property by Webbe and Hooper to another party, George Gibbs. Curiously enough, Gibbs enters into the transaction as a member of the first party in the leasing of the property to Webbe and Hooper and then as a member of the second party in the sublease. To explain the situation, some students of the problem consider Gibbs to be the agent or steward of the Shakespeares.[146]

The property involved in this transaction has been taken to be the same as that involved in the first transaction treated above, that is, the property eventually transferred to the Lamberts through foreclosure of mortgage, or sale. It is an interesting fact that the final agreement of this second transaction took place two or three days *before* the negotiation of the Lambert mortgage, and that the confirmation took place about two months *after*, as if the Shakespeares were desirous of making sure of certain arrangements before negotiating with Edmund Lambert for a mortgage. Interesting, too, is the coincidence of terminal dates. The sublease to George Gibbs was to begin on Michaelmas, 1580, the very day on which the Lambert mortgage fell due and was to be paid off.

But that the property is not exactly the same seems obvious from the fact that in this second transaction the property is described as "seventy acres of land, six acres of meadow, ten acres of pasture and common of pasture for all manner of animals, with the appurtenances, in Wilmcote,"[147] whereas the property mortgaged to Lambert on November 14, 1578, is described as "one messuage or tenement, one virgate of land and four acres of arable land with the appurtenances in Wilmcote."[148] A most important difference in the descriptions is the mention of the messuage or tenement in the mortgage and no mention of a messuage in the leases. It is not impossible, of course, that the two transactions involved parts of the same larger holding, with some overlapping.

To the theory of the poverty of John Shakespeare, this second, two-part transaction offers little support. There is no mention whatsoever made of money. The only consideration named is "one-half of a quarter of wheat and one-half of a quarter of barley," which George Gibbs was to pay "annually on the feast-day of the Nativity of our Lord" to "Thomas and Humphrey, and to the heirs of Thomas himself."[149] Whatever else the deal may have meant, it could not have been helpful in restoring the waning fortunes of John Shakespeare.

A third real estate transaction is the conveyance of an interest or "moitye" in a Snitterfield property by John Shakespeare to Robert Webbe for a consideration of £4. The date of the indenture is October 15, 1579. A bond guaranteeing fulfillment of the agreement bears the same date. The nature of the moiety is not defined, and the property is not clearly located in the documents.[150] Here again, considering the small amount of money involved, it is hard to understand how the transaction could have done much to repair the fortunes of John Shakespeare.

There may well be a direct connection between this third transaction and the last real estate transaction to be considered. This fourth deal is the conveyance of a sixth part of a Snitterfield property to Robert Webbe in the Easter term, 22 Elizabeth (1580), by John and Mary Shakespeare for a consideration of £40 This is a much larger transaction than the third. It involved "the sixth part of two parts of two messuages, two gardens, two orchards, sixty acres of land, ten acres of meadow, and thirty acres of heath and a brewery [?] with the appurtenances in three parts of divisions in Snitterfield. . . ."[151]

It is true that this Snitterfield property was originally Mary Arden's and that for John Shakespeare to dispose of it looks suspicious to advocates of the poverty theory, but there are other plausible reasons for his selling besides a dire need of money. The very size of the property tends to establish the opposite impression—namely, that John Shakespeare was a man of extensive property more than three years after he had resolved to withhold himself from public affairs.

In summary, the evidence of these four real estate transactions does not seem to compel the conclusion that John Shakespeare was desperately poor in the late 1570's.

(5) A fifth and rather general type of evidence presented to support the poverty theory is the economic condition of Stratford itself. Karl Elze, accepting the fact of John Shakespeare's poverty, writes:

> What the causes were that led to the continued decline of John Shakespeare's prosperity, we do not know; probably it was connected with the general state of depression that seems to have affected the whole town of Stratford at this time. That some such state of depression did exist, we know from irrefutable evidence, by the petition which the bailiffs [sic] and burgesses of Stratford addressed to the Lord Treasurer Burghley in 1590. The town, it is stated, had fallen "into much decay for want of such trade as heretofore they had by clothing and making of yarn, employing and maintaining a number of poor people by the same, which now live in great penury and misery, by reason they are not set to work as before they had been." Special mention is also made of the decline of the wool trade, otherwise so flourishing; hence, when tradition maintains—as is not unlikely—that John Shakespeare was a dealer in wool, we find here a very obvious connection between the decline of John Shakespeare's personal circumstances, and the state of the municipal affairs in general.[152]

First of all it may be said that for John Shakespeare wool dealing was auxiliary to the trade of glover and whittawer. Moreover, the alderman derived no small part of his income from farming or farm lands. Therefore, to suppose that the fortunes of John Shakespeare would be shattered by a decline of the wool trade is unwarranted.

In the second place it ought to be noticed that the petition which Elze cites is dated as late as October-November, 1590. It was in 1577, thirteen years earlier, that John Shakespeare is supposed to have been in such a parlous financial state as not to have the self-respect to show himself among his fellow aldermen.

So much then for the evidence educed to establish John Shakespeare's poverty. What about the other side of the matter? There are several indications that, instead of being very poor at the time he quit the Corporation, John Shakespeare was actually in a favorable financial position.

(1) The first indication is that in the Michaelmas term (November 2–28), 1575, the alderman purchased "two houses, two gardens, and two orchards with the appurtenances in Stratford-upon-Avon"[153] from Edmund Hall and Emma his wife for forty pounds sterling. These houses were in Henley Street, adjacent to the house John Shakespeare had bought in 1556. The purchase more than doubled the value of his real estate holdings in Henley Street. To put up the equivalent of $1600 in cash for the enlargement of his home was not to reveal poverty. John Shakespeare retained possession of his Henley Street properties until his death in 1601.

(2) A second indication is that the name of John Shakespeare "appeared near the top of the list of 'Gentlemen and Freeholders' in Stratford drawn up at the time of the Musters, April 1580."[154] At that time, therefore, John Shakespeare must have been considered a man of substantial means.

(3) A third indication is that upon two separate occasions John Shakespeare stood surety for others. On June 4, 1586, only three months before he was finally dismissed from the Corporation, John Shakespeare stood surety for a debt which his brother, Henry Shakespeare, owed Nicholas Lane. The original debt was £22, but only £10 remained unpaid on February 1, 1588, when Lane brought legal action against John Shakespeare to collect.[155] Beyond the fact that Shakespeare appealed to a higher court when the suit went against him, nothing is known of the outcome of the case. At any rate, John Shakespeare's acceptability as surety for a debt of £22 ($880) is enough to show that the delinquent alderman was far from being poverty-stricken in 1586.

The second instance is a matter of befriending a townsman in trouble. On July 11, 1587, less than a year after his name was crossed off the Corporation rolls, John Shakespeare went bail for £10 at Coventry for one Michael Pryce, a tinker of Stratford-upon-Avon.[156] Pryce proved himself unworthy of friendship, for he failed to appear and thus cost his benefactor approximately $400 in forfeited bail money.

When these several indications of John Shakespeare's satisfactory financial condition are considered, the plausibility of the theory of poverty is diminished. It does seem as if some explanation of John Shakespeare's withdrawal from public life other than poverty must be found. The field is left clear for other theories. Important among these theories, from the standpoint of John Shakespeare's religion, is the theory of conscientious protest.

B. The Theory of Conscientious Protest

This theory is developed by opposite sides. Carter, Fripp, Clark, and others, on the one side, argue for a Puritan protest; Bowden, Thurston, de Chambrun, and others, argue for a Catholic protest. Here again there is a tantalizing equilibrium in the debate.

Each side finds a reason for its views in the change in religious conditions in England and Warwickshire which took place in the early 1570's. The failure of the movement under the leadership of the Earls of Northumberland and Westmoreland to put the Catholic Mary Queen of Scots upon the throne of England in 1569 had driven Rome to extreme measures. In 1570 a papal bull excommunicating Queen Elizabeth was put into force by Pope Pius V. Adherents of the Queen were placed under "the sentence of anathema" and "cut off from the unity of the Body of Christ."[157] Roman Catholics who remained loyal to the Queen were thus threatened with severe Roman Church discipline.

Parliament did not take the excommunication lying down. An act was passed making it high treason "to declare the Queen to be Heretic, Schismatick, Tyrant, Infidel and Usurper, to publish or put in use the Pope's bull, to be reconciled to the Church of Rome, or to conceive absolution by virtue of them."[158] The issue between faithfulness to the Church and loyalty to the Queen became clear-cut, and the consequences of one's Catholic views much more serious. The followers of Rome were driven to cover.

If times were becoming difficult for Roman Catholics, so too were they becoming difficult for Puritans. The Puritan branch of English Protestantism had been growing in strength. Cheyney describes the development briefly:

The religious settlement introduced by Elizabeth was preserved with difficulty. The Puritans became constantly more numerous. Some of the bishops, many of the parish ministers, and an ever-increasing number of the people were opposed to the ceremonies of the established church and even to some of its doctrines and its mode of government. The Reformation in England began to interest the mass of the people. Many congregations and their pastors dropped the form of service required by law; "prophesyings," or meetings of clergymen and laymen for the discussion of religious subjects, were held and at London new congregations were organized which met not in the parish churches but in other buildings and followed other religious practices. In parliament a majority of the members of the House of Commons were Puritans and introduced law after law intended to make changes in the established church in the direction of more complete Protestantism.[159]

The Queen was not pleased with the development. To stem the tide of Puritanism which so seriously threatened the calm surface of English religious un ty, Elizabeth, in 1570, removed Thomas Cartwright, eloquent Puritan preacher and teacher, from his professorship at Cambridge. She forbade irregular religious meetings and broke up the Puritan congregations of London, imprisoning those who continued to attend them. She required clergymen to use the approved Prayer Book, in all religious services and to accept the Thirty-nine Articles as the doctrinal statement of their faith, or to be deprived of their benefices.[160] Temporarily the progress of the movement was stayed.

But repressive action could not stop Puritanism. It gathered new momentum during the period of diplomatic maneuvering through which Elizabeth went in connection with the French marriage suits. Hoping to soften the effects of her excommunication abroad and to offset a threat of invasion by Catholic powers, but at the same time realizing that she could not go through with the project, Queen Elizabeth entertained the suit of the French Catholic Henri de Valois, Duke of Anjou, afterwards King Henri III of France, for her hand in marriage. While considering the proposal, the Queen made a progress into Warwickshire, visiting the Earl of Warwick, Ambrose Dudley, at Warwick Castle, and the Earl of Leicester, Robert Dudley, at Kenilworth Castle. It was at Kenilworth on Friday, August 22, 1572, that the Queen announced her rejection of the suit on the grounds that her age and differences of religion were insurmountable obstacles to the marriage.

But the threat of a French Catholic marriage did not die with that. Seven years later it came strongly to life. The French Ambassador, Simier, spent nearly the whole year of 1579 in England negotiating a treaty and advancing the suit of François de Valois, Duke of Alençon. The Duke himself was at Greenwich in August of that year.

Protestant and Puritan opposition to the marriage was strong. John Stubbs of Lincoln's Inn wrote his famous pamphlet, *Discovery of a Gaping Gulf, whereunto England is like to be swallowed by another French Marriage, if the Lord forbid not the banns by letting her Majesty see the sin and punishment thereof*, and had his right hand chopped off for his pains. The Dudleys stood out against the match. The Privy Council warned the Queen of "great and increasing danger." Open rebellion seemed imminent.

In Warwickshire the air was tense. Musters were held at Warwick at Whitsuntide, 1579. Stratford, too, felt the uneasiness of the realm.

On 2 September [1579] it was resolved that proclamation be made on the morrow 'in the Market-place, that all persons coming to our market keep the Queen's Majesty's peace within our borough, and leave their weapons at their inns; and that all inhabitants assist the officers in keeping the peace, in pain of imprisonment and loss of their freedom'.[161]

The show of strength which the Puritans of the Midlands made during this decade of political and religious uncertainty displeased the Queen. Her resolution to stamp out the movement grew firmer. In April, 1576, she appointed a Grand Commission Ecclesiastical.

It was empowered to inquire by jury, witnesses, and other means into all infractions of the Four Statutes of Supremacy, Uniformity, Authority over states and subjects, and Reformation of disorders among ministers; into all singular, heretical, erroneous and offensive opinions, seditious books, contempts, conspiracies, false rumours, slanderous words, enormities, disturbances, misbehaviours, frays, etc., committed in any church, chapel, or churchyard; to order, correct, reform, and punish any persons wilfully and obstinately absenting themselves from church and service; the penalties prescribed for such misdemeanours to be levied by the churchwardens for the benefit of the poor, fine and imprisonment to be imposed by the commissioners, the obstinate being visited with excommunication and other ecclesiastical censures, bond or recognizance to be taken for the appearance of offenders.[162]

The effectiveness of the Grand Commission Ecclesiastical in Warwickshire as an instrument against Puritanism was considerably enhanced by the nomination in March, 1577, of John Whitgift, one of the Commissioners, to be Bishop of Worcester. Most of the Commissioners were more strongly anti-Catholic than anti-Presbyterian, but Whitgift was a Puritan-hater of the most fervent kind. He took his new responsibilities seriously. In the summer of 1577 he made a tour of his diocese, including Stratford, and complained in his report[163] that he got no information about recusants worth capture. The fault was not that there were no recusants, but that recusancy was condoned so generally by the people of the diocese that no one would inform against them.

It is evident, then, from the foregoing that both Roman Catholics and Puritans living in England from 1570 onward were in some danger and that their danger was proportionate to the prominence of their public status. Hence the withdrawal of John Shakespeare from public life in

1577 for reasons of religious faith, either Roman Catholic or Puritan, becomes possible.

It remains to be seen, however, whether the evidence makes the withdrawal on religious grounds *probable* and whether these religious grounds were Catholic or Puritan.

(1) John Shakespeare's failure (previously discussed) to pay the reduced assessment of 3s. 4d. made January 29, 1577/8, in connection with the muster of troops to support Elizabethan policies is taken to be an indication of Puritan disapproval on his part. (The *reduction* in the amount of the assessment cannot, of course, be explained on this basis.) But in the list of ten persons presented on March 11, 1578/9, for non-payment of this assessment, both Catholics and Protestants are represented, as Fripp himself points out.

(2) Likewise the real estate transactions entered into by John Shakespeare and discussed above in connection with the poverty theory are supposed by some to be proof of danger of religious persecution. All the property mortgaged, leased, or sold in those four transactions was located outside the limits of Stratford, hence most in danger of confiscatory action. That it later came to be a practice of those who owned property in danger of confiscation to dispose of that property to friends under the terms of conditional and secret agreements is clear from the *Lansdowne MSS.* After the Gunpowder Plot in 1607, when a new drive on recusants was initiated, investigating officers were forewarned of "preventions commonly" in "use to deceive," including these:

> Recusants demise their lands to tenants reserving certain rents, and the tenants stuff the grounds with their cattle; and when the commissioners come to seize goods, it is the tenants' goods, and the King is without remedy.

> Recusants convey all their lands and goods to friends, and are relieved by those which have the same lands.

> There are Recusants that labour with their friends to find their lands at small values and get one or other to rent the King's part at that rate, whereby the King is much deceived and the Recusant little hindered.[164]

The rather strange terms of some of John Shakespeare's real estate transactions sound like these "preventions." For example, the subleasing, late in 1578 or early in 1579, of the eighty-six-acre tract of land in Wilmcote to George Gibbs for the "peppercorn" consideration of a few bushels of wheat and barley, the lease to begin on Michaelmas, 1580, the very day when a mortgage for £40 held by Edmund Lambert on what may have been part of this tract was due, looks like a transaction intended to conceal the ownership of the property, or, if not to conceal ownership, to put the property into safe hands.

But even if John Shakespeare entered into this unusual transaction to safeguard his property, we cannot be sure whether he did it as a Puritan or as a Catholic. The two men to whom the lease was made, Thomas Webbe and Humphrey Hooper, are known only through their mention in the lease itself. Perhaps their very obscurity is an indication of the safety with which property might be entrusted to their hands—they did not make themselves conspicuous by religious and political partisanship. George Gibbs, to whom the sublease was made, may have been the Wilmcote farmer of that name whom Agnes Arden, the widow of Robert Arden and stepmother of Mary Arden Shakespeare, named as an over-seer of her estate when she made her will in 1579. But that identification helps little to determine whether Gibbs was befriending a Catholic or a Puritan John Shakespeare, if befriending him he was.

The mortgaging of the Wilmcote property to Edmund Lambert on November 14, 1578, does not offer much to prove evasion on John Shake-speare's part. In the first place, it looks as if the same property shortly after, in the Easter term of 1579, was sold outright to Lambert, so that John Shakespeare had cash in return for his property. Puzzling, however, is the fact that the alderman went to court in later years to undo the action. In the second place, though the transaction involved the inherit-ance of Mary Arden Shakespeare, it transferred ownership of the prop-erty to the husband of Mary's sister, Joan. The deal was strictly a family affair. If the intent was to avoid confiscation, would not someone outside of the Arden family have been a safer trustee? The Ardens were not apathetic toward the religious issues of the day, for only a few years later, in 1583, Edward Arden of Park Hall, Mary Arden Shakespeare's second cousin, lost his life for his part in a Catholic plot to kill the Queen.

And the two conveyances of property to Robert Webbe, nephew of John and Mary Shakespeare: one, in 1579, of a moiety in a Snitterfield property for £4, and another, in 1580, of a sixth part of a Snitterfield property for £40, do not suggest unmistakably the liquidation of property in danger of legal attachment. Here again, the probability that John Shakespeare was seeking to avoid the penalty of his religion is lessened by the fact that Robert Webbe belonged to the Arden family. His con-nection to Mary Arden Shakespeare was especially close, for his mother, Margaret Arden, was Mary's sister, and his father, Alexander Webbe, as a son of the widow of Robert Arden by a previous marriage, was Mary's stepbrother. The two conveyances may well have sprung from Robert Webbe's desire to build up a tract of land in his home parish of Snitterfield and from John and Mary Shakespeare's willingness to cooperate in the endeavor.

Not only are the rather peculiar *terms* of some of the real estate transactions cited to prove John Shakespeare's avoidance of confiscatory penalties, but the *grouping* of these transactions within the short space of one and a half years (November 14, 1578, to the Easter term, 1580) is taken to indicate undue pressure of a persecuting kind. Contenders on both sides of the debate are satisfied that this apparent hurry and this congestion in the real estate activities of John Shakespeare support their view of the alderman's religion.[165]

(3) A strange bit of deportment on the part of John Shakespeare in 1580 is thought by some to support the theory of conscientious protest. "He was . . . bound over in some local court to present himself at the Queen's Bench in Westminster on a day in Trinity Term (3–22 June) . . . with adequate sureties for his maintenance of the Queen's peace,"[166] but failed to present himself. As a consequence he incurred a fine of £20. Moreover, to this fine was added another of equal amount for his failure to produce one John Audley, a hat-maker of Nottingham, for whom he had gone surety and who likewise failed to appear.[167] John Shakespeare paid the fines. The receipt is recorded in the "Coram Regina Roll, Anglia 20[b], 21[a], Trinity Term 22 Elizabeth."[168]

John Shakespeare was not alone in suffering this heavy penalty for withholding himself. On the list in the Public Record Office there are 220[169] names of persons throughout the kingdom who were fined at the same time. There seems to have been some plan of concerted action in ignoring the court. Most of the persons named were from London, East Anglia, the Midlands, and the Welsh Marches—all known centers of Puritanism.

The exact nature of John Shakespeare's offence has not come to light. Fripp suggests the crime was "some indiscretion in word or act, probably a treasonable speech."[170] Since the French marriage had been very much in the wind in 1579, and since John Shakespeare committed his offence some time before June, 1580, there may have been a direct connection between the two events.

We cannot be sure that all of the persons fined with John Shakespeare were fined for religious reasons or that they were all of one religious faith. Though the Puritans, in their hostility to the French marriage, may seem to have had the greatest provocation to disturb the peace, there were also conforming Protestants, and even some Catholics, who did not like the match. And though the list was made up from recognized Puritan centers, it does not follow that all the offenders must have been Puritans.

Neither can it be made out that they were all Catholics.* It is, therefore, very difficult to draw any conclusion with respect to John Shakespeare's religion from the occurrence of his name on the list.

Mrs. Charlotte Stopes thinks that the John Shakespeare concerned was the shoemaker of that name in Stratford.[171] But the John Shakespeare on the list is identified as a "yeoman," something which the corviser was not. Besides, the shoemaker is not mentioned in any document as living in Stratford before 1584.[172]

As Joseph Quincy Adams suggests in his *A Life of William Shakespeare*,[173] the incurment of this heavy penalty of £40 just before Michaelmas, 1580, may explain why John Shakespeare was a little late in offering to pay the mortgage held by Edmund Lambert on the Wilmcote property. The amount of the fine was exactly that of the mortgage payment due. Perhaps the very money got together to satisfy the mortgage went to pay the fine.

The heavy and inconvenient fine may also explain the readiness of the Shakespeares to sell their Snitterfield property to Robert Webbe in the spring of 1580. Confronted with the necessity of raising money either to protect himself in the coming trial or to put up bond for his freedom, John Shakespeare would welcome the £40 he received in that transaction, again the exact amount involved in the court penalty.

(4) Fripp is of the opinion that John Shakespeare's doggedness in fighting the lawsuits to which he was exposed in that period is another indication of the alderman's conscientious protest as a Puritan against prevailing conditions. He mentions especially the suits of William Burbage (1582), John Browne (1585), and Nicholas Lane (1586–87), all against John Shakespeare for the collection of debt. It is Fripp's contention that John Shakespeare resisted doggedly not because he did not have the money to pay his debts, but because he was afraid of process.[174] Presumably an adverse turn in any of these suits would mean a judgment, and a judgment might mean costly liens against property, even confiscatory action.

But if John Shakespeare had the money to pay, as Fripp contends, he would be able to settle a judgment immediately and so avoid process. The late date of these suits cannot detract from their value as evidence from Fripp's standpoint, for his thought is that they confirm an attitude of protest which, though it manifested itself as early as 1577 or earlier, continued at least until 1592.

All in all, the argument based on John Shakespeare's doggedness does not seem to establish much. John Shakespeare never showed a readiness

* J. Semple Smart, in his *Shakespeare: Truth and Tradition*, pp. 68–72, believes in this instance that Shakespeare was persecuted as a Catholic.

to submit to suit; his determination in legal matters had been demonstrated before 1577.

(5) Fripp also thinks that the tardiness of John Shakespeare's effort to regain his property at Wilmcote from Edmund Lambert's son and heir, John Lambert, supports the theory of Puritan protest.[175] Plausibility is lent to the view by the fact that the Spanish Armada was scattered in late July and early August, 1588. The defeat of the Armada had the effect of releasing political and religious tension throughout England. The Spanish threat was over. Catholics and Puritans could breathe and move more freely. In the Michaelmas term of court just a few months later, John and Mary Shakespeare filed their first bill of complaint in the Wilmcote property case.

But a better reason for filing the complaint at that time seems to be the fact that Edmund Lambert died on March 1, 1587. Thus his estate was in the process of being settled during 1587 and perhaps the following year. It was the logical time for the Shakespeares to do something about their property.

Fripp's point about tardiness is made especially in connection with the long lapse of time between the filing of the first complaint and the second. It was not until November 24, 1597, nine years later, that the Shakespeares made their second attempt to recover the property. These years may have been years of hazard for John Shakespeare. If they were, he could be expected to exercise caution about exposure to legal processes. But there are weak links in the chain of evidence. The fact that the usual answer of the defendant and the usual replication of the complainant are not attached to the 1588 bill of complaint and that there is no documentary indication of the outcome of the case at that time suggests a private arrangement for postponement of the case. The second bill of complaint in 1597 may have been occasioned by the termination, or breakdown, of that arrangement.

When the evidence for the theory of conscientious protest as the reason for John Shakespeare's withdrawal from public life is carefully weighed, it does not compel one to accept that theory, nor does it determine whether John Shakespeare was a Catholic or a Puritan.

12. The Argument from the Recusancy Returns of 1592

Whatever the shortcomings of all the preceding arguments as determinants of the religious convictions and affiliations of John Shakespeare, in the eyes of both those who support the Catholic view and those who support the Puritan view the point is settled by the evidence of the recusancy returns of 1592.

The occasion for these returns and the nature of the documents themselves must first be examined.

During the 1580's the campaign against Puritan nonconformity was pressed. Whitgift was elevated to the archbishopric of Canterbury in 1583. He sought to gratify the Queen's wishes by instituting strenuous anti-Puritan measures. But Puritanism grew stronger, nevertheless.

That strength was manifest in Warwickshire. Cartwright, the deposed Puritan professor of Cambridge, in 1585 was appointed master of the Leicester Hospital in Warwick by the Puritan Earl of Leicester. He preached in the Guild Chapel at Stratford in 1586, on the invitation of the Corporation, and again in 1587.[176] The first time he was accompanied by Job Throgmorton, whose name is so closely linked with the "Martin Marprelate" tracts which began to appear in 1588.

But a blow was dealt English Puritanism, and particularly Warwickshire Puritanism, when the two Dudleys died: the Earl of Leicester on September 4, 1588, and the Earl of Warwick in February, 1590. Whitgift was quick to seize his opportunity. He summoned Cartwright before the Court of High Commission at London on the 20th of May, 1590. When Cartwright and fifteen others refused to take the oath *ex officio mero*, they were committed to the Fleet. There Cartwright stayed until May, 1592, when he was released through the influence of Lord Burghley. These events conspired to make the lot of the Puritan hard.

The lot of the Catholic nonconformist was equally hard. To keep the Catholic faith alive, priests educated in seminaries abroad began to filter into England as early as 1577. In 1580 the Roman Catholic movement was given further impetus by the arrival of the Jesuit mission under the leadership of Robert Persons and Edmund Campion. Though Campion was soon imprisoned and executed, and though Persons soon found it more healthful to return to the Continent, for a while the Jesuit mission enjoyed a good measure of success in revitalizing the Old Faith.

The resurgence of Catholic zeal was signalized by the attempt of John Somerville in 1583 to shoot the Queen. Somerville was the husband of Margaret Arden, daughter of Edward Arden of Park Hall, a relative of Mary Arden Shakespeare. Incited by Hugh Hall, the Park Hall priest, Somerville set out on October 25 for London, but the next day was arrested before he got there. The Park Hall household was soon implicated. Edward Arden was apprehended, tried, convicted, and on December 20th executed at Smithfield. Somerville hanged himself in Newgate the night before the execution. Anti-Catholic sentiment ran high and continued to rise during the following years. Tension mounted to its highest point just before the arrival off the coast of England of the Spanish Armada. When the Armada was repulsed, the tension snapped, and for a time there was a general feeling of relief.

But though the naval and military might of Catholic Spain had been broken, the subversive agents of Rome had not lost their zeal. The work of these agents, the Jesuits and seminary priests, became especially dangerous in the eyes of English statesmen in 1591–92. It was then that rumors, well-founded or not, ran through the realm telling of a renewal of effort on the part of Catholic Spain to invade England. Measures to discover and combat the work of fifth columnists became more and more aggressive.

From her manor of Richmond, on the 18th of October, 1591, Queen Elizabeth issued what Strype calls "A Declaration of great Troubles pretended against the Realm by a Number of Seminary Priests and Jesuits sent, and very secretly dispersed into the same; to work great Treasons under a false Pretence of Religion. . . ."[177]

In the "Declaration" the Queen outlined the situation which had developed since the defeat of the Spanish Armada. She lamented the renewed hostile activity of the King of Spain and pointed out the new threat to England's safety arising from the vassalage of the Pope to the Spanish King, the levying of forces in Italy to invade France, the apparent preparations for another Spanish Armada, and the work of the young men trained in foreign seminaries and secretly sent to England to persuade English citizens to renounce their allegiance to the Crown. To forestall the threat, the Queen called upon the ministers of the Church to be diligent in their teaching and example, and upon her subjects to see to it that there were sufficient forces by sea and land to resist invasion. "And . . . to withstand and provide speedy Remedy against the other fraudulent Attempts of the *Seminaries*, *Jesuits*, and Traitors," the Queen determined

> . . . by the Advice of our Council, to have speedily certain Commissioners, men of Honesty, Fidelity, and good Reputation, to be appointed in every Shire, City, and Port-Town, within Our Realms, to enquire, by all good Means, what Persons, by their Behavior or otherwise worthy to be suspected to be any such Persons, or have been sent, or that are employed in any such Persuading of Our People, or of any residing within our Realm, to Treason, or to move any to relinquish their Allegiance to Us, or to acknowledge any kind of Obedience to the Pope, or to the King of Spain; and also of all other Persons that have been thereto induced, and that have thereto yielded: . . .[178]

The proclamation continued with a description of the methods employed by the seminary priests and Jesuits and concluded with a charge to the officers and citizens of the realm to counteract the work of the traitors and to inform against them whenever possible.

Appended to the proclamation was a set of articles laying down the procedure which the commissioners were to follow. After each commission had organized itself and held its first meeting, it was to

make some Partitions among yourselves, to execute the Commission with more Ease: And yet you shall every forty Days, for this present year, assemble all together, to confer upon your several Proceedings: So as you may once every Quarter give Knowledge to her Majesties Council of your Actions.

Item, You shall send to the Bishop or Ordinary of the Diocese, and to the Chancellor or Official, and to the Archdeacon of the same, to certify you of all Persons, with their Dwelling-Places, whom they shall know to have been presented to them as Recusants, and that do so continue in their Recusancy. And the like Certificate you shall require from the *Custos Rotulorum*, or the Clark of the Peace, and from the Clark of the Assize of the County, to know such as have been presented and indicted as Recusants, as well Women as Men; and what Process hath been sent forth against them. And likewise you shall by any other Means inform yourselves of all such as within your County are commonly noted to be Receivers or Comforters of Persons that are suspected to have come from beyond Seas, as Seminaries, Priests, Jesuits, or Fugitives. . . .

Item, In your Examination of any Persons by vertue of this Commission, you shall not press any one to answer to any Questions of their Conscience for Matter of Religion, otherwise than to cause them answer whether they do usually come to Church, and why they do not. And if you shall perceive that they are wilful Recusants, then you shall examine them upon any Matters concerning their Allegiance to her Majesty, and of their devotion to the Pope, or to the King of *Spain;* or upon their Maintenance of any Jesuits, Seminaries, Priests, or other Persons, sent from *Rome*, or from any Parts beyond Seas, to dissuade any Subjects from their Obedience to the Queen's Majesty.[179]

The instructions then went on to give sample questions to be asked in the interrogation of those suspected of adhering to the Pope or to the King of Spain, to direct that especial attention be paid to persons who within the space of the past year had given or taken board and lodgings, and to require the commissioners of one shire secretly to send information to commissioners of other shires whither suspects had fled. The last article of instruction suggested that the commissioners employ the services of trusted persons, such as parsons and vicars known to 'be faithful, to help them

. . . observe all such as refuse obstinately to resort to Church. And such Persons you shall call before you, and, without dealing with them

for their Recusancy (for which they shall be otherwise by Law pun-
ished) you shall, as in your Direction think meet, (respecting the
Quality of their Persons) require them to answer to the two former
Questions, or to either of them.: For that by their Recusancy they do
give Cause to suspect to be disloyal in their Duties to the Queen's
Majesty and the State, or to favour the common Enemies.[180]

The first of "the two former questions" asked the recusant whether he
had "been moved by any, and by whom, and when, and by what Persuasion, to give Aid, or Relief, or to adhere to the Forces of the Pope or King
of *Spain*. . . ." The second asked him whether he had "been at *Rome*,
Rheimes, or in *Spain* within these five years," when he had returned to
England and why, and what he had been doing since.

On November 23, 1591, the Privy Council appointed the commissions
called for in the Queen's proclamation. Included, of course, was a commission for Warwickshire. The notification of appointment reiterates the
intention of the Queen's proclamation. It reads:

> Elizabeth &c. To our dere cosin Henry Erle of Huntingdon, lord
> president of the North partes, and to the Reuerend ffather in god
> William Bushop of Couentry and Lichfield, and to our right trustie and
> welbeloued Henry Lord Berkeley, William Lord Compton, and to our
> trustie and welbeloued Sr Thomas Lucy Knight, Sr Fowke Grevell
> Knight, Sr John Harrington Knight, Sr Henry Goodyer Knight,⸱ S^r
> William Leigh Knight, Sr Thomas Leigh Knight, John Puckering &c
> Greeting . . . to enquire what persons haue come from beyond the
> seas since the ffeast of St Michaell tharchangell in the xxxijth yere of
> her maties reign, or of any other persons that do recide in any parte of
> the Countie of Warwick or els where and all partes thereof aswell
> within the liberties as without that probablie by their behauior and
> manner of life or otherwise may be suspected to haue come from beyond
> the seas in the qualitie and vocacion of Seminaries, Priestes, Jesuites
> or Fugitiues . . . &c. And in lyke manner shall cause inquisicion and
> examinacon to be made of all persons that haue heretofore geuen or
> shall hereafter geue assistance, succour or reliefe in diet, lodging, pen-
> sion, reward or in anie other sort to anie of the aforesaid malefactors.
> Dated xxiij daie of Nouember in the xxxiiij yere of her ma^{ties} reigne.
> Articles annexed for a further Instruction to the Commissioners how
> to proceed in thexecution thereof.[181]

The Warwickshire Commission met at Warwick on February 27, 1592.
t made its First Certificate at Easter (*c*. March 25). That part of the
report which deals with Stratford-upon-Avon appears as Appendix I in

this work. In it, as part of a list of nine persons absenting themselves from church for fear of process, is the name of "Mr John Shackspeare."

Meetings of the Commission were held during the summer of 1592, and a Second Certificate was issued at Michaelmas (September 25). The preamble and parts relating to Stratford-upon-Avon are reproduced as Appendix II in this work. Once more the name of "Mr John Shackespere" appears in a list of nine who "it is sayd . . . coom not to Churche for feare of processe for Debtte."

The appearance of John Shakespeare's name in the recusancy returns has been variously interpreted.

Mrs. Stopes represents a group of scholars who are inclined to pin the guilt on another man. Feeling somewhat uncertain in the matter, she writes: ". . . it is quite possible it [the return] might refer to John Shakespeare the shoemaker, who, having been Master of the Shoemakers' Company, *might* have been called 'Mr'."[182] To reassure herself, she adds in a footnote: "It remains a fact that John Shakespeare, shoemaker, is heard of no more in Stratford-on-Avon, and shortly afterwards his house was tenanted by another man."[183]

Joseph Quincy Adams likewise suggests that "the recusant may have been the shoemaker" and relegates the whole matter of the recusancy returns to a footnote.[184]

Interestingly enough, this theory of mistaken identity is supported by the circumstantial evidence that John Shakespeare's name does not appear on a later return made by the Bishop of Worcester in 1596. If the name in the early return did refer to the shoemaker, the later omission would be explained by his removal from Stratford. The shoemaker left Stratford in 1594, going back to Warwick whence he came and dying there in February, 1624. But militating against the view is the fact that the title of "Mr"—a title not given casually in the 16th century but reserved for men of special position—would not likely be given to a master of a guild by commissioners who themselves enjoyed social and political distinction and who would thus be inclined to maintain distinctions. An officer of a guild gained no right to the title of "Mr" by virtue of his office, as did certain officers of a civil corporation. In the case of John Shakespeare, the poet's father, the title of "Mr" automatically devolved upon him when he was chosen high bailiff in 1568, and it is exactly because a distinction is thenceforth consistently made in the Corporation records between "Mr. John Shakespeare" and "John Shakespeare" that the two men can be kept apart. It seems hard to avoid the conclusion that the Mr. John Shakespeare of the recusancy returns was the father of the dramatist.

Fripp, Carter, Clark, and others are certain that John Shakespeare's appearance on these two reports means Puritan recusancy. Carter flatly says:

> The section upon which the names appear is that devoted to Puritan Recusants, not to that occupied by Jhesuites, seminarye preestes, fugitives, and Papists.
>
> The names are those of persons who were forbearing attendance at their parish church, and who unless they could show a lawful excuse would be imprisoned as nonconforming Puritans. Such terms would not, and could not be used of the Roman Catholics. Papists were persecuted for being Papists, not for forbearing attendance at the parish church. The names quoted are considered by the presenters to be *bonâ-fide* members of the Established Church who are breaking the law which insisted on a monthly attendance at Church services, and the excuses tendered might possibly have been of service to a non-attending Puritan, but would not have been accepted for one moment from a Papist.[185]

Carter's statement is less convincing than it might be, because it is based in part upon an historical inaccuracy. A few pages before that on which the statement appears, Carter says (pp. 160 ff.) that the Warwickshire Commission was appointed in 1592 under the Recusancy Act of that year, an act which, as Carter correctly affirms on pages 152 ff., was directed primarily against Puritans. But as Bowden points out, the anti-Puritan measure to which Carter refers and on which he bases his argument for a Puritan recusancy

> . . . was the first act of the *thirty-fifth* year of Elizabeth. The Parliament which passed it only sat three months, from February 19, 1592 [1592/3], till April 10, 1593. On the other hand, the return of the Commissioners for Warwickshire is dated in the heading "25 September, *in the thirty-fourth* year of her Majesty's most happy reign," or 1592. We must therefore leave Mr. Carter to explain how the Warwickshire Commissioners were appointed by an Act of Parliament passed five months *after* they had sent in their return. He has failed to realize that as, according to the old style, the year 1592 began on 25th March, September 1592 was four months earlier than February of the same year, which ended March 24.[186]

Chambers also calls attention to the confusion of dates and says: "So far as the recusancy returns of 1592 are concerned, the position is clear. They had nothing to do, as has been suggested by a confusion of dates, with the anti-Puritan legislation of 1593."[187]

But Carter's statement loses all its value as a result of the fact that the names of Squire William Clopton and his wife, than whom there were no stronger Catholics in Stratford, are presented in the First Certificate in the section immediately preceding that referred to by Carter "for not Comminge to the Church . . . monthly."

Fripp also is dogmatic about the Puritan recusancy of John Shakespeare. He says that some of the forty-one persons named on the First Certificate were

> . . . unmistakably puritans, Master John Wheeler, John his son, Master John Shakespeare, Master Nicholas Barnhurst, Thomas James or Jones *alias* Giles, William Baynton, son-in-law of Adrian Quyney, Richard Harrington, William Fluellen, and another son-in-law of Adrian Quyney, George Bardell.[188]

The list of examples of Puritans is identical with the list of nine absenting themselves for fear of process.

But if Carter and Fripp believe in the Puritan recusancy of John Shakespeare, Bowden, on the other side, believes with equal firmness in a Catholic recusancy. Says he:

> Such then is the Recusancy-return, and its impartial perusal can leave no doubt, we think, that it includes none but Catholics, and that John Shakespeare was at that time a Popish recusant, sheltering himself under the excuse of debt.[189]

Also on the Catholic side is Chambers, who, while he does not say that the recusants reported were all Catholics, implies that it is much more likely that they were Catholics than Puritans. In his analysis of the situation leading to the returns, Chambers says, "Clearly Catholics alone, and not Puritans, were in danger."[190]

The wording of the Queen's proclamation leaves little doubt that the object of the investigation throughout the realm was to discover Catholics who were functioning as fifth columnists. Since fifth columnists would be hard to detect, a simple and technical expedient had to be devised to catch them in a dragnet. But the very simplicity and technicality of the expedient would mean that a great many persons innocent of subversive activities and loyal to the Crown would also be caught. However, that unavoidable result would present no insurmountable difficulty. Once caught in the first great draft, the agents of Spain and of Rome could easily be separated from the honest citizens of the kingdom by further investigation. The simple and technical test adopted was church attendance. Not everyone irregular in church attendance was a Catholic or an agent of Spain, but every agent of Rome or Spain would be irregular in church attendance. Clearly, then, in the early reports of the commissioners all sorts of people would be included: Catholics, Protestants, and Puritans. So it must have been in the case of the Warwickshire returns.

The religious faith of the nine among whom John Shakespeare was listed is especially hard to determine. Those nine gave the most colorless of excuses: "fear of process." Bowden maintains that this is "the stereotyped excuse with nonconforming Papists"[191] and supports his contention by citing a return furnished by Bishop Cheyney of Gloucester to the Privy Council on October 24, 1577 (fifteen years earlier, it is to be noted), in which the Bishop divides the recusants in his diocese into three groups:

> First, those who refused to come to church, or open, obstinate recusants; secondly, some supposed to savour of Papistry [who] alleged sickness, some others debts, and therefore refused fearing process; the third sort, commonly called Puritans, [who refused] as not liking the surplice.[192]

Bowden concludes: "Here then it is Papists, not Puritans, who allege the excuse of debt, for the latter were only too willing to express their repugnance to anything in their eyes savouring of Papistry."[193]

Fripp agrees that "fear of process" is "an old and recognized excuse,"[194] but with Carter[195] believes it to be more fitting to Puritans than to Catholics. He is strengthened in his belief that the excuse is stereotyped by observing that a repetition of the excuse "in the case of the *same* nine, *after an interval of six months*, is more than suspicious."[196] These men were not poor and had no reason to fear process. They must have been leniently dealt with by "friendly churchwardens" and "tolerant magistrates."

> So conscious, indeed, are the commissioners of the unreliability of the statement that they throw the responsibility for it, should it be challenged, on the presenters. They are careful to record '*it is said* that these come not to church for fear of process for debt' and '*they are thought* to forbear the church for debt.'[197]

Fripp's inference that John Shakespeare and his eight fellow recusants received preferential treatment at the hands of the Commission needs a little examination. At its inception the Commission was composed of Lord Henry Berkeley of Caludon (near Coventry) who functioned as a kind of chairman in calling the meetings; the Earl of Huntingdon, brother-in-law of the Puritan Dudleys; Bishop Overton of Coventry; Lord William Compton of Winyates; Sir Thomas Lucy; Sir John Harrington of Combe Abbey; Sir Henry Goodere of Polesworth; Sir Thomas Leigh of Stoneleigh; John Puckering; and Sir William Leigh, the high sheriff of the county.[198] The signers of the Second Certificate are "Thomas Lucy, Fowlke Grevyle, Clem: Fissher, Tho: Dabrygecourt, H. Goodere, John Haryngton, Thomas Leigh, Edw. Holte and Robert Burgoyn."[199]

It is clear from this list that the Commission was not made up of men eager to hunt down Puritans. Sir Thomas Lucy was certainly a strong Protestant, and perhaps a Puritan. It was his father, Squire William Lucy, whose vicar, Edward Large, had caused such a stir at Hampton Lucy in 1537. Sir Fulke Greville was the father of the friend of Sir Philip Sidney and was an active Protestant, at least politically. In a list of strong Protestant families in Warwickshire in the early years of Elizabeth's reign, Fripp includes "the Fishers of Packwood."[200] The "Clem. Fissher" of the Commission may have been of that family, though there were Warwick Fishers who were Catholic. In the same list is "Henry Goodyer of Polesworth" and "Robert Burgoyne of Wroxall." The sincerity of Burgoyne's Puritanism is attested by the fact that he had Thomas Cartwright baptize his daughter, Elizabeth, at Wroxall Abbey just ten days before Cartwright was summoned to London by the Ecclesiastical Commission in 1590.

But too much should not be inferred from a possible Puritan bias in the personnel of the Commission. The Privy Council, in keeping with the purpose of the whole investigation, would hardly choose Catholics to form the Warwickshire Commission. The Council had sent a letter to Lord Berkeley under date of December 19, 1591, cautioning him "to be privately advertised whether any in the commission was known or suspected to be unsound in religion or had wives, children or any known to be recusants or did harbour persons backward in religion."[201] The first qualifications of a commissioner would be conformity to the Church of England and loyalty to the Crown. From the nature of the Warwickshire report, it seems plain that the commissioners, as representative public men, "were content to make examples of a few contumacious Romanists, and to let off the rest, Catholics and Protestants, their peaceable neighbours."[202] The very small number of indictments made between the first and second returns seems to indicate that the recusancy of Puritans and Catholics alike was not taken very seriously by the Commission. Only in cases of clear-cut cooperation with the agents of Rome and Spain were the commissioners conscientious to act punitively.

The omission of John Shakespeare's name in the later recusancy report, previously mentioned, needs further comment. The return was made by the new Bishop of Worcester, Thomas Bilson, on July 17, 1596, just a few weeks after his consecration on June 13th. In "forty several parishes" the Bishop found "nine score recusants of note, besides retainers, wanderers and secret lurkers" and "six score and ten households, whereof about forty are families of gentlemen, many of them not only of good wealth but of great alliance." Of these wealthy recusants the Bishop named, among others, "John Wheeler, gentleman, and Elizabeth his wife," "John Smith, gentleman,"* and "Thomas Greene, gentleman," all prominent Stratfordians. Among nineteen "gentlewomen that refuse the Church though their husbands do not," he named "Joan, wife of Thomas Barber, gentleman," and "Frances, wife of John Jeffreys, gentleman."[203]

Of these, John Wheeler must have been the son reported with his father in the list of nine in both certificates of 1592, for the elder John Wheeler had died in 1592. Mistress Wheeler, the wife of the elder John, had also been reported on both 1592 returns, and presumably the Bishop referred to her when he reported the "wife" of John Wheeler, gentleman, though she really was the latter's mother. Joan Barber and Frances Jeffreys had also been reported in both 1592 returns, the latter being reported in the Second Certificate as indicted for wilful recusancy. Other than these, there seem to be no names of the 1592 returns repeated in the 1596 return.

The omission of John Shakespeare's name is, therefore, in no sense of the word, singular, for it was the inclusion of 1592 names rather than the omission of them which was unusual. As a matter of fact the 1596 report was something quite different from the 1592 returns. The 1596 report was made by a new bishop, not a political commission. As a church officer, the bishop was perhaps more concerned about religious grounds for recusancy than political grounds. His return seems more like a report of a survey than of a special investigation. The bishop does not even bother to name many of the wealthy recusants, and he groups "the meaner sort" into "fourscore and ten several households, where the man or wife or both are recusants, besides children and servants," without mentioning a single name.

Fripp's comment to explain the omission of John Shakespeare's name, that "the Poet's father, near seventy years of age, probably was left in peace as incorrigible,"[204] is not wholly satisfying, for a few years added to a man's life after sixty do not make much difference in his incorrigibility. It would be more reasonable to explain the omission on the grounds of religious complacency than of religious incorrigibility, for those who

* An interesting point here to be noted is that John Smith may have been named after John Shakespeare. His father, William Smith, haberdasher and a neighbor in Henley Street, is thought to have been the godfather of John Shakespeare's eldest son, William, the future poet, and the conjecture is made that Neighbor Smith returned the compliment when his eldest son, John, came to be baptized. See Fripp, *Shakespeare: Man and Artist*, I, 39.

were included in both the 1592 and 1596 reports were exactly those who remained incorrigible in recusancy.

In the light of all the foregoing, it does not seem possible to conclude with certainty that John Shakespeare's name appeared on the recusancy returns of 1592 because he was a man of ardent nonconforming faith, or that his faith was clearly of one kind, Puritan or Catholic. All that can be safely concluded is that the elderly ex-alderman was irregular in church attendance.

13. The Argument from the Shakespeare Coat-of-Arms

A final line of argument on which Puritans and Catholics take opposite sides in regard to the religion of John Shakespeare concerns the Shakespeare coat-of-arms. When John Shakespeare was elected high bailiff of Stratford on September 4, 1568, he became eligible, by virtue of his office, for a coat-of-arms. It would be necessary for him as a new bailiff to take the initiative in applying for one, but it was the duty of the Heralds of the College of Arms to grant the application once it was made. Sir John Ferne states the case as follows:

> If any person be aduaunced, into an office or dignity, of publique ad-
> ministration, be it eyther Ecclesiasticall, Martiall, or Ciuill; . . . the
> Herealde must not refuse, to deuise to such a publique person, vpon
> his instant request, and willingnes to beare the same without reproche,
> a coate of Armes: and thenceforth, to matriculate him, with his inter-
> mariages, and issues discending, in the register of the Gentle and Noble.
> . . . In the ciuill or politicall estate diuers offices of dignitie and
> worship, doe merite coats of Armes, to the possessour of the same
> offices: as . . . and Bailiffes, of Cities and, auncient Boroughes, or
> incorporated townes.[205]

Whether or not John Shakespeare took advantage of his eligibility immediately is problematical. There seems to be no doubt that he eventually made application, but the date of the application appears to be five or six years later. We learn about this application from a draft for a grant of arms to John Shakespeare dated 1596. Two copies of this draft exist today in the College of Arms *Vincent MS 157*. In the second and revised copy there is a note reading:

> This Joh[n] sheweth [?] A patierne therof vnder Clarent Cooks hand.
>   [in] paper. xx years past
>   Towne officer & cheffe of the Towne
> A Justice of peace that And was Baylif ∧ of Stratford vppo[n] Avon
> xv or xvj years past[206]

If "xx years past" in the note is accurate, the first application must have been made in 1576. But in 1576 John Shakespeare was not "bailiff and chief of the town of Stratford," though he was "a justice of the peace" by virtue of being a past bailiff and past chief alderman. If the statement in the note: "A Justice of peace and was Bailiff officer and chief of the Town of Stratford-upon-Avon xv or xvj years past" applies to the application of 1596 and not to the pattern under Clarenceux Cook's hand, the chronology is even farther off, for in 1580 or 1581 John Shakespeare was well into his period of delinquency as an alderman.

In favor of the view that John Shakespeare made an almost immediate application for a coat-of-arms is the fact that Robert Cook, Clarenceux King-of-Arms, had Warwickshire in his province in 1567 and "had had his visitation committee in Warwickshire in 1568, the very year in which John Shakespeare became High Bailiff of Stratford."[207]

Regardless of when it was made, this first application has some bearing upon the problem of John Shakespeare's religion, since the application was apparently withdrawn and since the reason for the withdrawal remains conjectural.

Fripp believes that John Shakespeare withdrew the request as part of his conscientious Puritanic objection to the policies of the Corporation and Queen Elizabeth.[208] But if John Shakespeare declined "gentlehood" in *1576* for reasons of conscience, it is hard to justify his attempt to gain gentlehood in *1596*, only a few years after being twice reported for what Fripp believes was Puritan recusancy. Lee calls attention to the un-Puritan conduct of John Shakespeare in applying for a coat-of-arms:

> The Elizabeth puritans . . . according to Guillim's *Display of Heraldrie* (1610), regarded coat-armour with abhorrence, yet John Shakespeare with his son made persistent application to the College of Arms for a grant of arms.[209]

Adams offers another explanation of the withdrawal, namely, financial stringency. He writes:

> To secure a coat of arms . . . was an expensive undertaking. . . . Without money . . . the honor could not be secured; and according to Sogliardo, in *Every Man out of his Humor*, the fees charged amounted to not less than £30. If John actually made the application in 1576, his sudden pecuniary reverses might explain the fact that he failed to carry the project through.[210]

It is not necessary to go so far as to posit extreme poverty as the cause for the discontinuation of the project. Fripp points out that the former high bailiff would have to meet a number of exacting requirements:

To become 'John Shakespeare gentleman' he must give evidence of his ability to live without 'manual labor', and 'bear the port, countenance and charge of a man of substance'. His wife must dress well and keep servants, have time for visiting and recreation, attend town functions and make merry with friends at christenings, churchings, and weddings, as well as duly take part in a funeral.[211]

If John Shakespeare's circumstances were straitened in 1576, as they may well have been, it would have been hard for him to meet these requirements. The theory of temporary financial stringency fits in well with the renewal of the application in 1596, after son William had made a success in London and might be willing, for his own sake as well as his father's, to give financial aid to the undertaking.

The 1596 application for a grant of arms is of significance for the problem of John Shakespeare's religion also because that application is the basis of a later request for an impalement of the Arden coat-of-arms upon the Shakespeare arms. This later request was made in 1599. The fact that the request was made at all proves that the grant of 1596 was executed. There could be no request for impalement if no coat-of-arms existed originally.

The interesting and significant thing in this document[212] from the standpoint of John Shakespeare's religion is the tricking, or sketch, of the proposed impalement, in the upper left-hand corner. The Shakespeare coat-of-arms is sketched above. It is like that coat-of-arms sketched in the first and second drafts of 1596. The description of the Shakespeare arms in the text of the 1599 document is almost identical with the description in the 1596 documents. The coat-of-arms sketched and described is that which is regularly depicted today as the Shakespeare arms.

Below the tricking of the Shakespeare coat-of-arms is a sketch of a first attempt at the impalement of the "Auncyent Arms of (the said) Arden. of Willingcote." The shield is divided vertically into two halves. The left half is the Shakespeare arms: a gold field with a diagonal, dull black band in which a silver-tipped gold spear is inserted. The right half is a white field; in it is a "fess chequey," that is, a horizontal crossband made of squares of alternating azure and gold, like a checker-board. This is the Park Hall Arden shield. But the fess chequey has been scratched out, and alongside of the whole shield a new half-shield has been drawn. This half-shield is *gules* (blood red) in color and has across the top of it a *chief* (band) of gold. In the red shield are distributed three *crosslets Or fitchée*, that is, three gold crosses sharpened at the bottom and crossed at the top and ends so as to form three small crosses on each large cross.

In the gold band at the top of the shield is a blood-red *martlet,* or English swallow, without feet.

Advocates of the Puritanism of John Shakespeare say that this revised shield, intended to supplant the Park Hall half-shield, is the arms "of the only Arden who was a Protestant, namely, John Shakespeare's old contemporary Simon Arden, still living and resident at Longcroft, Yoxall, in Staffordshire. . . ."[213]

The argument is an interesting one and, if valid, strengthens the Puritan side of the debate. But the argument seems to be completely refuted by information which Mrs. Stopes and others offer with regard to the coat-of-arms shown in the revised impalement. It seems that the arms substituted are not those of Simon Arden, but of another Park Hall family. Mrs. Stopes makes the point that ". . . the reason [for the substitution of one Arden arms for another] lay in no breach of connection, but in the fact that Mary Arden was an heiress, not in the eldest line, but through a *second son.*"[214] This second son would be Mary's grandfather, Thomas Arden, the second son of Walter Arden of Park Hall.[215]

The theory is that in their search for a suitable coat-of-arms already in existence to represent Mary Arden, the Heralds of the College of Arms considered the advisability of using some modification of one of three existent Arden coats-of-arms: that of the Earls of Warwick, that of the Beauchamp branch of the Warwick family, or that of an older branch of the Park Hall Ardens. The familiarity of the first two coats would make an adaptation of either of them inadvisable, and so the Heralds tricked in the arms of the older branch of the Park Hall Ardens.* But a second thought reminded them of the inappropriateness of a fess chequey for a descendant of a second son, and a search was then instituted for something appropriate. The search revealed the existence of an arms of "Arden or Arderne gu., three cross crosslets fitchée or; on a chief of the second a martlet of the first. . . ."[216] that is, a shield with a blood-red field in which were distributed three sharp-bottomed crosses of gold, each having its top and side-pieces crossed to form smaller crosses, the field being surmounted by a crossband of gold containing a blood-red martlet. This coat-of-arms presumably appealed to the Heralds as a usable one for impalement.

But a disqualifying detail in this coat-of-arms was the martlet, the conventional heraldic difference to represent a fourth son, not a second. A second son should have a crescent. But the crescent was already in use

---

* Stephen I. Tucker, in his *The Assignment of Arms to Shakespeare and Arden* (London, 1884), p. 4, suggests that the connection of John Shakespeare's wife with the Warwick Ardens, though asserted, could not be proved, and that therefore the Heralds would have to go to the Park Hall Ardens for a proper arms to impale.

in the arms of the Alvanley Ardens in Cheshire. To indicate a difference merely by the omission of the crescent was not possible either, because the Alvanley coat-of-arms *without* the crescent was already the coat-of-arms of Simon Arden of Longcroft, the first cousin of Mary Arden's father. Confronted with the necessity of committing an inaccuracy, the Heralds chose to represent a second son as a fourth rather than as a first. The Park Hall Arden arms employing the martlet for a difference was therefore tricked in as the revised impalement. In the revision there was no rejection of a Catholic Arden arms and the substitution of a Protestant Arden arms. Both the rejected and the substituted arms were of Catholic Ardens.

It seems, then, that the attempt to impale the Arden arms upon the Shakespeare arms offers no evidence for the Puritanism of John Shakespeare.

14. Summary

In the preceding pages we have reviewed the most important evidence in the major arguments advanced to prove the nature of John Shakespeare's religion and have sought to show how delicately balanced the issue is. Only through the discovery of further documentary evidence does it seem possible to settle the question one way or the other.

A document which can settle the question is at hand. It is not new, for it has been known to scholars for almost two hundred years. But it has been considered spurious. It is the Spiritual Last Will and Testament of John Shakespeare. To present this document in a fresh light and to evaluate it as proof that John Shakespeare was a Catholic in his religion is the object of the next part of this work.

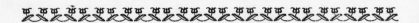

PART TWO

THE SPIRITUAL LAST WILL AND TESTAMENT
OF JOHN SHAKESPEARE

SOMETIME after the 14th day of June, 1784, the printer of the *Gentleman's Magazine* in London received a packet of mail from Stratford-upon-Avon. It contained a letter from John Jordan, wheelwright and amateur antiquarian of that place, explaining an enclosed copy of a spiritual last will and testament of one John Shakespeare. About the original document, Jordan wrote

> . . . there are two sentences and a half lost at the begginning;—it is wrote in a fair and legible hand, and the spelling exactly as I have sent it to you;—it was found by Mr. Joseph Mosely, a bricklayer of this town, some years ago under the tileing of the house where the poet was born, and carefully by him preserved till he most generously gave me the original manuscript the 8th day of June, 1784, where any gentleman who chuses to call on me shall be welcome to the perusal.[1]

The printer of the magazine examined the copy of the will and then rejected it as spurious. Thus the first critical judgment passed upon the document which is to be the subject of this chapter was unfavorable.

But though the rejection of the manuscript by the editor of the *Gentleman's Magazine* left Jordan's "wishes and curiosity . . . unsatisfied," the ends of scholarship were not completely frustrated, for the original document had found its way into the hands of Edmond Malone, the great Shakespearean scholar of that day. The earliest *published* information we have of John Shakespeare's Spiritual Last Will and Testament appears in Malone's *An Historical Account of the Rise and Progress of the English Stage* in his 1790 edition of Shakespeare's works. Malone there tells of the finding of the document and gives the text of the manuscript. The information is quoted below from the reprint which appears in the fourth Johnson-Steevens edition of Shakespeare's works, revised by Isaac Reed. Malone says:

About twenty years ago, one Mosely, a master-bricklayer, who usually worked with his men, being employed by Mr. Thomas Hart, the fifth descendant in a direct line from our poet's sister, Joan Hart, to new-tile the old house at Stratford, in which Mr. Hart lives, and in which our poet was born, found a very extraordinary manuscript between the rafters and the tiling of the house. It is a small paper-book, consisting of five leaves stitched together. It had originally consisted of six leaves, but unluckily the first was wanting when the book was found. I have taken some pains to ascertain the authenticity of this manuscript, and after a very careful inquiry am perfectly satisfied that it is genuine.

The writer, John Shakspeare, calls it his *Will*; but it is rather a declaration of his faith and pious resolutions. Whether it contains the religious sentiments of our poet's father or elder brother, I am unable to determine. The handwriting is undoubtedly not so ancient as that *usually* written about the year 1600; but I have now before me a manuscript written by Alleyn the player at various times between 1599 and 1614, and another by Forde, the dramatick poet, in 1606, in nearly the same handwriting as that of the manuscript in question. The Rev. Mr. Davenport, Vicar of Stratford-upon-Avon, at my request endeavoured to find out Mr. Mosely, to examine more particularly concerning this manuscript; but he died about two years ago. His daughter, however, who is now living, and Mr. Hart, who is also living, and now sixty years old, perfectly well remember the finding of this paper. Mosely some time after he found it, gave it to Mr. Peyton, an alderman of Stratford, who obligingly transmitted it to me through the hands of Mr. Davenport. It is proper to observe that the finder of this relique bore the character of a very honest, sober, and industrious man, and that he neither asked nor received any price for it; and I may also add that its contents are such as no one could have thought of inventing with a view to literary imposition.

If the injunction contained in the latter part of it (that it should be buried with the writer) was observed, then must the paper which has thus fortuitously been recovered, have been a copy, made from the original, previous to the burial of John Shakspeare.

This extraordinary will consisted originally of fourteen articles, but the first leaf being unluckily wanting, I am unable to ascertain either its date or the particular occasion on which it was written; both of which probably the first article would have furnished us with. If it was written by our poet's father, John Shakspeare, then it was probably drawn up about the year 1600; if by his brother, it perhaps was dated some time between that year and 1608, when the younger John should seem to have been dead.

[Since the sheet which contains the will of John Shakspeare was printed I have learned that it was originally perfect, when found by Joseph Mosely, though the first leaf has since been lost.[9][*] Mosely transcribed a large portion of it, and from his copy I have been furnished with the introductory articles, from the want of which I was obliged to print this will .n an imperfect state. They are as follows:

I.

"In tl 2 name of God, the father, sonne, and holy ghost, the most holy and blessed Virgin Mary, mother of God, the holy host of archangels, angels, patriarchs, prophets, evangelists, apostles, saints, martyrs, and all the celestial court and company of heaven, I John Shakspear, an unworthy member of the holy Catholick religion, being at this my present writing in perfect health of body, and sound mind, memory, and understanding, but calling to mind the uncertainty of life and certainty of death, and that I may be possibly cut off in the blossome of my sins, and called to render an account of all my transgressions externally and internally, and that I may be unprepared for the dreadful trial either by sacrament, pennance, fasting, or prayer, or any other purgation whatever, do in the holy presence above specified, of my own free and voluntary accord, make and ordaine this my last spiritual will, testament, confession, protestation, and confession of faith, hopinge hereby to receive pardon for all my sinnes and offences, and thereby to be made partaker of life everlasting, through the only merits of Jesus Christ my saviour and redeemer, who took upon himself the likeness of man, suffered death, and was crucified upon the crosse, for the redemption of sinners.

II.

"*Item.* I John Shakspear doe by this present protest, acknowledge, and confess, that in my past life I have been a most abominable and grievous sinner, and therefore unworthy to be forgiven without a true and sincere repentance for the same. But trusting in the manifold mercies of my blessed Saviour and Redeemer, I am encouraged by relying on his sacred word, to hope for salvation and be made partaker of his heavenly kingdom, as a member of the celestial company of angels, saints and martyrs, there to reside for ever and ever in the court of my God.

*Reed's footnote 9 says: "The lost articles, &c. (here inclosed in crotchets) are supplied from Mr. Malone's *Emendations and Additions* in his Vol. I, Part II. p. 330-31."

III.

"*Item*, I John Shakspear doe by this present protest and declare, that as I am certain I must passe out of this transitory life into another that will last to eternity, I do hereby most humbly implore and intreat my good and guardian angell to instruct me in this my solemn preparation, protestation and confession of faith,] at least spiritually, in will adoring and most humbly beseeching my saviour, that he will be pleased to assist me in so dangerous a voyage, to defend me from the snares and deceites of my infernall enemies, and to conduct me to the secure haven of his eternall blisse.

IV.

"*Item*, I John Shakspear doe protest that I will also passe out of this life, armed with the last sacrament of extreme unction: the which if through any let or hindrance I should not then be able to have, I doe now also for that time demand and crave the same; beseeching his divine majesty that he will be pleased to anoynt my senses both internall and externall with the sacred oyle of his infinite mercy, and to pardon me all my sins committed by seeing, speaking, feeling, smelling, hearing, touching, or by any other way whatsoever.

V.

"*Item*, I John Shakspear doe by this present protest that I will never through any temptation whatsoever despaire of the divine goodness, for the multitude and greatness of my sinnes; for which although I confesse that I have deserved hell, yet will I stedfastly hope in gods infinite mercy, knowing that he hath heretofore pardoned many as great sinners as my self, whereof I have good warrant sealed with his sacred mouth, in holy writ, whereby he pronounceth that he is not come to call the just, but sinners.

VI.

"*Item*, I John Shakspear do protest that I do not know that I have ever done any good worke meritorious of life everlasting: and if I have done any, I do acknowledge that I have done it with a great deale of negligence and imperfection; neither should I have been able to have done the least without the assistance of his divine grace. Wherefore let the devill remain confounded; for I doe in no wise presume to merit heaven by such good workes alone, but through the merits and bloud of my lord and saviour, jesus, shed upon the crose for me most miserable sinner.

VII.

"*Item*, I John Shakspear do protest by this present writing, that I will patiently endure and suffer all kind of infirmity, sickness, yea and the paine of death it self: wherein if it should happen, which god forbid, that through violence of paine and agony, or by subtilty of the devill, I should fall into any impatience or temptation of blasphemy, or murmuration against god, or the catholike faith, or give any signe of bad example, I do henceforth, and for that present, repent me, and am most heartily sorry for the same: and I do renounce all the evill whatsoever, which I might have then done or said; beseeching his divine clemency that he will not forsake me in that grievous and paignefull agony.

VIII.

"*Item*, I John Shakspear, by virtue of this present testament, I do pardon all the injuries and offences that any one hath ever done unto me, either in my reputation, life, goods, or any other way whatsoever; beseeching sweet jesus to pardon them for the same: and I do desire, that they will doe the like by me, whome I have offended or injured in any sort howsoever.

IX.

"*Item*, I John Shakspear do heere protest that I do render infinite thanks to his divine majesty for all the benefits that I have received as well secret as manifest, & in particular for the benefit of my Creation, Redemption, Sanctification, Conservation, and Vocation to the holy knowledge of him & his true Catholike faith: but above all, for his so great expectation of me to pennance, when he might most justly have taken me out of this life, wher. I least thought of it, yea, even then, when I was plunged in the durty puddle of my sinnes. Blessed be therefore and praised, for ever and ever, his infinite patience and charity.

X.

"*Item*, I John Shakspear do protest, that I am willing, yea, I do infinitely desire and humbly crave, that of this my last will and testament the glorious and ever Virgin mary, mother of god, refuge and advocate of sinners, (whom I honour specially above all other saints,) may be the chiefe Executresse, together with these other saints, my patrons, (saint Winefride) all whome I invocke and beseech to be present at the hour of my death, that she and they may comfort me with their desired presence, and crave of sweet Jesus that he will receive my soul into peace.

XI.

"*Item*, In virtue of this present writing, I John Shakspear do likewise most willingly and with all humility constitute and ordaine my good Angel, for Defender and Protectour of my soul in the dreadfull day of Judgement, when the finall sentence of eternall life or death shall be discussed and given; beseeching him, that, as my soule was appointed to his custody and protection when I lived, even so he will vouchsafe to defend the same at that houre, and conduct it to eternall bliss.

XII.

"*Item*, I John Shakspear do in like manner pray and beseech all my dear friends, parents, and kinsfolks, by the bowels of our Saviour jesus Christ, that since it is uncertain what lot will befall me, for fear notwithstanding least by reason of my sinnes I be to pass and stay a long while in purgatory, they will vouchsafe to assist and succour me with their holy prayers and satisfactory workes, especially with the holy sacrifice of the masse, as being the most effectuall meanes to deliver soules from their torments and paines; from the which, if I shall by gods gracious goodnesse and by their vertuous workes be delivered, I do promise that I will not be ungratefull unto them, for so great a benefitt.

XIII.

"*Item*, I John Shakspear doe by this my last will and testament bequeath my soul, as soon as it shall be delivered and loosened from the prison of this my body, to be entombed in the sweet and amorous coffin of the side of jesus Christ; and that in this life-giveing sepulcher it may rest and live, perpetually inclosed in that eternall habitation of repose, there to blesse for ever and ever that direfull iron of the launce, which, like a charge in a censore, formes so sweet and pleasant a monument within the sacred breast of my lord and saviour.

XIV.

"*Item*, lastly I John Shakspear doe protest, that I will willingly accept of death in what manner soever it may befall me, conforming my will unto the will of god; accepting of the same in satisfaction for my sinnes, and giveing thanks unto his divine majesty for the life he hath bestowed upon me. And if it please him to prolong or shorten the same, blessed be he also a thousand thousand times; into whose most holy hands I commend my soul and body, my life and death: and I beseech him above all things, that he never permit any change to be made by me John Shakspear of this my aforesaid will and testament. Amen.

"I John Shakspear have made this present writing of protestation, confession, and charter, in presence of the blessed virgin mary, my Angell guardian, and all the Celestiall Court, as witnesses hereunto: the which my meaning is, that it be of full value now presently and for ever, with the force and vertue of testament, codicill, and donation in 〈c〉ause of death; confirming it anew, being in perfect health of soul and body, and signed with mine own hand; carrying also the same about me; and for the better declaration hereof, my will and intention is that it be finally buried with me after my death.

> "Pater noster, Ave maria, Credo.
> "jesu, son of David, have mercy on me.
> Amen."[2]

Malone's favorable judgment was a considered one. As he recounts in the above passage, he had written to the Rev. James Davenport, vicar of Stratford-upon-Avon after 1787, "to examine more particularly concerning this manuscript." The nature of his doubts are plain from the letter, which he wrote on October 21, 1789.

I have some doubts concerning the very curious paper you were so good as to transmit to me, which you may, perhaps, be able to dispel;— it appears to me that the handwriting is at least thirty years more modern than the year 1601, when John Shakspeare, the father of our poet, died; and the spelling is in many places not sufficiently ancient;— thus we frequently find the words *mercy, majesty,* etc.—the name Shakspeare is written throughout with* a final *e,* a practice which began to prevail in the middle of the last century, but of which I have not found a single instance before in any instrument whatsoever;— the pointing throughout is remarkably correct, but perhaps this may have been by Mr. Payton or by you;—it is very unlucky that the first leaf is lost, as in the first article we probably should have found a description of the occupation of the writer and the time when it was drawn up;—is there the most remote chance of finding it now?—how long had he [Mosely] this little relique in his possession before he gave it to Mr. Payton, and did he ask any price for it?—did Mr. Thos. Hart ever hear of it?—it is very remarkable that among the children of old John Shakspeare recorded in your register, there is not one of the name of John.—I have sometimes been inclined to think that there was an elder son of that name born before the commencement

---

*In his note marked * the editor, Halliwell-Phillipps, calls attention to the mistake by Malone or by a transcriber in writing *"with* a final *e"* for *"without."* In Malone's text, based on the original, the name is spelled "Shakspear," without a final *e.*

of the register; and if such a one there was, and he lived to the year 1630, or thereabouts, this paper might have been written by him, and this would solve some of the difficulties which I have stated; yet to find a person so deeply tinged with popery at that late period, appointing the blessed Virgin his executress, appears strange also;—if there even was a younger John, he must have died, I think, before 1608.— I beg to know whether there is any tombstone within or without your church that marks the place where John Shakspeare was buried.—I have been able to make out the whole of the last leaf of this curious paper, in which the ink is very faint, and some of the words almost obliterated, except one line, concerning which I have some doubts; —the passage is in the thirteenth article, and runs thus;—'there to blesse for ever and ever the direful iron of the launce, which *like a charge in a censore*, formes so sweet and pleasant a monument within the sacred breast of my lord and Saviour;'—the words underscored are those I doubt about—are the contents of a censor called anywhere in the sacred writings its *charge?*—in the last article the writer desires that his will, as he calls it, may be buried with him;—perhaps that request may have been complied with, and this may have been a copy made previous to his interment;—to investigate this would be curious. —I beg to know whether the numerals III, V, etc., prefixed to the articles, were originally prefixed, or were added since?—I have this moment observed that in the twelfth article he exhorts his *parents* to pray for him, another circumstance which leads us to a younger John.[3]

The results of this inquiry allayed the doubts of Malone, for he decided to publish the document in his forthcoming edition of Shakespeare's works and had the manuscript set up into type. The printer proceeded to print the pages.

Then occurred the experience which Malone reports in his *Emendations and Additions* and which Reed prints "inclosed in crotchets." In a small quarto book belonging to Jordan and forwarded by him through Dr. Davenport to Malone, Malone found the text of the spiritual will of John Shakespeare *complete*. Naturally he was surprised, for he had seen the original manuscript only in a mutilated form, and through his inquiries he had been led to believe that the manuscript had been found mutilated. Puzzled, he wrote to Jordan on March 10, 1790, as follows:

You have inserted a copy of this religious testament of John Shakespeare, whom I believe to have been the poet's eldest brother. The original of this was, some time ago, transmitted to me by Mr. Davenport, but the first leaf was wanting, containing the first two articles and part of the third, in consequence of which I have been obliged to

print it imperfect. On my writing to Stratford on this subject I understood that Mr. Hart said it wanted the first leaf *when originally found*;
and Mr. Payton, I think, concurred in the same account. How, then,
have you made a copy of the first two articles and part of the third?
When was your copy made and from whom did you obtain the original?
And did you some years ago send a copy of this paper to the printer of
the *Gentleman's Magazine?*[4]

Jordan replied to Malone in a long letter dated March 19, 1790, and
made a full account of all he knew about the manuscript. He wrote:

I think myself much honoured by your agreeable letter, and am pleased
with the queries you have proposed therein, and I shall therefore answer them as well as my poor abilities will enable me to do; querie
first,—The religious will of John Shakspeare, whom I believe to have
been the poet's father, and not his elder brother, as you seem to have
suggested by an interpolation, was given to me in June, 1785,* by
Joseph Mosely, a bricklayer of Stratford, who said he found it in 1757;
—I observed to him that the beginning was wanting; he answered it
was, but it was perfect when he found it; he said that soon after he
discovered it, he shewed it to old Mr. Payton, who read it over, and
returned it to him, saying he wished the name had been William
instead of John; and that there was no farther notice taken of it, but
it had been thrown about the house in a careless manner till he had
mentioned it to me;—I asked him if he had ever shewed it to Thomas
Hart; he said he had not;—Thomas Hart never knew of this till I told
him of it, which was thirty years after it was found.—I told him I
should be glad to have it perfect; he answered he would endeavour to
find what was wanting and would help me to it;—after this I saw no
more of him for a long time, during the interval of which I shewed it
to Mr. Keating, the bookseller, who desired a copy, which I gave him,
who shewed it to several gentlemen for their opinion, some whereof
looked upon it as authentick while others thought it a fiction; among
the latter was the Rev. Jos. Greene, A. M., rector of Welford, near
Stratford, who is a gentleman possessed with much classical knowledge
and antiquarian sagacity, with whom I had a good deal of conversation
upon the matter;—I told him I should like to have the opinion of the
publick; he advised me so to do; accordingly I sent it in the state it
then was to the printer of the Gentleman's Magazine for that purpose,
who rejected it as spurious; therefore my wishes and curiosity remained
unsatisfied;—after this I applied to Mosely for what was wanting,

*Note the discrepancy in the date here with the date given in Jordan's letter to the
editor of the *Gentleman's Magazine.* i.e., 1784.

who put me off from time to time till the autumn of 1786, when he came to me, and asked me to lend it to him to shew to Mr. Tomkins, the mercer, and said he would seek for what was wanting and return it to me again in a few days; but not performing his promise, some time after I asked him for it, and he said he had given it to Mr. Payton of Shottery, from whom I knew it was irrecoverable;—I then desired to know whether he had found the rest part of it, and he answered in the negative, and promised that, as soon as he did find it, I should have the first sight of it; this past on without any occurence till after Michaelmass in 1788, when he was taken ill in a decline, and, as I was going by his door he called me in and said he had found what was wanting of the writing, and I might copy it if I pleased, which I accordingly did, and was desirous of keeping the original, which was very much worn and torn, but he was very unwilling, and said he would give it to Mr. Payton, who had the rest part of it, but whether he ever did or not, I cannot say, for he died about Christmass following, so that if he never gave it to Mr. Payton it is intirely lost;—on the top of the outside leaf was the following memorandum,—'found the 29 of April, 1757';—this is all the information I am able to give of this matter, so beg leave to submitt it to your superior judgment to make of it what use you please.[5]

Still not perfectly satisfied with Jordan's explanation, Malone wrote him another letter on March 25, 1790.

Sir, I received your packet safe by the coach, and request to know whether the first copy which you made of John Shakespeare's will, and which you have inserted in your small quarto book, was taken from the original found by Joseph Mosely, or from a copy made by him or any other person, and whether the leaf which Mosely gave you shortly before his death, containing the first and second articles, was of the same size, and written in the same manner with the rest. The few leaves which were sent to me were very small, tacked together by a thread; the size the eighth part of a sheet, and the upper part of the last page but one almost illegible.

When did Mosely first mention his having found this paper (I mean the will) to any one?

Why should he ask you to lend him your copy to show Mr. Tompkins when he had himself the original?

Was the copy in your book made from that you gave Mr. Keating or from the original papers?[6]

Whatever the nature of Jordan's reply, if he made one, Malone came to the conclusion that the text of the missing paragraphs was authentic, and he published that text in the *Emendations and Additions* to make the Spiritual Last Will and Testament complete.

But Malone did not rest quiet with his judgment in the matter. He continued to study the problem. New documents came to his hand. He became interested in other miscellaneous papers alleged to be the work of Queen Elizabeth, of Henry, Earl of Southampton, and of William Shakespeare, the genuineness of which he suspected and the forgery of which by William Ireland he believed he could prove. While dealing with these Ireland forgeries, Malone may have felt more than usually cautious. At any rate he finally concluded that the Spiritual Will of John Shakespeare was not just what he had thought it to be. He announced his "retraction," as it is sometimes called, in his *An Inquiry into the Authenticity of Certain Miscellaneous Papers*, published in 1796. Speaking there in connection with the Profession of Faith of William Shakespeare, an Ireland forgery, Malone says:

> The Profession of Faith before us was manifestly formed on a Confession of Faith written by one John Shakspeare, which I published for the first time in the end of the year 1790.[118] It was found about the year 1770, by one Mosely, a master bricklayer, who usually worked with his men, being employed by Mr. Thomas Hart, (the fifth descendant in a direct line from our poet's sister, Joan Hart,) to new-tile the old house in Stratford, in which Shakspeare, on no good authority, is supposed to have been born. The paper was discovered between the rafters and the tiling of the house; and the evidence respecting its authenticity transmitted to me by my friend the Rev. Dr. Davenport, Vicar of Stratford-upon-Avon, appeared to me sufficiently satisfactory to warrant its publication. But in my conjecture concerning the writer of that paper, I certainly was mistaken; for I have since obtained documents that clearly prove it could not have been the composition of any one of our poet's family; as will be fully shewn in his Life.[7]

Malone never completed his *Life of William Shakspeare*. In preparation for its appearance in the *Third Variorum* edition of Shakespeare's works in 1821, James Boswell, the editor, finished the biography as well as he could from Malone's memoranda. Among those memoranda was a reiteration of Malone's retraction of the Spiritual Will, with an interesting modification. Speaking of William Shakespeare's legal will, Malone says:

> It commences with a pious declaration of his religious principles, but affords not the slightest countenance to a notion which has been

started, of Shakspeare being a Roman Catholick. To this supposition, I myself may have given some support by the publication some years ago, of a singular manuscript, purporting to be the confession of faith of John Shakspeare, whom I conjectured to have been either the father or brother of the poet; but I am now convinced that I was altogether mistaken. I have already, I trust, satisfactorily proved, p. 53, that he had no brother of the name of John, and I have as little doubt that the person by whom this paper was drawn up, was not his father.[8]

To the above passage Boswell adds a footnote:

Mr. Malone has already expressed this opinion, in his Detection of the Ireland forgery; and has there mentioned, that he had obtained documents which clearly proved that this confession of faith could not have been the composition of any one of our poet's family. I have not been able to discover this documentary evidence, but I suppose it may have been connected with his discovery of John Shakspeare the shoemaker, whom he mentions in the commencement of this Life, and who has been hitherto confounded with the poet's father. It is highly improbable, indeed, that the latter, who held the situation of Bailiff of Stratford, should have been a Roman Catholick.[9]

It does seem as if the documents which came to light had something to do with handwriting and authorship rather than with the contents of the will, for Malone specifically says that he was mistaken in his "conjecture concerning the writer of that paper" and that the documents "clearly prove it could not have been the composition of any one of our poet's family." The retraction is a limited one, and seems to be based on an uncertainty with regard to the script itself and to the author of it. Malone does not attack the contents of the script, as if he questioned their authenticity.

The earliest defender of John Shakespeare's will to take to print after Malone's retraction is George Chalmers. In his *An Apology for The Believers in the Shakspeare-Papers* (London, 1797), a reply to Malone's *Inquiry*, Chalmers takes Malone to task for inconsistency in logic in his rejection of William Shakspeare's Profession of Faith.

In the same strain, he [Malone] (b) [the "(b)" in Chalmers' text referring to "Inquiry, 197–8,"] objects, that though John Shakspeare made a confession of faith, in the reign of Elizabeth, it is improbable, William Shakspeare should make a profession of his faith, in the reign of King James. He had himself produced to the public, in 1790, the confession of John Shakspeare, which was found in the *hiding-hole* of the house of Shakspeare. From the sentiment, and the language, this confession appears to be the effusion of a Roman Catholic mind, and was probably drawn up by some Roman Catholic priest (c). If these premises be granted, it will follow, as a fair deduction, that the family of Shakspeare were Roman Catholics; a circumstance this, which is wholly consistent with what Mr. Malone is now studious to (d) inculcate, viz. "that this confession could not have been the composition of any of our poet's family." The thoughts, the language, the orthography, all demonstrate the truth of my conjecture, though Mr. Malone did not perceive this truth, when he first published this paper, in 1790. But, it was the performance of a *Clerke*, the undoubted work of the family priest.[10]

But in spite of Chalmers' ready defense of the Spiritual Will, by far the majority of later Shakespeareans rejected the document as a forgery.

Thus Charles Knight, in presenting the confession of faith of John Shakespeare, writes:

We have no hesitation whatever in believing this document to be altogether a fabrication. . . . We not only do not believe that it was "the composition of any one of our poet's family," nor "the undoubted work of the family priest," but we do not believe that it is the work of a Roman Catholic at all. It professes to be the writer's "last spiritual will, testament, confession, protestation, and confession of faith." Now, if the writer had been a Roman Catholic, or if it had been drawn up for his approval and signature by his priest, it would necessarily, professing such fulness and completeness, have contained something of belief touching the then material points of spiritual difference between the Roman and the Reformed Church. Nothing, however, can be more vague than all this tedious protestation and confession; with the exception that phrases, and indeed long passages, are introduced for the purpose of marking the supposed writer's opinions in the way that should be most offensive to those of a contrary opinion, as if by way of bravado or seeking of persecution. . . . in this his last confession, spiritual will, and testament, he calls upon all his kinsfolks to assist and succour him after his death "with the holy sacrifice of the mass," with a promise that he "will not be ungrateful unto them for so great a benefit," well knowing that by the Act of 1581 the saying of mass was punishable by a year's imprisonment and a fine of 200 marks, and the hearing of it by a similar imprisonment and fine of 100 marks. The fabrication appears to us as gross as can well be imagined.[11]

George Gilfillan, in his *The Poetical Works of William Shakespeare and the Earl of Surrey*, published in 1856, also rejects the document, writing as follows:

A silly attempt was made in the last century, by the fabrication of a MS., stated to be from the pen of John Shakespeare, to palm on the public the belief that Shakespeare's father was a Catholic, and that the poet, consequently, was brought up in that persuasion. This, however, has been shown conclusively to be false. John Shakespeare, in 1568, when the poet was four years old, was the chief magistrate of Stratford; and no chief magistrate at that period could have been a Papist.[12]

Halliwell-Phillipps, to whom we owe the earliest complete collection of documents related to the problem, likewise adopts a negative attitude. ". . . there can be no doubt," he writes, "that the whole of the paper is a modern fabrication."[13]

Karl Elze, in his *William Shakespeare: A Literary Biography*, published originally in 1876, rejects the document, writing "that the supposed will of John Shakespeare, found under the roof of Shakespeare's birthplace in 1770, is nothing but a gross piece of forgery. . . ."[14]

Throughout his various editions from 1898 to 1915 of *The Life of Shakespeare*, Sir Sidney Lee includes an appendix, "The Sources of Biographical Knowledge," in which he writes:

> Much notoriety was obtained by John Jordan (1746-1809), a resident at Stratford-on-Avon, whose most important achievement was the forgery of the will of Shakespeare's father. . . .[15]

In a report on "Recent Shakespearean Research" published in *The Quarterly Review* for October, 1921, C. R. Haines keeps up the barrage of condemnation when he writes: ". . . the so-called will of John Shakespeare, an absurd rigmarole found like a dead mouse behind the wainscot of the birthplace, still meets with ardent champions among Roman Catholics."[16]

Latest among the detractors of the document is B. Roland Lewis, who in his *The Shakespeare Documents* mentions the Birmingham Free Public Library, Birmingham, England, as one of the repositories of Shakespeare documents and says:

> Its chief manuscript possessions are the John Jordan manuscripts which, in part at least, appear to be forged. Among these are (a) the ballad of Sir Thomas Lucy, supposedly written by the youthful Shakespeare, (b) the Spiritual Last Will and Testament of John Shakespeare reputed to have been found under the tile roof of the Birthplace property. . . .[17]

A long list of biographers, including Joseph Hunter, George Russell French, Edward Dowden, Henry N. Hudson, James Walter, George

Brandes, William J. Rolfe, Frank Harris, Henry C. Beeching, Walter Raleigh, Max J. Wolff, George Saintsbury, William A. Neilson, Alois Brandl, Joseph Quincy Adams, and Edgar I. Fripp, make no mention of the document whatsoever and by their silence dismiss it as spurious. Carter, of course, interested in the Puritanism of John Shakespeare like Fripp, gives the will no place in his treatment of John Shakespeare's religion.

The ranks of the defenders of the document are very thin indeed. After George Chalmers, the first notable defender was Nathan Drake, M. D., who in his *Shakspeare and His Times*, first published in 1817, reproduced the text of the testament as he found it in Reed's edition of Shakespeare's works (Vol. iii, p. 199 *et seq.*), and supported Chalmers' opinion of the document. Drake wrote:

> This conjecture of Mr. Chalmers appears to us in its leading points very plausible; for that the father of our poet might be a Roman Catholic is, if we consider the very unsettled state of his times with regard to religion, not only a possible but a probable supposition: in which case, it would undoubtedly have been the office of the spiritual director of the family to have drawn up such a paper as that which we have been perusing. It was the fashion also of the period, as Mr. Chalmers has subsequently observed, to draw up confessions of religious faith, a fashion honoured in the observance by the great names of Lord Bacon, Lord Burghley, and Archbishop Parker.[18]

Between Drake's work and the end of the nineteenth century there was no voice to speak for the document. Then, in 1896, John Pym Yeatman, barrister of Lincoln's Inn, came forward with his *The Gentle Shakspere*, in which he included a chapter in vindication of "John Jordan, the Stratford Poet,"[19] published the will of "John Shakspere" as taken from Jordan's works,[20] and made an impassioned, if not scholarly, defence of its authenticity.[21]

Another recent champion of the document is H. S. Bowden, who, in one of the chapters of *The Religion of Shakespeare* written by himself and not edited from the writings of Richard Simpson, makes out a case for the will. He considers the "practice of making these spiritual testaments" as "common with catholics." He recalls that Malone never questioned the authenticity of the will itself. He points out the difficulties which Jordan would have had to overcome in successfully forging the document, since Mosely and Payton had both seen the original and would have checked him in his deceit. He asks what possible motive there could have been for forgery and suggests that there could have been none, as there was in the case of the forgery of William Shakespeare's Profession of Faith by Ireland. He concludes:

> The genuineness of the will is guaranteed by a chain of witnesses during some thirty or forty years, and its contents are in complete agreement, as has been shown, with the spiritual testaments drawn up by Catholics at that period. Against the evidence, internal and external, in favour of the will, the unsupported assumption of its forgery is not, we think, tenable. The will has therefore a right in our judgment to be regarded as genuine till further evidence to the contrary be adduced, and thus we leave it as forming the last witness to John Shakespeare's religious belief.[22]

Most notable of modern Shakespeare scholars who accept the will as authentic is Sir Edmund K. Chambers. In his *William Shakespeare: A Study of Facts and Problems*, he cautiously writes:

> Beyond the return itself [the recusancy return of 1592], the only document which may bear upon John Shakespeare's religion is the devotional will or *testamentum animae* found in the roof of one of his Henley St. houses in the eighteenth century. I do not think that this is a forgery, but if the John Shakespeare who made it was the poet's father, it probably dates from his early life, and carries little evidence as to his religious position under Elizabeth.[23]

Chambers explains his view more fully in an appendix, in which he characterizes Jordan as "a self-educated man of literary tendencies" who could not be thought "capable of any fabrication which required scholarly knowledge."

> . . . I cannot believe that he was responsible for the text of John Shakespeare's 'spiritual will' . . . . it is most unlikely that Jordan or anyone else in the 18th-century Stratford would reproduce the language of what certainly reads like the devotional exercise of a professing Catholic. . . . Even if the will is genuine, it does not quite follow that Shakespeare's father wrote it, although the discovery in his house points to this. If he did, it must have been in comparatively early life, as the writer refers to his 'parents'. He names as a patron St. Winifred, whose well at Holywell in Flintshire was a famous resort for pilgrims.[24]

Credit for a major contribution to the solution of the problem of John Shakespeare's will should go to Herbert Thurston, S. J. In an article published as long ago as May, 1882, in *The Month*,[25] Thurston expressed his dissatisfaction with the prevailing interpretation of the document as a forgery by Jordan and affirmed his confidence in the original opinion of Malone that the document was an authentic bit of late sixteenth- or early seventeenth-century writing. Thirty years later Thurston wrote another article for *The Month*, entitled "The Spiritual Testament of John Shakespeare,"[26] in which he gave a full account of the history of the document, with transcriptions of Malone's version of the complete will; Malone's first account of the finding of the will and of his investigation of its authenticity; Malone's "emendation" after the discovery of Jordan's complete text; Malone's letter to Davenport, October 21, 1789; Malone's two letters to Jordan, March 10 and March 25, 1790; and finally Malone's retraction in his *Inquiry*, 1796. Thurston had not come upon Jordan's reply to Malone's letter of March 10, 1790, until after the article was written, and he could only mention the reply in a concluding footnote. Though Thurston confessed misgivings with regard to the first two articles and part of the third, he felt more than ever convinced that Malone's original opinion with regard to the remainder of the document was correct.

At length his confidence was rewarded. By great luck in 1923, or shortly before, he found, in the British Museum, a Spanish version of a spiritual testament consisting of fourteen articles and corresponding, phrase for phrase from the middle of Article III to the end, with the Spiritual Testament of John Shakespeare. Here is his account of the discovery:

It was . . . a matter of some satisfaction when, after long search, I at last stumbled upon the original of this curious paper [John's testament]. Strange to say, I met it first under conditions as remote as possible from any suggestion of Elizabethan recusancy. Happening to open a tiny booklet of half a dozen leaves, printed in the city of Mexico, A. D. 1661, I came upon the following title page:

TESTAMENTO O ULTIMA
VOLUNTAD DEL ALMA

hecho en Salud para assegurarse el christiano de las tentaciones del Demonio, en la hora de la muerte; Ordenado por San Carlos Borromeo, Cardenal del Santa Praxedis, y Arcobispo de Milan.
(rude woodcut of the crucifixion)
Con licencia. En Mexico.
Por la Viuda de Bernardo Calderon, en la calle de San Agostino. Año de 1661.

[Translation by Thurston, in footnote:]

The Testament or Last Will of the Soul, made in health for the Christian to secure himself from the temptations of the devil at the hour of death, drawn up by St. Charles Borromeo, Cardinal of St. Praxedis and Archbishop of Milan. With licence. At Mexico by the widow of Bernard Calderon, St. Augustin's Street, 1661.

A brief examination showed at once that the form therein printed was a Spanish version of the document which in Malone's copy was associated with the name of John Shakespeare. Every phrase in the English text—imperfect, it will be remembered, at the beginning— finds its counterpart in this Mexican leaflet.[27]

The testament was signed in ink by "Juan Phelipe Hernandez" in a blank space provided for the purpose in the first article only. (In the will of John Shakespeare, all fourteen articles contain the testator's name.)

Thurston also uncovered other versions of the same testament: one, a "copy of the same Spanish text, written throughout by hand, which is bound up in MS. Egerton 443, also at the British Museum . . . . apparently made before the year 1690 by some professional scribe for the use of one Maria Teresa de Cardenas";[28] another, printed in the Romansch dialect at Barraduz, [*sic* in Thurston] (Switzerland) in 1741;[29] and still a third, an Italian text of the document, printed as an appendix in the *Life of St. Alessandro Sauli* by Francesco Saverio Maria Bianchi (edition of Bologna, 1878, though the work itself is older).[30] And a seventeenth-century French testament "on the same lines" was found in the Bibliothèque Nationale by Clara Longworth de Chambrun, who quotes a part to compare it with Article XII of John Shakespeare's will to show the close similarity.[31]

Thurston's fortunate discovery has come to serve a number of purposes in explaining "the very curious paper" which Malone first introduced to the world.

(1) In the first place it proves the document to be a formula of devotion. Chalmers had hinted as much when he called the testament "the performance of a *Clerke*, the undoubted work of the family priest." Drake had strengthened Chalmers' presumption that it was a formula of devotion by emphasizing the fact that it was the fashion of the times "to draw up confessions of religious faith" and citing instances of confessions by Bacon, Burghley, and Parker. Yeatman and Bowden also had insisted upon the formulary nature of the document. Bowden, deriving his information from Thurston's earliest article in *The Month* (May, 1882), had pointed to "forms for the *Testamentum animae*" which "are to be found in English Primers of the sixteenth century" and with which

the Shakespeare document "corresponds in matter and style."[32] Bowden had cited Father Gaspar Loarte's *Exercise of the* [sic] *Christian Life*, which had been translated into English and printed as early as 1579, and "two other brief forms of spiritual wills englished from the *Sarum Horae* of 1508" as found in Maskell's *Monumenta Ritualia Ecclesiae Anglicanae*.[33]

In his 1911 article, before his own discovery, Thurston himself had quoted an example of a devotional formula suitable for use in prospect of death from Loarte's *Exercise of a* [sic] *Christian Life* and had called attention to the *Manual of Prayers* of 1596 and to the *Enchiridium* compiled by Verepaeus, of contemporary date, as circumstantial evidence of the formulary nature of the Shakespeare will.[34] His discovery of a printed copy of the formula clinched the argument. Objections, such as those raised by Chambers,[35] to the effect that the devotional formulas cited by Bowden and Thurston do not exactly correspond to the Shakespeare document in that they are not of a testamentary character, fall away in the presence of the Spanish duplicate. The assumptions of Chalmers, Drake, Bowden, and Thurston himself, founded on a knowledge of Catholic customs and on a kinship with the Catholic spirit, were vindicated.

The formulary nature of the document helps to explain Malone's difficulties with regard to handwriting, spelling, and punctuation. As quoted above, Malone thought the handwriting was "thirty years more modern than the year 1601," and his reasons for thinking so were that "the spelling is not sufficiently ancient;—thus we frequently find the words *mercy, majesty,* etc. [instead of merc*ie* or merc*ye* and majest*ie* or majest*ye*]—the name Shakspeare is written throughout with[out] a final *e*, a practice which began to prevail in the middle of the last century [17th], but of which I have not found a single instance before in any instrument whatsoever;—the pointing throughout is remarkably correct. . . ."

With regard to the spelling of *"mercy"* and *"majesty"* as being too modern, it needs only to be remarked that "mercie," "mercye," and "mercy" and "majestie," "majestye," and "majesty" occur repeatedly throughout *The Prayer Book of Queen Elizabeth* issued in 1559.*

From the spelling of the name "Shakspear" without the final *e*, little can be inferred. In the first place there was no uniformity among the Shakespeares in the spelling of the name. The research of Joseph Hunter

---

*For "mercy" see "The Ordre for the Administracion of the Lordes Supper, or Holy Communion," p. 93. In the "Te Deum" (p. 45) the spellings "mercy" and "mercie" occur in the same line. For "majesty" see "Te Deum" (p. 44), "A Prayer for the Queenes Majesty" (p. 58), and "The Collect" for the First Sunday of Advent (p. 61).

(*New Illustrations*, 1845) revealed no fewer than twenty-six spellings in contemporary materials and as many as fifty-five different spellings in all. Later research by others has revealed even greater variety: Edmund Chambers (*William Shakespeare*, 1930) reports eighty-three variants; B. Roland Lewis (*The Shakespeare Documents*, 1940) lists more than one hundred.[36]

In the second place, instances of the name spelled without the final *e* occur long before Malone was able to find them: "Shakesper" at London in 1506 and at Nottinghamshire in 1549;[37] "Shakyspear" in a Wroxall will in 1539;[38] "Shaxper" at Balsall in 1575 and at Warwick in 1577.[39] The earliest instance of the spelling of "Shakspear" (the spelling of the Spiritual Testament) which Lewis cites is at London in 1605.[40]

Since there is no signature of John Shakespeare extant, we cannot know which of the many variants John himself preferred. But it is illuminating to consider that Richard Simons, the town clerk of Stratford, adopted the spelling "John Shakspeyr" as early as October 1, 1557,[41] and used it repeatedly throughout the minutes of the Stratford Corporation.[42] The variant adopted by Simons' deputy when the good town clerk was absent was "Shacksper," the spelling found in the records of meetings of the Corporation held August 30, September 6, and September 27, 1564.[43] In the official copies of the accounts of John Shakespeare and his fellow chamberlain John Taylor, made by Simons, John's name is spelled "John Shakspeyr."[44] The same is true for the accounts rendered by the two men as acting-chamberlains.[45] May this not suggest John Shakespeare's own preference for spelling his name without a final *e*? The suggestion is made stronger by the fact that in the chamberlains' account submitted January 10, 1563/4, by John Taylor and John Shakspeare an item of expenditure reads: ". . . payd to shakspeyr for a pece tymbur."[46] Though the copy is made by Simons, would he not be disposed to spell the name of the man who made the report the way he found it in the report itself? At least, the successor of Richard Simons, Henry Higford, adopted a spelling without a final *e* in recording the newly elected high bailiff as "John Shakysper"[47] and in a few other entries.[48] Higford's favorite spelling of the name, however, was "Shakyspere." Henry Rogers, who succeeded Higford in 1570, adopted the spelling "Shakespere," with the variant "Shaxpere" appearing in his later records. But the name without the final *e* frequently occurs throughout the records of these later clerks and in other documents. The minutes of a Corporation meeting held November 3, 1574, written in a strange hand, have "John shaksper."[49] Again in December, 1579, "Johannes shaxper"[50] appears. In the book of gentlemen and freeholders in the County of Warwick, 1580, the alderman of Stratford is listed as "John

Shaxper."[51] Corporation minutes for January 31, 1581/2, note the absence of "Johannes shaxper."[52] When the delinquent alderman presents himself on September 5, 1582, to vote for John Sadler for bailiff, he is listed as "Johannes Shaxper."[53] The spelling on November 16, 1582, is "Johannes Shackesper."[54] Again, on January 23, 1582/3, it is "Shaxper."[55] On February 1, 1582/3, it is "Shackeser."[56] This spelling recurs on August 21, 1583.[57] "Shaxper" appears on October 4 and October 16, 1583.[58] On April 10, 1584, "Shackesper" occurs.[59] But when the alderman was eventually dismissed from the Corporation, he was written off as "John Shaxpere," *with* the final *e*.[60] Although as a recusant in the recusancy returns of 1592, the poet's father was reported as "John Shackspeare," and "John Shackespere," both spellings with a final *e*, in that very same year, on August 21, his name is spelled "John Shaksper senior," *without* the final *e*, in an inventory of the goods of Henry Field, made by Thomas Trussell, Master John Shakespeare, Richard Spooner, and others.[61] Most interesting of all, the burial entry in the Stratford Parish Register reads:

1601, Septembr 8. Mr Johañes Shakspear.[62]

In the light of these many exceptions, unknown of course to Malone, it is no longer necessary to consider the document under discussion as being of a late date because of the spelling of "Shakspear" without a final *e*.

And the "remarkably correct" pointing throughout the document, *too* correct to assure Malone, is also satisfactorily explained by the fact that the document is a devotional formula. The original had been drawn up by a scholar on the Continent where pointing was more regular, and translations and copies had been made by educated Catholic priests. This very regularity is an argument in favor of the authenticity of the document rather than against it, for, as Thurston has pointed out,[63] forgers of Elizabethan documents tended to exaggerate the irregular spelling of the period. The manuscript was, as we now believe, a copy of a model manuscript or of a printed form in general circulation, and nothing less than regularity, both in spelling and in pointing, could be expected in it.*

It should not be forgotten that Malone himself, after expressing early doubts with respect to the handwriting in 1789, became better satisfied, for in publishing the text he wrote:

The handwriting is undoubtedly not so ancient as that *usually* written about the year 1600; but I have now before me a manuscript written

---

*The formulary character of the document also explains the apparent inconsistency in the insertion in Article X of the name of only one patron "(saint Winefride)" after the plural form "patrons."

by Alleyn the player at various times between 1599 and 1614, and another by Forde, the dramatick poet, in 1606, in nearly the same handwriting as that of the manuscript in question.

(2) Thurston's fortunate discovery discloses the original source of the manuscript copy. Three of the four cognate versions of John Shakespeare's will known to Thurston: the Mexico City Spanish copy of 1661, the Spanish version in MS. Egerton 443 dating before 1690, and the Romansch dialect copy printed in Switzerland in 1741, bear a preamble or head ascribing the testament to St. Charles Borromeo, Cardinal Archbishop of Milan. The Italian copy does not carry such a heading, but it appears as an appendix in the biography of Alessandro Sauli, a friendship with whom, "begun in student days at Pavia and . . . renewed at Mantua . . . was one of the deepest of Charles' life."[64] Although Francisco Adorno, S. J., was Borromeo's spiritual adviser at the time of the Cardinal's death on November 3, 1584, Borromeo had made "a general confession of his whole life" to the "learned and saintly Barnabite friar, Alessandro Sauli."[65] The relationship between the two men was intimate enough to warrant the assumption that the confession in the appendix of Sauli's *Life* is not his own, but that of his venerable superior.

There is no reason for doubting the ascription of authorship to Borromeo. An excellent occasion for his writing the devotional formula would have been the "Plague of St. Charles," which struck Milan during the years 1576–78 and carried off an estimated 17,000 souls. So eminent was the leadership of the Cardinal Archbishop in those dreadful years that the plague has come to bear his name.[66]

Borromeo's authorship of the testament helps explain the presence of copies in England during the last years of the life of John Shakespeare. The document was taken there, in all probability, by the Jesuit missionaries who, under the leadership of Father Edmund Campion and Father Robert Persons, reached England in 1580. The missionary party, for the moment consisting of ten priests and two laymen,* on its way from Rome to England, stopped at Milan early in May, 1580.

*Members of the party were: "Three of the Society, Fr Campian, Fr Persons and Ralph Emerson, lay brother. . . . Five of the English Seminary, three priests and two scholars, Mr. Ralph Sherwin, Luke Kirby, Edw. Rishton, Thomas Brisco, and John Paschal. . . . Four ancient grave priests, Mr Edward Brombery, D. D., Mr Will. Giblet, Mr Thos Crane, Mr Will. Kemp. . . ." Robert Persons, *Vita Campiani* (fol. 106), cited by J. H. Pollen in Catholic Record Society *Miscellanea* (London, 1906), II, 26, footnote **. Pollen is citing the quotation in Father Christopher Grene's *Douay Diaries*, p. 172. Dr. Thomas Goldwell, Bishop of St. Asaph, was a member of the party when it left Rome, but had gone on ahead.

St. Charles Borromeo received our pilgrims into his house, and kept them there for eight days. He made Sherwin preach before him, and he made Campion discourse every day after dinner. "He had," says Parsons, "sundry learned and most godly speeches with us, tending to the contempt of this world, and perfect zeal of Christ's service, whereof we saw so rare an example in himself and his austere and laborious life; being nothing in effect but skin and bone, through continual pains, fasting, and penance; so that without saying a word, he preached to us sufficiently, and we departed from him greatly edified and exceedingly animated.[67]

That this visit of the Persons-Campion missionary party was not the only contact between St. Charles Borromeo and English Catholics is demonstrated by other evidence. An entry for September, 1580, in the "Annals or Diary of the English College, Rome" reads:

In September we sent to England for the help of the souls there led astray, the Revv. George Birket, John Gore, Antony Tirill, Edward Gratley, in priest's Orders.[1] [Footnote reference is in text] . . . .
(They were entertained by St. Charles Borromeo at Milan, as appears from his letter to Father Alphonsus Agazzari, dated September 29, 1590.) [In the handwriting of Father Grene][68]

The missionary technique of the Jesuits in England is described by Persons in his *Of the Life and Martyrdom of Edmund Campion*, written in 1594 and left unfinished.

We entered for the most part as acquaintance or kinsfolk of some person that lived within the house, and when that failed us, as passengers or friends of some gentleman that accompanied us, and after ordinary salutations we had our lodging by procurement of the Catholics within the house, in some part retired from the rest, where putting ourselves in priest's apparel and furniture, which ever we carried with us, we had view and secret conference with the Catholics that were there, or such of them as might conveniently come, whom we ever caused to be ready for that night late to prepare themselves to the Sacrament of Confession, and the next morning very early we had Mass and the Blessed Sacrament ready for such as would communicate, and after that an exhortation, and then we made ourselves ready to depart again, and this was the manner of providing when we stayed least, but when longer and more liberal and full stay was, then these exercises were more frequented.[69]

This account is supplemented by a report sent by Edmund Campion to the General of the Society of Jesus in a letter the probable date of which is November, 1580.

I ride about some piece of the country every day. The harvest is wonderful great.* On horseback I meditate my sermon; when I come to the house I polish it. Then I talke with such as come to speak with me, or hear their confessions. In the morning, after Mass, I preach; they hear with exceeding greediness and very many go to the sacraments, for the ministration whereof we are ever well assisted by the priests, whom we find in every place, whereby both the people is well served and we much eased in our charge. The priests of our country themselves being most excellent for virtue and learning, yet have raised so great an opinion of our Society that I dare scarcely touch the exceeding reverence all Catholics do unto us.[70]

The use of such a formula as a spiritual last will and testament by the Jesuit missioners and by other priests as they came in contact with the Jesuits would be occasional. There are two expressions which occur in the correspondence of Jesuits of the period which hint at the use of the formula in England.

The first appears in another part of the letter of Campion quoted above. Estimating the fruits of his labor and that of his comrades, Campion wrote: "Very many even at this present are being restored to the Church, new soldiers *give up their names* while the veterans offer their blood; by which holy hosts and oblations God will be pleased, and we shall, no question, by Him soon overcome."[71] The italicized expression hints at the signing of a formula, though if the "new soldiers" were new converts, the tactlessness of having new converts sign last wills and testaments favors the conclusion that such formulae were not meant.

A better bit of evidence is found in a letter of Dr. William Allen, rector of the English College in France, to Father Alphonsus Agazzari, rector of the English College at Rome, the starting point of the Jesuit mission to England and a close point of contact with the Italian Church. On June 23, 1581, Allen wrote from Rheims:

We have heard from England, by a letter of F. Robert Parsons, S. J., that the persecution still rages with the same fury, the Catholics being

---

*Just how "wonderful" the harvest was cannot be determined, but Martin P. Harney, S. J., in his *The Jesuits in History* (New York, 1941), p. 148, says that Campion and Persons "brought back in the one short year of their hazardous apostolate at least 10,000 souls. Some have placed the number much higher." Dr. William Allen, rector of the English College at Rheims, writing to Father Agazzari, rector of the English College at Rome, June 23, 1581, said, ". . . it is supposed that there are twenty thousand more Catholics this year than last." (Cited by Richard Simpson, *Edmund Campion*, p. 210.)

haled away to prison and otherwise vexed, and the Fathers of the Society being most diligently looked for; but they are still, by God's singular providence, at liberty. . . .

Father Robert wants *three or four thousand or more of the Testaments*, for many persons desire to have them. . . .[72]

Just what are the "Testaments" requested by Father Persons? The first impression is that they are *New* Testaments, in the Rheims translation. But one fact makes the impression erroneous. The date is wrong. Dr. Allen's letter was written June 23, 1581, at least nine months too early for it to refer to the Rheims New Testament. *The First and Second Diaries of the English College, Douay* (London, 1878) reveal that, though the translation of the Vulgate New Testament into English was begun at Rheims by Gregory Martin on or about October 16, 1578,[73] the work was not completed until March, 1582, under which date appears the entry, "Hoc ipso mense extrema manus Nouo Testamento Anglice edito imposita est."[74] The title-page shows the book to have been "printed at Rhemes by John Fogny, 1582."[75]

Not only is the date of publication against the assumption that Dr. Allen was forwarding a request for Rheims New Testaments, but the size and cost of that New Testament are also against it. Pope describes the book as a "handsome quarto volume,"[76] in which the text alone filled 742 pages (3–745), and "the very lengthy preface" and "supplementary pieces"[77] occupied forty-nine more. Three or four thousand copies of an 800-page quarto volume to be transported from Rome to England would present a problem in logistics knotty enough to baffle even the ingenious Jesuits. And though the problem of transportation were solved, the risk of getting such bulky merchandise past the port officers of England would be so great as to compel hesitation about going forward with the matter. Then, assuming that the New Testaments actually got to England, the priests would still have great trouble in disposing of them, for the price was high. Pope estimates that the cost of publishing was £4 [$20] a copy.[78] In view of this high cost, though Pope says, ". . . it is tempting to suppose that the edition was . . . not a small one,"[79] it is scarcely probable that the original edition ran large enough to fill a request for three or four thousand copies at any single source.

Finally, since the New Testament was printed at Rheims, there would be little point in Dr. Allen's sending a request for copies from Rheims to Rome.

All this, of course, while it proves the Testaments asked for were not Rheims New Testaments, does not prove that they were testaments of the sort made by John Shakespeare. But when it is recalled, first, that the English College at Rome was the generative point of the Jesuit missionary effort in England; second, that more than a year had elapsed between the visit of the missionary party with Cardinal Borromeo at Milan and the request for copies of testaments to be sent from Rome (thus allowing time for the exhaustion of any small supply of Italian versions which the Jesuits may have brought with them for actual use in profession, or as a basis for translating manuscript copies into English, and for the making of arrangements for the unhindered printing of copies of an English translation at Rome); and, third, that the testaments when printed would make a small* booklet of no more than six pages, it is not unreasonable to assume that spiritual last wills and testaments were meant.

If the three or four thousand testaments were of the sort devised by Cardinal Borromeo and if, in response to Father Robert's request, they got to England in reasonable time, it is easy to see how some copies reached Warwickshire and Stratford-upon-Avon.

A question, however, arises in connection with the fact that the original of John Shakespeare's testament was in manuscript form throughout. Two possible answers suggest themselves. The first is that John Shakespeare's will was a priest's copy of a printed *English* model. It is easy to understand that three or four thousand printed copies sent from Rome to Persons would hardly meet the demand in every quarter of England during the first years of missionary success. Not only did "many persons desire to have them," but problems of distribution kept printed copies from those who wanted them. A good executive like Persons would see to it that printed copies were distributed among key priests, so that these priests could themselves make manuscript copies for use among the Catholic adherents of their neighborhood. And as the Jesuit mission lost momentum through the execution of Edmund Campion and the departure of Persons for the Continent, the probability diminishes that the supply of testaments was renewed. Printed copies sent from Rome in 1581 would soon all have been signed and hence rendered useless for others. The secret presses which the Jesuits managed to set up would be kept busy printing books of greater importance. The formula might have been kept in use then through manuscript copies written out by priests from the few precious printed copies remaining in their hands. One of these could have been signed by John Shakespeare.

The second answer suggested is that John Shakespeare was among those reached by the Jesuits early in their mission, before the arrival of the printed testaments from Rome. In that case a manuscript transla-

---

*Malone said his manuscript original was "the size of the eighth part of a sheet." See his letter to Jordan, March 25, 1790.

lation would have been made from the *Italian* version supplied by Borromeo. Somewhat in support of this suggestion is the tradition mentioned
by J. H. Pollen that "Person's harvest . . . included John Shakespeare,
the father of the poet."[80]

(3) The question of whether John Shakespeare himself performed the
physical act of signing the testament must remain unanswered. Malone
does not tell us whether the signature was in a different hand from the
remainder of the testament. In this connection, Malone's expression of
regret that the first sheet had been lost is especially appropriate. If a
signature was to be placed anywhere, it would certainly be upon the
first sheet of such a document. Thereafter, the transcribing priest might
well write the name of the testator as an integral part of his transcription. In view of the fact that Malone was troubled about the handwriting
of the manuscript, it seems probable that the signature and the profession were in the same hand and that Malone, coming to believe that
John Shakespeare could not write, concluded that the testament was not
his. Since the days of Malone, however, the literacy of John Shakespeare
has been accepted by many Shakespearean scholars,[81] so that if Malone's
doubts were of this sort, they were needless. However, the fact of John
Shakespeare's ability or lack of ability to sign his own name is not pertinent here, since the first sheet of the original document was never seen
by any Shakespearean scholar and since the remaining sheets could have
been written by a clerk. Hence it is that Thurston's discovery serves a
third purpose in dispensing with the necessity of proving or assuming
John Shakespeare's literacy.

(4) A fourth purpose happily served by Thurston's discovery is the
solution of certain textual difficulties.

First of these are the difficulties which Malone proposed. In writing to
Davenport before publishing the text of the document, Malone said
that the ink was very faint on the last leaf, but that he had been able to
make out the whole of it

> . . . except one line, concerning which I have some doubts;—the
> passage is in the thirteenth article, and runs thus;—'there to blesse
> for ever and ever the direful iron of the launce, which *like a charge in a
> censore*, formes so sweet and pleasant a monument within the sacred
> breast of my lord and Saviour;'—the words underscored are those I
> doubt about—are the contents of a censor called anywhere in the
> sacred writings its *charge*?

Jordan had seen the original of this passage five or six years earlier
than Malone. In his version he wrote *"like a sharp-cutting razor."*[82] The
Spanish version at this point reads *"a modo de sincel agudo,"* and the

Italian version, *"a guisa di scalpello pungente."*[83] It becomes evident immediately that Jordan's transcription was the correct one and that Malone's doubts were founded on a misreading of the illegible text.

A second difficulty raised in the mind of Malone by the text is the use of the words "parents" in Article XII. In his letter to Davenport he wrote: "I have this moment observed that in the twelfth article he exhorts his *parents* to pray for him, another circumstance which leads us to a younger John." The difficulty here is not with the reading of the word "parents" but with its meaning. In the English version the word occurs in the phrase "all my dear friends, *parents*, and kinsfolks." The parallel phrase in the Italian and Spanish versions is *"amigos y parientes."* *"Parientes,"* derived from the Latin *parens*, here means *relatives*. John Shakespeare could have used the word in the Romance sense long after his father and mother were dead. Malone need not have looked for "a younger John."

A third textual difficulty removed by Thurston's discovery is one of which Malone was not aware. In Malone's 1790 printed version of the document, a passage in Article IV beseeches pardon for ". . . all my sins committed by seeing, speaking, *feeling*, smelling, hearing, touching or by any other way whatsoever." This passage as rendered by Jordan contained the word "justing" for Malone's *"feeling."* Both transcribers erred in this case, for the word in the original was "gusting," an Elizabethan word for "tasting." The whole article has to do with the testator's request for "the last sacrament of extreme unction." Thurston points out that "in the ritual form of the Sacrament the priest when anointing the lips prays that God may forgive *quidquid per gustum et loquelam deliquisti, i. e.*, the sins committed by 'speaking and gusting' (tasting.)"[84]

(5) The major textual difficulty which Thurston's discovery solves is, of course, the contents of the original first two and a half articles. The restoration of this part of the document is so important as to deserve separate treatment.

The text of the first two articles and part of the third, as supplied by the Mexican and Italian versions of the Spiritual Testament, translated by Herbert Thurston, is as follows:

Preamble (*Cabeza*) of the Testament

The dangers to which human life is exposed being countless, and I, Juan Phelipe Hernandez, knowing that I am a mortal man, born only to die, without knowledge of the hour at which this debt will have to be discharged, in order that I may not be taken unprepared [and that my flight may not be in winter or on the sabbath day, as our Saviour says in the gospel]* have taken thought with the divine aid to prepare myself for that uncertain hour, since God now gives me the time; and so with my whole heart being prostrate before the feet of Christ our Lord, as He hangs upon the cross, I declare unto the world my last will in the following form.

In the name of the Father, and of the Son, and of the Holy Ghost.

In the first place as the foundation of all salvation, I, Juan Phelipe Hernandez, declare and confess in the presence of Almighty God, Father, Son and Holy Ghost, three Persons in one God, of the most holy Virgin and all the Court of Heaven, that I wish to live and die obedient to the Holy Roman Church, firmly believing all the fourteen articles of the Faith* taught by the holy Apostles, all the interpretations and declarations made upon them by the Holy Catholic Church, and all that the same Catholic Church, guided by the Holy Ghost, has taught, defined and declared.

Item. I protest in this same form that at the end of life I desire to receive the most holy Viaticum, in order to unite me perfectly and peacefully with my Lord Jesus Christ by means of so divine a Sacrament; the which if by some accident I should be unable then to receive, I now declare in view of that time that it is my purpose to receive it. . . .[85]

This text is quite different from Jordan's version as printed by Malone. It is different in content and in style and tone. The difference in content is obvious. The most notable difference in style and tone is between the verbose extravagance of Jordan's text and the restraint of the Spanish and Italian texts.† The Jordan text seems excessive in its very first sentence, opening the testament with an elaborate list of witnesses: "In the name of God, the father, sonne, and holy ghost, the most holy and blessed Virgin Mary, mother of God, the holy host of archangels, angels, patriarchs, prophets, evangelists, apostles, saints, martyrs, and all the celestial court and company of heaven," whereas the Borromeo text seems reverently simple, making the confession "in the presence of Almighty God, Father, Son and Holy Ghost, three Persons in one God, of the most holy Virgin and all the Court of Heaven." The Jordan text seems influenced by the redundancy of secular legal instruments and employs such expressions as "sound mind, memory, and understanding," "all my transgressions externally and internally," "sacrament, pennance, fasting, or prayer, or any other purgation whatever," "of my own free and voluntary accord," "make and ordaine," "will, testament, confession, protesta-

†Thurston's discovery proves that the Jordan version is a sixth longer than the Borromeo original translated into English.

tion, and confession of faith." There is no such legal redundancy in the Borromeo text, either in these early articles or in those which follow. While it must be admitted that there is a certain wordiness throughout the Borromeo testament, that wordiness is not the wordiness of a lawyer seeking to close the last legal loophole, but the wordiness of a priest seeking to attain the solemnity of a ritualistic formula.

How can these differences in content, style, and tone be accounted for? Malone, we remember, was eager for a satisfactory explanation of Jordan's possession of the text of these early articles. He wrote to Jordan on March 10, 1790, asking, "When was your copy made and from whom did you obtain the original?" Jordan's answer in his letter of March 19, 1790, is not without its discrepancies. He said the will "was given to me June, 1785," whereas he had submitted a copy of it to the *Gentleman's Magazine* in June of the preceding year. This may have been a slip of memory or of pen, readily enough excused. Also he said that Mosely, in reply to a direct question, acknowledged never having shown the document to Thomas Hart in whose house it was found. Yet Malone, in his 1790 account of the paper, said that Mr. Hart, still living, "perfectly well remember[s] the finding of this paper." Also Jordan said, in his letter to the *Gentleman's Magazine*, dated June 14, 1784, that the original manuscript of the will had come to his hand only six days previously, on June 8th. But in his letter to Malone, March 19, 1790, Jordan said that after requesting the missing first page from Moseley, "I saw no more of him for a long time, during the interval of which I shewed it [the original booklet] to Mr. Keating, the bookseller, who desired a copy, which I gave him, who shewed it to several gentlemen for their opinion." Among these gentlemen, said Jordan, were some who thought the document "a fiction," notably "the Rev. Jos. Greene." Jordan was not satisfied with Greene's adverse judgment and said he would like to submit the will to the opinion of the public. Greene advised him to do so; "accordingly I sent it in the state it then was to the printer of the Gentleman's Magazine for that purpose. . . ." Thus Jordan seems to contradict himself: in one letter he speaks of a six-day interval; in the other he speaks of a long time.

These discrepancies, however, are not nearly so suspicious as Mosely's strange inability to find the missing part and his rather miraculous discovery of it just before his death. Mosely's apparent failure to give the original text of the first page to Payton, as he professed it his intention to do after Jordan had made a copy of it, is likewise suspicious. If Payton had received the original first page, he would have shown it to Dr. Davenport, to whom he had already shown, or was about to show, the remainder of the document, and Dr. Davenport would have forwarded that page to Malone along with, or after, the other pages.

Malone's second inquiry made March 25th in reply to Jordan's letter of the 19th has in it a hint of suspicion of forgery. Malone requested "to know . . . whether the leaf which Mosely gave you shortly before his death . . . was of the same size, and written in the same manner with the rest. The few leaves which were sent to me were very small. . . ." Can it be that a study of the proportion of Jordan's copy of the first two and a half articles to the rest of the document led Malone to believe that the first page which Mosely had lately discovered must have been larger than the five pages which Malone himself had seen and studied?*

At least one later student of these first articles suspected their forged nature. Writing in 1911, before he had discovered the Borromeo version of the document, Thurston said that the first articles seemed less authentic. He noted that they contain several suspicious phrases, such as "an unworthy member of the Holy Catholic religion"; "Evangelists, Apostles, Saints, Martyrs" instead of either "Apostles, Evangelists, Martyrs and Confessors," or at least "holy martyrs"; "do in the holy presence *above specified*"; and "my good and guardian angel" as a redundancy in view of "my good Angel" in Article XI. Moreover, they make several suspicious omissions, such as the failure to mention the holy Viaticum and the Mass, and to affirm loyalty to the Apostolic See. Finally, Thurston pointed out that the connecting sentence in Article III is "purposeless and clumsy."[86]

This final suspicion of Thurston's is remarkably confirmed by a comparison of the artificial linkage of Jordan's first paragraphs with the Borromeo version, on the one hand, and the smooth transition of thought in the Borromeo version itself, on the other. In the parallel columns below, the Jordan version of the first part of the third paragraph is given on the left side and Thurston's translation of the Mexican Borromeo version on the right. Below the two parallel columns is the text of the Malone version (Englished Borromeo version) of the remainder of the third paragraph.

Jordan's version	Mexican version
Item. I John Shakspear doe by this present protest and declare, that as I am certain I must passe out of this transitory life into another that will last to eternity, I do hereby most humbly implore and intreat my good and guardian angell to instruct me in this my solemn preparation, protestation, and confession of faith	*Item.* I protest in this same form that at the end of life I desire to receive the most holy Viaticum, in order to unite me perfectly and peacefully with my Lord Jesus Christ by means of so divine a Sacrament; the which if by some accident I should be unable then to receive, I now declare in view of that time that it is my purpose to receive it

at least spiritually, in will adoring and most humbly beseeching my saviour, that he will be pleased to assist me in so dangerous a voyage, to defend me from the snares and deceites of my infernall enemies, and to conduct me to the secure haven of his eternall blisse.

Nothing could be more strained than the connection at the left; nothing more natural than that at the right. A forger's imagination was not equal to the task. A literary deceit stands exposed.

The identity of the forger is not as easy to establish as the fact of forgery. Malone does not indict Jordan. He does not even say that he believes a forgery was perpetrated. It is not the genuineness of the paper which he calls into question but its authorship by John Shakespeare, or any member of his family. Malone's faith in Jordan's integrity is demonstrated by the continued cordiality between the two men. As late as 1799, Malone entertained Jordan at London. In a letter dated July 1st of that year Jordan tells Mr. Payton of Stratford:

I breakfasted, dined, drank tea, and supped at Mr. Malone's last Thursday, and I am happy to inform you that I was treated in the most respectable and genteel manner by that truly great, good and honourable gentleman.[87]

Charles Knight believes in the forgery of the *whole* document, but does not believe Jordan the guilty one. He cryptically accuses "a rival editor." In a "Note on John Shakspere's Confession of Faith," Knight writes:

We doubt exceedingly whether Jordan fabricated the one or the other [the Spiritual Testament or the drawing of New Place, both of which Malone published in his 1790 edition]: but there was a man who was quite capable of prompting both impositions, and of carrying them through; one upon whom the suspicion of fabricating Shaksperian documents strongly rested in his lifetime; one who would have rejoiced with the most malignant satisfaction in hoaxing a rival editor. We need not name him.[88]

Must he not mean William Ireland?

Even Halliwell-Phillipps, who also believes the *whole* document a hoax, is not dogmatic in calling Jordan the forger. He writes:

If Jordan himself was, as is most likely, the forger of the document, there are no means of ascertaining the degree of risk that he incurred by naming Mosely as its discoverer. That individual died towards the end of the year 1787, and nothing is known respecting the state of his mental health in 1784, or if it is within reasonable conjecture that his illiteracy enabled Jordan to substitute a fabrication in the place of a manuscript of another description that may have been found at the Birth-Place, or whether he was a person likely to have been a confederate with his Shakespearean friend in the imposition.[89]

Sidney Lee makes the flat statement that John Jordan's "most important achievement was the forgery of the will of Shakespeare's father."[90]

The forger may have been Jordan. But why did he not attempt the forgery *before* sending the document to the *Gentleman's Magazine*? If it was because Mosely was still alive and could check the fraud, why, after Mosely was dead, did Jordan bother to tell Malone that Mosely had shown a *complete* original to Payton, by which gentleman Malone could easily verify the story and from whom Malone might get sufficient information to expose a fraud? Surely a forger would endeavor to lead others away from sources of damaging information rather than lay a trap for himself. As has already been remarked, Mosely's conduct is more suspicious—it suggests a late resolution to make a good story better by supplying the missing part which Jordan so insistently asked for. If it be objected that Mosely was only a bricklayer, it must be rejoined that Jordan was only a wheelwright. Mosely had regained possession of the truncated original in the autumn of 1786, under pretext of showing it to Mr. Tomkins, the mercer. Jordan never saw the original again, for Mosely told him he had given it to Payton. With the original to consult, it would be easy for Mosely to fabricate an article or two, remotely similar in tone and apparently appropriate in content. The difficulty here is that most of what we know about Mosely we learn from Jordan.

In truth, it would not be hard for Mosely, Jordan, or any artisan to commit the hoax. The first article is patently modelled upon the *Notificatio* of a conventional will, forms for which were easily available. No better comparison can be made of the first article than with the *Notificatio* of the authentic will of William Shakespeare, John's own son. (It is a curious fact that the finder of William's will in the Doctors' Commons, London, in 1747, was the very man who sometime in 1784 judged John Shakespeare's will to be spurious, namely, the Rev. Joseph Greene of Stratford-upon-Avon.[91]) Note the striking similarity of the opening sentences of the two documents:

William Shakespeare's authentic will	John Shakespeare's spurious will
In the name of God, Amen! I William Shackspeare, of Stratford upon Avon in the countie of Warr., gent., in perfect health and memorie, God be praysed, doe make and ordayne this my last will and testament in manner and forme following, that ys to saye, ffirst, I commend my soule into the handes of God my Creator, hoping and assuredlie beleeving, through thonelie merites, of Jesus Christe my Saviour, to be made partaker of lyfe everlastinge, ...[92]	In the name of God, the father, sonne and holy ghost, [etc.] . . . , I, John Shakspear, an unworthy member of the holy Catholick religion, being at this my present writing in perfect health of body and sound mind, memory, and understanding . . . do . . . make and ordaine this my last spiritual will, testament, [etc.] . . . hopinge hereby to receive pardon for all my sinnes and offences, and thereby to be made partaker of life everlasting, through the only merits of Jesus Christ my saviour and redeemer. . . .

Lewis points out that the *Notificatio* of William's will is virtually identical with a form of will given in William West's *Simboleographie* (1605), "a volume of typical legal forms widely used in his day."[93] Similar volumes, if not that very one, must have been accessible in the latter half of the 18th century to Mosely, or Jordan, or whoever the fabricator was. While it is true that models of Catholic wills might not be quite so accessible, it would not be hard for a forger to make touches suggestive of Catholicism.* As Thurston remarks, some of these touches are off-color to the initiated eye.

It is worth noting the rather marked Protestant character of the second paragraph in the spurious version. Such expressions as "a most abominable and grievous sinner" suggest Geneva more than Rome. In fact the religious sentiment of the whole spurious portion is Protestant, not Catholic. A rapid reading of the following excerpt from the will of Sir Nicholas Pelham, dated February 6, 1559, will substantiate this. In publishing the will of Pelham in his *Testamenta Vetusta*, Sir N. H. Nicolas explicitly says: "This Will . . . is introduced as an example of the religious sentiments expressed in Testaments after the Protestant became the authorized religion in this Country."[94] The testator deposes as follows:

*Whatever their religious coloring, it is interesting to observe that the words "cut off in the blossome of my sins" (Article I) are almost exactly the words of the ghost in *Hamlet* (I, v, 76).

In the name of God, Amen. I Sir Nicholas Pelham, of Laughton, otherwise Laston, in the county of Sussex, . . . being whole of bodie, and of good and perfecte memory, our Lord God be praised, knowing and considering the brittleness of this short transitory lyef, do make this my present testamente and laste wille . . . in manner and forme hereafter following. . . . First, knowledginge my self a grevus offender and sinner against the lawes and commaundiments of Almighty God, through the frailetie of this mortal flesh, and suerdley trusting unto his most swete and comfortable promise, that in whatsoever hour the sinner doth bewaile and repent his synnes, that he will graciously here hym, and receive him to his Savior. I, hartely repenting my sinful lyef, and being in parfecte love and charitie with all men, do righte so aske of Almightie God, mercies and forgiveness of my said offences and sinnes, certainely believing, that through the merits of Christ's blessed passion, to be accompted and received among his elect, and chosen to the most joyus and everlasting kingdom of God, according to his licke promis made unto all them which faithfully believe in him; of which number, I trust dughtless to be one. . . .[95]

Until Herbert Thurston's discovery of the genuine text of the early articles of John Shakespeare's will, the incongruity of such Protestant sentiments prefixed to a Catholic confession of faith escaped notice.

(6) Besides accounting for the nature of John Shakespeare's will as a formula of devotion, disclosing the author of that formula as St. Charles Borromeo, making the literacy of John Shakespeare a question beside the point, solving several textual difficulties, and proving the Jordan version of the first two and a half articles to be a forgery, the Thurston discovery meets many miscellaneous objections made by detractors of the document.

There are, for example, the objections raised by Charles Knight in his *William Shakspere: A Biography* (1842). Knight did not believe the Spiritual Testament to be the work of a Roman Catholic at all. One of his reasons for so believing was that ". . . if the writer had been a Roman Catholic, or if it had been drawn up for his approval and signature by his priest, it would necessarily, professing such fulness and completeness, have contained something of belief touching the then material points of difference between the Roman and the Reformed Church."[96] But once it is understood that the confession is a devotional formula drawn up by an Italian archbishop for Italian Catholics threatened with death by the plague and not concerned with the fulminations of theological and ecclesiological disputes, Knight's objection melts away.

Knight is also convinced that he finds in the testament "phrases, and indeed long passages, . . . introduced for the purpose of marking the supposed writer's opinions in the way that should be most offensive to those of a contrary opinion, as if by way of bravado or seeking of persecution."[97] As examples, he cites, and quotes in part, Articles IV, X, and XII, all of them in the genuine portion of Malone's version. The twelfth article is worst of all.

> This last item, which is the twelfth of the paper, is demonstrative to us of its spuriousness . . . . he calls upon all his kinsfolks to assist and succour him after his death "with the holy sacrifice of the mass," with a promise that he "will not be ungrateful unto them for so great a benefit," well knowing that by the Act of 1581 the saying of mass was punishable by a year's imprisonment and a fine of 200 marks, and the hearing of it by a similar imprisonment and a fine of 100 marks. The fabrication appears to us as gross as can well be imagined.[98]

Here again, what Knight did not know was that these expressions of Catholic devotion originated in the mind and heart of an *Italian* churchman and that Italian parishioners who signed the testament could not be concerned with Elizabethan acts of religious repression. The specific Act of 1581 had yet to be passed when Borromeo wrote the document. It is even possible that John Shakespeare signed the testament before that Act was passed.

Finally, Knight does not accept the document as being Roman Catholic because of apparent exaggerations of diction "which mark the work of an imitator of the language of the sixteenth century, rather than the production of one habitually employing it. . . ."[99] He singles out Article XIII as containing some of the worst exaggerations and, quoting the article, italicizes *sweet and amorous* in the expression "to be entombed in the sweet and amorous coffin of the side of Jesus Christ," *life-giving sepulchre* in the expression "that in this life-giving sepulchre it may rest and live," *direful iron of the launce* and *like a charge in a censor* in the expression "there to bless for ever and ever that direful iron of the launce, which, like a charge in a censor, forms so sweet and pleasant a monument within the sacred breast of my Lord and Saviour." He concludes, "Surely this raving is not the language of a man in earnest."[100] But now it appears that Knight was mistaken in his judgment. What words are more natural to the spirit of Charles Borromeo than *sweet and amorous*? The thought of a *life-giving sepulchre*, aside from being common in Catholic devotions, was particularly appropriate and comforting in the presence of thousands of new graves opened in Milan to receive the victims of the Black Death. *Like a charge in a censor* was, as we have seen, Malone's misreading of an illegible text and needs no comment here. As for the *direful iron of the launce*, Thurston and Bowden both point out that the expression is derived from the line *"quae vulnerata lanceae mucrone diro"* of the ancient hymn, "Vexilla Regis,"[101] so that here again Knight is mistaken in his judgment of the Catholic spirit.

So much then for the contribution which Thurston's discovery makes to the solution of the problem. There remain, however, several questions the answers to which must be found elsewhere by the study of other evidence.

(1) First of all there is the question: Is the signer of the will *John* Shakespeare? Thurston himself is not certain that the signer is a man and is inclined to think that "Jhon"* stands for "Joan." His argument is as follows:

> The house in which the discovery was made was certainly that in which the poet's sister, Joan Hart, *née* Shakespeare, lived until her death in 1646. Now the testament, in Section X, names only one patron, St. Winefride, a female saint; whence it would be natural to infer that the form was originally copied for a woman. The name Joan, in Elizabethan times, was, of course, written in several different ways, Jone, Johne, Joane, etc.—if I mistake not, I have even seen it written John. It might well be, therefore, that the testament was originally transcribed for Joan Shakespeare in her girlhood. Whether Jordan, by a touch or two, thought it worth while to alter the name into John; or whether as the spelling of the whole paper seems to suggest, the five leaves discovered by Mosely were only a copy of an older original, it is in either case possible that John Shakespeare's name has come to replace that of his daughter. I can readily conceive that somewhere about 1660 one of the Harts, finding the perishing original in an old drawer, might copy the paper just for the curiosity of the contents. There can be no doubt that at that date they held the name of Shakespeare in much veneration. A son born in 1666, was christened Shakespeare Hart, and a generation later we find a William Shakespeare Hart. The substitution of John for Joan might in that case be a simple blunder of the copyist.[102]

The details of Thurston's argument need to be treated in turn. The house was truly that in which Joan Hart lived until her death, but just as truly had it been the house of her father until his death. It is true, too, that the testament names only one patron, St. Winefride, a female saint. But while it may seem natural to infer that the testament was therefore copied for a woman, this conclusion does not necessarily follow. Men did

*So Thurston spells the name. I do not know upon what authority. Malone, in first publishing the document in 1790, spelled the name "John."

have female saints for patrons. A single instance will suffice to prove the point. Sir Thomas Wyndham made his will at his manor of Felbrigge, 22 October, 1521, and said:

> Also to the singular mediacions, and prayers of all the holy company of hevyn, aungells, archaungells, patriarches, prophets, apostells, evangelists, martyres, confessoures, and virgynes; and specially to myn accustomeed advourrys, I call and crye, Saint John Evangelist, Saint George, Saint Thomas of Canterbury, Saint Margaret, Saint Kateryn. and Saint Barbara, humbly beseche you, that not onlye at the houre of deth, soo too ayde, socour, and defend me. . . .[103]

There was, therefore, nothing unnatural in John Shakespeare's naming St. Winefride.

Who, then, was St. Winefride? According to *The Catholic Encyclopedia* she was born at Holywell, in the northeastern part of Wales about 600. Under the tutelage of St. Beuno, her uncle, Winefride prepared to consecrate herself to God. But her beauty attracted Caradoc, the son of neighboring Prince Alen. Caradoc called at her home to pay court. Finding her alone while her parents attended Mass, the young suitor became so ardent in his avowals of love that Winefride, only fifteen years old, fled. Angered by the rebuff, Caradoc pursued her and with his sword struck off her head. The head rolled down a slope, and where it came to rest a spring of water welled up. St. Beuno, somehow made aware of the tragedy, discontinued the celebration of the Mass and went to where the murdered girl lay. He covered the severed head and the body with his cloak and went back to the church to finish the Holy Sacrifice. When the saint and his communicants returned to the body and removed the cloak, they found Winefride restored to life. Only a thin white line on her neck marked the path of the decapitating sword. Winefride, now holier than before, became a nun. A convent was built upon her father's land, and there she lived eight years. She then moved to Gwytherin, farther west in Wales, to escape the invading Saxons and there established a religious community. She remained abbess of the community until her death on November 3, 660. The spring at Holywell became the resort of pilgrims, and many miracles of healing were performed there.[104]

The question immediately arises: Why did John Shakespeare choose St. Winefride for a patron saint? Nothing in her story seems peculiarly appropriate to John Shakespeare. Holywell was in Wales, more than a hundred miles distant from Stratford-upon-Avon. The explanation may be found in a special relationship which existed between St. Winefride and the Jesuit mission of 1580. The episcopal head of that mission was Dr. Thomas Goldwell, the Bishop of St. Asaph. The episcopal seat at the town of St. Asaph was only ten or twelve miles from Holywell. Dr. Goldwell was officially interested in St. Winefride. He "obtained from the sovereign pontiff the confirmation of certain indulgences granted by Martin V (1417–31) to pilgrims who visited the well."[105] It is true that Bishop Goldwell fell sick at Rheims on his way to England and never reached that island, but no other bishop was sent in his place.[106] In such discussions of procedure as presumably were held by the missionary party before leaving Rheims, the virtues of St. Winefride and of Holywell must have been commended by the episcopal head of the party. It would be quite natural for a member of that party, once in England carrying on the work of confirming Catholics in their faith, to recommend St. Wine-fride as a patron saint to any signer of a testament like that of John Shakespeare who may have shown hesitancy in the choice of a patron. This connection* between St. Winefride and the mission of 1580 makes the rather unusual inclusion of the patroness's name in John Shake-speare's will an argument for its authenticity and for its being the will of John, not of Joan, Shakespeare. The Joan Shakespeare who survived infancy was born in 1569 and would have been only eleven or twelve years old when the missioners arrived, a rather tender age at which to be signing last wills and testaments. John, on the other hand, was near, if not past, fifty.

Thurston's comment upon the irregular Elizabethan spelling of the name Joan as removing a possible objection to the view that Joan signed the testament loses much of its effectiveness when we recall that Malone had every opportunity to examine the manuscript, and he seems never to have doubted that the signature was that of a man, John, not of a woman, Joan. All of those who saw the original document—Mosely, Jordan, Keating, Greene, Hart, Payton, Davenport—seem not to have doubted either. They all knew about Joan Shakespeare, especially since Thomas Hart was her direct descendant. In the face of their consensus and in view of the weakness of the position which prefers to take "Jhon" to mean "Joan"† when it is so much more regularly a spelling of "John," Thurston's conjecture does not seem valid. In his rather forced effort to account for the later history of Joan's testament, Thurston, as previously quoted, says that he could "conceive that somewhere about 1660 one of the Harts, finding the perishing original in an old drawer, might copy the paper just for the curiosity of the contents." But if the document

---

*The English Province of the Society of Jesus established a Residence of St. Wine-fride, for the records of which see H. Foley, S. J., *Records of the English Province of the Society of Jesus*, Series X, Part II, 528–37 and Series XII, 932–46.

†In the Parish Register entry of the baptism of Joan, April 15, 1569, her name is spelled "Jone." See Lewis, *op. cit.*, I, 128.

was known at that time and a copy of it was made, why should that copy be discovered under the rafters of the Hart house a century later? After 1660 no Hart would have needed to hide the document. And in 1757 or 1770 no Mosely or Jordan could have perpetrated the pretense of finding either the original document or a copy hidden in the rafters, for the Thomas Harts would have known about the 1660 original found in the old drawer and the copy made for curiosity's sake.

With regard to the theory that the signer of the testament was a woman named "Joan," something must be said about an ephemeral aunt of William Shakespeare who was a nun. Madame de Chambrun, writing of another matter in her *Shakespeare Rediscovered*, says that

> . . . John Shakespeare's sister had been a nun at Wroxall until the forced dissolution of the Convent, after which the inmates were sent back to their families or thrown upon the world, the sole exception being the prioress who was allowed a slender indemnity from the Crown. Domina Shakespeare who died in Stratford when her nephew was fourteen certainly must have influenced his childhood. . . .[107]

The basis of Madame de Chambrun's statement is probably the mention in the register of the Guild of St. Anne of Knowle at Wroxall, under date of 1525, of a "Domina Jane Shakspere" who was the sub-prioress of Wroxall Abbey.[108] No further unmistakable trace has been left by "Domina Jane," but the register of Hatton, under date of October 21, 1571, contains the entry: "Mortua et sepulta erat Domina Jana aliquando una monicarum Wraxall."[109] Both Wroxall and Hatton are in Warwickshire. These points suggest the possibility of Domina Jane's being the aunt of William and, as a Catholic nun, a plausible signer of a Catholic last will and testament.

But there are hindrances to the hypothesis. The nun's name is twice given as "Jane," not "Joan." The convent at Wroxall was dissolved in 1535.[110] Where could Aunt Jane have kept herself from that date until 1571, thirty-six years later? She is nowhere mentioned in any of the now numerous Shakespeare documents. Again, when she died in 1571, William was not fourteen, as Madame de Chambrun says, but only seven years old. Moreover, in 1571 the Jesuit mission had nine years to wait before bringing the Borromeo testament with it to England. It does not seem as if the Wroxall Jane Shakespeare could have signed the document in question.

Most damaging of all to the theory is the fact that recent students of the Shakespeare genealogy deny any relationship between the Wroxall Shakespeares and the Snitterfield-Stratford Shakespeares. Charles Elton says: ". . . so far as the inquiries have as yet proceeded, it cannot be said that there is any evidence of the poet's ancestors having come from Wroxall."[111]

Lewis writes: "Try as one will, in the light of the present evidence, one is unable to demonstrate that John Shakespeare's ancestral connections were with the Wroxall family of that name."[112]

And E. K. Chambers says:

Shakespeares were thick on the ground in sixteenth-century Warwickshire, particularly in the Woodland about Wroxall and Rowington to the north of Stratford. A Richard Shakespeare was in fact bailiff of Wroxall manor in 1534, but his after-history is known, and excludes a suggested identity with Richard of Snitterfield.[113]

In addition to the Jane Shakespeare of Wroxall, there may have been a Joan Shakespeare of Snitterfield. Fripp, in discussing the family of Richard Shakespeare, mentions two sons, John and Henry, "and perhaps a daughter, Joan."[114] Speaking of this conjectural daughter in another context, Fripp says: "Joan Shakespeare, of whom we hear, if she were Henry Shakespeare's sister, may have lived with him before and after his marriage with one Margaret. They all died in 1596–7."[115] This date allows for Aunt Joan's being alive during the Jesuit mission, but it makes William Shakespeare thirty-two or thirty-three at the time of his aunt's death. There is no evidence of Joan's ever having become a nun or of her ever having lived in Stratford. It seems unlikely, then, that William Shakespeare had a Catholic aunt on his *father's* side to tutor him in Catholicism until his fourteenth year or to sign the last will and testament ascribed to his father.

(2) But what of the conjecture of Boswell[116] that Malone might have had the discovery of the existence of John Shakespeare the shoemaker in mind as the reason for his rejection of the testament? It being accepted that the signer of the document was a *man* by the name of *John* Shakespeare, could it have been the corviser and not the father of the poet?

From information presented by Malone,[117] Halliwell-Phillipps,[118] Fripp,[119] and Chambers,[120] we learn that Shoemaker Shakespeare was "a trustworthy and unembarrassed tradesman" who arrived in Stratford "in or very shortly before 1584, being then a young man."[121] He probably was the son of Thomas Shaxper, shoemaker of Warwick, to whose business he succeeded when another son, William, was drowned in the Avon on July 6, 1579. He probably was the "Saxper *alias* Demayles" who married Joan Webbe on July 17, 1579, at St. Nicholas, Warwick. He was living in the Market Place, Warwick, as late as February, 1582. The first notice of his presence in Stratford is a Parish Register entry recording his marriage on November 25, 1584, to Margery Roberts, the daughter or widow of Thomas Roberts, shoemaker, of Back Bridge Street, to whose business John Shakespeare, shoemaker, seems to have succeeded. In 1585 he was elected an aletaster of the Corporation. In 1586 he was admitted as a freeman into the Company of Shoemakers and Sadlers. The large fee of £3 which he paid for his freedom (the receipt of half of this, as the Corporation's share, is recorded in the minutes of the Corporation and in the chamberlains' accounts for 1585–86) proves him not to have been a native of Stratford. In the fall of the same year he was appointed one of the town constables. He was re-elected the following year. Evidence of his good character is given by the extension to him by the Corporation in 1587 of a loan of £5 from the Thomas Oken fund, a fund set up to aid honest and industrious young businessmen. In that same year, John's wife, Margery, died. That he remarried is proved by baptismal entries for three of his children in the Stratford Parish Register: March 11, 1588/9, a daughter, Ursula; May 24, 1590, a son, Humphrey; and September 21, 1591, a son, Phillip. As Chambers points out, these three children were once taken to be the children of the poet's father by a second wife. In October, 1588, Shoemaker John accepted the guardianship of two sons of Thomas Roberts: Thomas Jr. and Richard. A Court of Record entry shows him to have been sued in 1591 by Richard Tyler for the collection of a debt of £4. In 1592 he was listed as surety for Thomas Fourde, who had borrowed money from the Bakers fund, and for Philip Grene, who had borrowed money from the Oken fund. An entry in the records of the Council, June 30, 1592, shows that at the time Shoemaker John was the Master of the Company of Shoemakers. Hereupon, he disappears from Stratford records. Probably he had left Stratford by 1595 and is the John Shakespeare buried at St. Mary's, Warwick, on 7 February, 1624.

The important detail to be noticed about Shoemaker John is his place of residence in Stratford. According to Halliwell-Phillipps

Thomas Roberts . . . lived on the north side of Back Bridge Street, holding extensive premises there under a lease from the Corporation that had been granted to him in 1578 for thirty-one years at the annual rental of twelve shillings. At some unascertained period after the death of this individual in September, 1583, the house was occupied by Shakespeare the Corvizer, who was certainly the tenant a few years afterwards, his name occurring in a list, drawn up in October, 1589, of those who had paid three quarters of their annual rents, in his case nine shillings out of twelve,—"Jhon Shackespere, ix.*s*., . . . xij.*s*." He is also noted in another manuscript as having regularly discharged the quarterly claim for the tenement in Bridge Street throughout the year 1590; Misc. Doc. i. 109. "Brydge Strett Warde, John Shaxpere, xij.*s*.," manuscript list dated January, 1590–1. After June, 1592, he is heard of no more in the records of Stratford, and he appears to have left the neighborhood at some time before 1595, in which year his dwelling is noticed in an official rental as tenanted by another person.[122]

None of this suggests that a spiritual testament signed by the shoe-maker could be expected to be found in the house in Henley Street. As long as Malone thought the John Shakespeare of the testament to be John Shakespeare Jr., the eldest son of the alderman, he could accept the naturalness of its being found in the Henley Street house, but when he discovered that no John Jr. ever existed (at least beyond non-documented infancy) and that the John Shakespeare he thought was John Jr. was the shoemaker and not a member of the alderman's family, his judg-ment concerning the authorship of the document was modified.

(3) We now come to the last question to be discussed: Does the known history of the Henley Street house present any obstacles to the conclu-sion that the Spiritual Last Will and Testament was hidden there be-tween 1580 and 1601 and that it remained there undisturbed until its accidental discovery in 1757 or 1770?

No evidence has come to light to disprove the accepted view that John Shakespeare, the poet's father, lived in Henley Street from 1552, or earlier, until his death in 1601. A view of frank pledge dated October 2, 1556, shows that in that year John Shakespeare bought two houses: one in Greenhill Street from George Turner, another in Henley Street from Edward West.[123] Whether the house in Henley Street was the one in front of which John Shakespeare had made a dunghill in 1552 cannot be determined, but it is just as reasonable to assume that it was not. The fact that John Shakespeare had already been living in Henley Street before he purchased a house there in 1556 makes it more probable that he lived with his bride in the new, or identical, Henley Street house after 1556, rather than in the Greenhill Street house, though there is nothing to disprove the latter alternative. That the house bought in Henley Street was what later became the east end of the Birthplace is indicated by an entry in the *Inquisitio post mortem* of the Earl of Warwick, October 6, 1590, where the chief-rent is noted as being "vj^d"[124] the same as men-tioned in the view of frank pledge certifying the purchase of 1556.

A foot of fine, Michaelmas term, 1575, records the purchase by John Shakespeare of "two houses, two gardens, and two orchards with the appurtenances in Stratford-upon-Avon" from Edmund Hall and his wife for forty pounds.[125] The street location of the two houses is not mentioned in the foot of fine, but in the *Inquisitio* mentioned above the property is listed under Henley Street, immediately after the property purchased in 1556, with a chief-rent of "xiij^d."[126] These two newly acquired houses were immediately adjacent to the eastern house and were incorporated with it to become the middle and western houses of the Birthplace.

From 1575 onward each of the three houses had its separate history. The East and Middle houses became the enlarged home of John and his family, with the older East House perhaps providing such space as John needed for the conduct of his business. The two parts were united by internal doorways. The West House was leased to one William Burbage as an independent dwelling. The Great Fire of 1594 either reached the West House so that it was partly destroyed, or so seriously threatened it that it was partly pulled down by fire hooks. John Shakespeare did not rebuild this portion. We conclude this from the fact that when he sold a strip of land at the west end of his property to his neighbor George Badger in 1596–97, he described it as a "toft,"[127] that is, "land where once stood a messuage 'that is fallen or pulled down'."[128] The deed of this transaction, dated January 26, 1597, offers indisputable proof that John Shakespeare was then living in the Henley Street house. It identifies John Shakespeare as a "yeoman, of Stratford-on-Avon," and reads:

> . . . I have confirmed to the aforesaid George Badger his heirs and assigns all that toft and parcel of land of mine with its appurtenances adjacent to and lying in the aforesaid Stratford-on-Avon, in a certain district likewise called Henley Street, between the free tenement of mine, aforesaid John Shakespeare on the east side and the free tenement of aforesaid George Badger on the west side, . . . ; *and is now in the tenure and occupation of me* the aforesaid John Shakespeare.[129]

When William Shakespeare married Ann Hathaway in November, 1582, he brought her to live with him most likely in the back part of the Middle House. There the family of William lived until the purchase of New Place in 1597. William's sister Joan and her husband, William Hart, a hatmaker, then took up residence in the Middle House. Upon the death of John Shakespeare in 1601, the whole estate fell to William Shakespeare, subject to his mother's dowry. William leased the East House to a Lewis Hiccocks, of Welcombe, who in 1603 made it into an inn, probably called "Maidenhead." The Middle House, now combined with what was left of the West House, was leased to Joan and William Hart at a nominal rent of 12d. William Hart died in 1616, but Joan continued to live in the Middle-West House until 1646, when she died. Her son Thomas and his family continued to live there. When the last direct descendant of William Shakespeare, his granddaughter, Elizabeth Hall (Lady Barnard), died in 1670, the Harts inherited the Birthplace. The succession of Hart descendants living in the Middle-West House was unbroken until 1757, or 1770, whichever may be the date when the Spiritual Will of John Shakespeare was found. At either of these times the Birthplace belonged to George Hart, to whose son Thomas (1729–93) the property passed in 1778. It is this long association of the Hart family with the Middle-West House that accounts for the tradition, current since the middle of the eighteenth century, that a bedroom in the Middle-West House was the room in which William Shakespeare was born.[130]

It is apparent from the foregoing that nothing stands in the way of assuming the document's being concealed in the attic of the Henley Street house by John Shakespeare and of its being found where it was reported to have been found: "under the tileing of the house where the poet was born," as Jordan says in his letter to the *Gentleman's Magazine*; or "between the rafters and the tiling of the house," i.e., "the old house at Stratford, in which Mr. Hart lives [1790], and in which our poet was born," as Malone writes in his 1790 edition of Shakespeare's works. The Birthplace tradition was already full-blown: "In the Jubilee of 1769, a precise 'Birthroom' was indicated. . . ."[131] Both Jordan and Malone could have had only the Middle-West House in mind.

The expression "between the rafters and the tiling" occasions comment. Was the roof in John Shakespeare's day covered with tile? Lewis writes:

> If the Birthplace in the time of John Jordan (as he so says in his questionable account of his discovery of the spiritual last will and testament of John Shakespeare) was covered with tiles, they have long since disappeared; and at present it has a heavy shingle roof. The likelihood is that John Shakespeare's home had had a thatched roof continuously from the much earlier period of its erection.[132]

Proof that the Birthplace carried a tile roof in the days of Jordan and Malone is furnished by a lithograph of "Shakespeare's Birth Place, as it appeared at the time of the Jubilee," 1769, reproduced opposite page 14 in R. B. Wheler's *A Guide to Stratford-upon-Avon*, published in 1814. The print unmistakably shows the roof to be tiled. It must have been the roof shown in this print which was "new-tiled" by Mosely in 1757, or 1770, when the document was discovered. Mentioning this improvement in his 1790 account, Malone uses the verb "new-tile." What did he mean by "new-tile"? If he meant that a new roof of tile had been put on by Mosely to replace one of thatch, he would be strengthening the plausibility of the discovery, for it is easy to understand how, upon the baring of the rafters, anything previously hidden between them and the thatch of the roof would come to light. If he meant that Mosely merely renewed the tile, then he would be corroborating Jordan's report to the *Gentleman's Magazine*, for, of course, to need retiling at that time the roof must have been covered with tile for a good many years before 1757, or 1770.

How long before, it is impossible to determine. But it is important to establish a strong probability that the roof was of tile from the time of John Shakespeare's hiding his will to the time of the finding of the will, for if during that interim a change had been made from thatch to tile, the hidden booklet must inevitably have been discovered.

There are several considerations which suggest that John Shakespeare had the roof of his Henley Street house tiled at some time before his death. In 1575 he bought the two houses to enlarge his Henley Street home. He was in a mood for improvement. Extensive alterations must have been undertaken to make the old East House and the new Middle House into a unit-dwelling and to make the West House a suitable tenement to be rented to others. If the roof were not already tiled, what more natural step than to tile it as part of these alterations? Again, in 1582, William Shakespeare was married, and it may have been necessary to remodel the Middle House to provide a home for him and his bride. In the course of these alterations, the roof may have been tiled. Then, the Great Fire of 1594 suggests one of two possibilities. First, the fire was a fierce one, destroying many houses, but it was stopped short of consuming the Shakespeare home. May not a tile roof have aided in stopping the fire? Secondly, if the Shakespeare home was thatched at the time of the fire, the narrow escape from destruction may have led John Shakespeare to have his roof tiled before the next fire. A second great fire did come in 1597, but spared the Shakespeare residence. Other serious fires followed in 1598 and 1614. That these fires accelerated a trend toward tiled roofs in the borough is shown by an action taken by the Corporation early in the seventeenth century. When it seemed as if Stratford was having more than its share of serious fires, the civic leaders reasoned that thatched roofs were the cause. Thereupon the town officials "forbade any more houses to be built with thatched roofs; indeed, ordered the thatch of old houses to be exchanged for the greater safety of tiles and slate."[133]

The foregoing considerations show John Shakespeare had ample incentive and opportunity for tiling the roof of his house. Between "the rafters and the tiling" of that roof he could have hidden his Spiritual Last Will and Testament, and in that hiding place the document could have remained concealed until Mosely found it.

Here, then, we must close this discussion. All that remains to be done is to emphasize anew the determinative value of the document which was found there. As Halliwell-Phillipps, in his note on the assumption that John Shakespeare was "secretly attached to the old religion," himself admits:

> There would be direct and conclusive evidence of this assumption were any reliance to be placed upon the statement that the poet's father authorized . . . the long confession of faith of "John Shakspear, an unworthy member of the Holy Catholick religion,". . . . [134]

Much more reliance can now be placed upon the statement and the document itself. The document offers strong evidence that John Shakespeare was a Catholic throughout his life and that his household was infused with the spirit of the Old Faith. It makes reasonable the conclusion that when John and Mary Shakespeare sought to instil religious sentiments and foster religious values in the minds and hearts of their children, those sentiments and values were of the Catholic tradition. It is now more certain that William Shakespeare was brought up in a Catholic home.

It will be interesting to see where and how in the writings of William Shakespeare a Catholic parental influence is apparent and in what respects Catholicism contributed to the molding and inspiration of the greatest poetic genius in England's literary history.

PART THREE

THE RELIGIOUS TRAINING OF WILLIAM SHAKESPEARE

BEFORE discussing the elements of Catholicism in the plays of William Shakespeare, we ought first to consider the nature and extent of his religious training during boyhood. Three institutions contributed to that training: the home, the school, and the church. We believe that the influence of the home was Catholic, of the school both Catholic and Protestant, and of the church, Protestant. These interacting influences would tend to cultivate in the boy William a spirit of understanding. The result in the mature dramatist was a tolerant attitude toward all religions. For himself, Shakespeare came to adopt a religion which rose above creeds and church organizations. Transmuted into art, that religion gave depth, fullness, and meaning to the conflicting despairs and aspirations of universal man.

1. The Home

If William was born and reared in a Catholic household, what sort of religious training would he have received in it? We cannot say with certainty, for there is no way of knowing what went on in the Henley Street household between 1564 and 1582, that is, from the year of William's birth to the year of his marriage. We can only generalize about the typical Catholic household of the period, assuming that some, if not all, of the generalizations apply to the home of young William.

Even to generalize about the typical Catholic home of the early Elizabethan era is not easy. It was an era during which Catholicism was being driven into secrecy. The traditions of Catholicism were disintegrating. Just how far the disintegration had gone in English home life at any one decade in the period is difficult to say. But it can be said that banned traditions are more susceptible to decline in their public manifestations than in their private and domestic practice. If the English Catholic Church was made over rather rapidly to conform outwardly to Edwardian and Elizabethan Protestantism, the English Catholic home must have persevered longer in the old Catholic ways. It is not assuming too much, therefore, to say that the Catholic home of 1564–82 was, in the main, the Catholic home of pre-Reformation days. Such generalizations as we shall make, therefore, will be based upon what is known about the pre-Reformation Catholic household of the fifteenth and early sixteenth centuries.

(1) First, it can be said that Catholic parents were themselves instructed in the fundamentals of the Old Faith, so that through home training they could impart those fundamentals of belief and practice to their children. Parents were not so ignorant of religious matters as is too commonly supposed. There were many agencies and practices operative throughout the medieval period of English religious history to give natively intelligent English laymen a rather good grounding in the Catholic faith.

(a) There was, for example, the required instruction of the people by the parish priest at stated periods four times a year. As early as 1281 Archbishop Peckham, through the Constitution adopted that year at the Synod of Oxford, ordered

> . . . that every priest having the charge of a flock do, four times in each year (that is, once each quarter) on one or more solemn feast days, either himself or by some one else, instruct the people in the vulgar language simply and without any fantastical admixture of subtle distinctions, in the articles of the Creed, the Ten Commandments, the Evangelical Precepts, the seven works of mercy, the seven deadly sins with their offshoots, the seven principal virtues, and the seven Sacraments.[1]

In the next century, in 1357, Cardinal Thoresby, Archbishop of York, followed the example of Peckham and went even farther, for, in issuing similar injunctions, he required the instruction to be given as often as every Sunday. He prepared a manual of instruction in Latin and had it translated into the Northern dialect and expounded by the monk Garryk (Gaytrige or Gaytryk). This manual was later produced in an expanded form in the Midland dialect by Wyclif, who had been a friend of Thoresby and who had not yet arrived at his more extreme opinions.[2]

Injunctions of this sort were still being issued in the early days of John and Mary Shakespeare. About 1536–38 Edward Lee, Archbishop of York, required " 'curates,' etc., to teach their parishioners the *Pater* and *Ave* in English, 'at Mattens times, and betwene Mattens and Laudes,' and the articles of the *Credo* after the Creed at Mass, as well as the Ten Commandments 'betwene Evensonge and Completorie' on holy days."[3]

No doubt there was a wide gap between theory and practice in this matter of priestly instruction, but that the regulation was generally recognized and to a large extent complied with is shown by the fact that during the fourteenth and fifteenth centuries a great many manuals intended to help parish priests in the performance of this duty appeared. With the invention of printing that number increased markedly. John Myrc's *Instructions for Parish Priests*, written in the fifteenth century (*c.* 1420), presupposes such periodical teaching. H. Maynard Smith points out ". . . that the Yorkshire parish of Kirkby Malsherd in 1500 presented their parson at a visitation for not expounding the fundamental truths," thus proving ". . . that the people expected it" and suggesting ". . . that neighbouring parishes were more fortunate in their parsons."[4] The parishes of Snitterfield and Aston Cantlow, home parishes of John Shakespeare and Mary Arden respectively, may have been unfortunate in having ignorant priests incapable of fulfilling their office with respect to the periodical instruction of their people, but some effort must have been made in this direction by the incumbents during the youth of John and Mary, with unascertainable results.

(b) Even the most ignorant priests conducted Mass, and through the service of the Mass the English people learned something of the tenets of Catholicism. There were explanations of the Mass in the vernacular, many of which have survived. Some of them were in verse to make them more easily memorized. Lydgate, the Monk of Bury, begins his versified exposition with this prayer:

> God of Heaven that shook earth and hell
> Give me grace some word to tell
> To the lewd who cannot read
> But Paternoster and the Creed.[5]

Deservedly popular and widely used was *The Lay Folks Mass Book*, translated from the twelfth-century French of Dan Jeremy, Canon of Rouen and Archdeacon of Cleveland, the latest version dating from the middle of the fifteenth century.[6] For those who could read, it paraphrased the *Confiteor*, the *Gloria in Excelsis*, and the Lord's Prayer in verse. It put the Nicene Creed into simple language. It expanded the Canon of the Mass and brought its meaning home to the people.

(c) Those laymen who had no access to explanations of the Mass in the vernacular or to copies of *The Lay Folks Mass Book* could still learn much from English parts of the church services. Parts of the Mass itself, notably the Bidding of the Bedes, were said in English and were often expanded to suit the occasion. There were English Litanies in use. The services for Baptism, Marriage, and the Visitation of the Sick were partly in English. The service of the shriving pew or confessional offered opportunities for the inculcation of religious ideas and principles in English. The sermon, as part of the High Mass, was in English. Even though the parish priests of some communities seem to have been utterly incapable of preaching a sermon, there were few communities which were not, at some time, regaled by the sermons of friars and other itinerant preachers. The value of the sermon as a medium of popular religious instruction in pre-Reformation days can be underestimated.

> The nature of the sermon would depend, as it still does, upon the nature of the preacher; the lazy could buy volumes of sermons ready-made, the conscientious might deliver learned discourses, but often the sermon was more of a personal talk, enlivened with stories, frequently humorous, fables, or comparisons drawn from popular books of natural history. It was from the pulpit that the people received their religious instruction, and although preaching never in pre-Reformation days held such a place in the services as it did in Puritan times, it did play a very important part.[7]

(d) In addition to the regular services of the church there were special ceremonial services, performed periodically, which contributed to the religious enlightenment of the common people.

At Candlemas the congregation marched round the church with their lighted candles remembering the aged Simeon and in honour of Him Who is the Light of the World. All received ashes on Ash Wednesday that they might understand the defilement of sin, and remember that the day was coming when it would be said of them, "earth to earth, ashes to ashes, dust to dust." On Maundy Thursday, great men washed the feet of the poor, typifying the reversal of human values in the light of the Incarnation. On Good Friday men crept to the Cross in humble adoration of Him Who died for them. On Easter Eve the new fire was hallowed from which the Paschal candle was lighted, and the cold hearths of every home were kindled anew. At Rogationtide the fields were blessed and religion consecrated the daily toil. At Whitsuntide the dove descended from the roof of the church, while clouds of incense perfumed the air. At Corpus Christi time were the glad processions of those rejoicing in Emmanuel, God with us. At Lammas the loaf, being the first fruits of the harvest, was presented as an act of thanksgiving to Him Who hears our prayer "Give us this day our daily bread." On All Hallows five boys in surplices with amices drawn over their heads chanted *"Venite omnes virgines sapientissimae"* in honour of those who had gone in to the marriage supper of the Lamb. On St.

Nicholas Day or Holy Innocents a boy pontificated, reminding all of the command to turn and become as little children.[8]

(e) One of the most dreadful and awe-inspiring special services of the medieval church was the pronouncement of the Great Sentence. It was performed on Sundays at least twice a year—in some churches as often as four times a year. The scene of the pronouncement was either the church or the churchyard. As to the manner of reading the Sentence, Myrc enjoins the priest:

> Thou shalt pronounce this hideous thing
> With cross and candles and bell knelling
> Speak out redely for noght thou wonde
> That all may thee understonde.[9]

The form of the ceremony seems to have been somewhat elastic. One version of the form taken by W. Maskell from a copy of the Sarum Manual in the Bodleian Library and reproduced in his *Monumenta Ritualia Ecclesiae Anglicanae*[10] begins with a long exposition in English and then pronounces the anathema in English as follows:

> But be autoritie of our Lorde God Almighty, and our lady saynt Marie, and of all heven, of angeles and archangeles, patriarkes and prophetes, apostles and evangelistes, martyres, confessores and virgines, and also bi the power of all holi chirche, that our Lorde Jesu Christe gaue unto seynt Peter, we denounce all the openly acursed that we have rekened unto you, and all tho that mainten them in theyr sinnes, or geve them to help or counseil, so that they be departed fro God and al holi chirche, and that they haue no part of the passion of our Lord Jesu Christ, ne of no sacrament that is in holy chirche, ne no part of the prayer amonge cristine folke, but that thei ben acursed of God and holy chirche, fro the sole of the foot unto the crowne of the heed, slepinge and wakynge, sythynge and standinge, and in all their wordes and werkes, and but yf (*unless*) they have grace of God, for to amende them here by they lyve, for to dwelle in the peynes of hell for ever withouten ende: fiat, fiat. Amen.[11]

The form proceeds in Latin with the absolution "*et modo et auctoritate absolvendi a sententia excommunicationis majore et minore.*" Another form, given by Myrc, after eight lines of verse of which four are quoted above, plunges directly into the anathema, lists the kinds of sinners that come under the curse, pronounces the formal sentence in an even more comprehensive way than the Sarum form of Maskell, and instructs the priest to conclude the ceremony in this manner:

>Than thou thi candell shalt cast to grounde
>And spet therto the same stound
>And lete also the belles knylle
>To make her hortes the mor grylle.[12]

The long list of sinners, not exhaustive, as Myrc hints, must have made the hearers of the Great Sentence look apprehensively inward to examine themselves. It included all persons who broke the peace of the church or robbed it, who withheld tithes or did anything to avoid payment; all slanderers, fire-raisers, thieves and receivers of stolen goods, heretics, usurers; all such as lent out cattle in the hope of getting a higher price at pay-day than they could at loan-time; all forgers of papal bulls; all clippers of the King's money, users of false weights and measures, bearers of false witness against matrimony or testaments; all traitors, disturbers of the peace, stealers of holy things, destroyers of the church's goods; all who helped Jews or Saracens; all destroyers of children, born or unborn, with drinks or witchcraft; all eavesdroppers, house-breakers, and man-quellers; all who communed wittingly with accursed persons; all makers of experiments, witches, and charmers; all those who struck priests or defiled sanctuaries; all false executors, and all those who abandoned their children at church doors or otherwise.[13]

Although in those parishes most strongly influenced by Protestant reformers the reading of the Great Sentence began to be replaced, as early as 1538, by the reading of Deuteronomy 28, a step which prepared for the eventual substitution of the milder Protestant Commination,[14] it seems almost certain that John Shakespeare and Mary Arden heard this solemn curse repeatedly in their youth. In them, as in other hearers, the Great Sentence must have quickened a sense of sin and a dread of its frightful consequences.

(f) Another instrument of popular religious education was the Prymer, "of all the books of the Middle Ages . . . the most common and best known."[15] It was a sort of lay Prayer Book, consisting of the Hours of the Blessed Virgin, the Seven Penitential Psalms (Pss. 6, 32, 38, 51, 102, 130, and 143), the Fifteen Gradual Psalms (Pss. 120–134), the Litany, the Office of the Dead (i.e., *Placebo* and *Dirige*, not the Burial Service), and the Commendations (Ps. 119, etc.)[16] In many instances other devotional material was added. In later editions the Psalter was sometimes combined with the Prymer.

That the Prymer was used by all classes of people is shown by the fact that extant copies exist in forms varying from large, beautifully ornamented, and costly, to small, very plain, and inexpensive editions. Though the greatest number of extant Prymers are in Latin, a considerable number are in English. The book is also found in both Latin and English. Editions are numerous, at least as many as twenty-nine having been printed between the years 1534 and 1547, the very years during which John Shakespeare and Mary Arden were growing up.[17]

The Prymer was eventually Protestantized, of course, William Seres being granted an exclusive license to print it by Edward VI in 1553,[18] but Catholic versions continued in use throughout the reign of Queen Mary and even after. The Prymer was primarily a book of private devotions, in many cases so highly treasured by its possessors that it was bequeathed as a legacy in their wills. No doubt the book was also taken to church for use in the service, especially for the Office of the Dead,[19] and the medieval church pew retained its book-rests for this and other reasons,[20] but "the traces of thumb marks so often found on the lower corners of the leaves" tell "a tale most vividly of long and continued holding, which can have only been for devotional purposes."[21]

(g) To Catholic laymen of the early sixteenth century there would also be available a considerable body of printed religious literature from which they could gain a rather comprehensive knowledge of the faith they professed. For example, there were the meditations of the great mystics of the fourteenth century, whose writings were never more popular than just before the Reformation. One of the first books printed at Oxford by Theodoric Root was Richard Rolle's *Explanation of Job*. It appeared in 1483. Other works by Rolle, or thought to be by him, were put into print in the early days of the press, three of them alone by Wynkyn de Worde in the first decades of the sixteenth century. Walter Hilton's *Scale of Perfection* was another mystical treatise early available. It first appeared in print in 1490, coming from the presses of de Worde. Later editions followed: in 1507, one by Julian Notary; in 1521, one by Pepwell and another by Wynkyn de Worde; and in 1533, still another by de Worde. Also available was *The Mirror of Simple Souls*, translated from the French, which went through four editions between 1507 and 1526. The *Imitation of Christ* by Thomas à Kempis was published in English by Pynson in 1503 and by de Worde in 1517. Portions of Margery Kempe's *Contemplations* were printed by Wynkyn de Worde in 1501 and by Pepwell in 1520.[22]

For persons of a less mystical and less pious bent of mind there were religious writings of a more entertaining nature. Of such are *The Golden Legend*, *Dives et Pauper*, and *The Floure of the Commaundements of God*. The first is too well known to need comment, but the other two deserve a paragraph each.

According to H. G. Pfander, "*Dives et Pauper* is . . . the only elaborate didactic treatise, written originally in English prose and built on a framework of the Ten Commandments that has been presented to us from the Middle Ages."[23] It was early printed and enjoyed great popularity.[24]

The work contains a Prologue and ten Books, one for each Commandment or Precept. The Prologue in its fullest form contains ten chapters, and the ten Books are divided into approximately 255 chapters. Thus we see that the treatise is of considerable length. The Prologue, as well as the ten Books, is written in the form of a conversation between a rich man and a poor, but Pauper does most of the talking, making the conversation very lop-sided. . . . The Prologue treats of the virtues of poverty as expounded by Pauper who, although a learned man, goes about the world in poverty and meekness, bringing salvation to both rich and poor by his preaching. Each Commandment is treated in its proper order, but the exposition is much expanded and contemporary disobedience much deplored.[25]

The *Floure of the Commaundements of God* is likewise a didactic treatise in English prose built on the framework of the Ten Commandments and coming to us from the Middle Ages. Hence it is an exception to Pfander's statement about *Dives et Pauper*, and Pfander himself confesses the oversight in a footnote and gives credit to A. W. Pollard for calling the work to his attention. Pfander writes:

This work is divided into two parts, the first being an objective treatment of the Commandments with much quotation from the Bible and Church Fathers, with numerous *exempla* scattered throughout, and with many cross-references to the second part of the work which is a compilation of over 500 *exempla* drawn for the greater part from the sermon series and *Promptuarium* of the Dominican John Herolt, of Nuremberg, who died in 1468. The treatise fills 125 folios (in the Wynken de Worde edition of 1510) and the *Exemplayre*, 134 folios. The Prologue of the *Exemplayre* says that the work was composed in Latin, translated into French, and then into English from the French (in 1509, according to the colophon of the edition of 1510). . . . The English translation of 1521, printed by Wynken de Worde, bears the Chertsey arms and name on the last page, and a Pope, a Bishop, and a Friar appear in the woodcut of the titlepage.[26]

The mere existence of all this mystical, didactic, and entertaining religious literature does not prove that any of it was read by the Shakespeares, but its general availability does prove that the literate Catholic layman of their day need not have been ignorant of his faith.

(h) Those Catholic folk who could not read the religious literature of their day could still learn much about their traditional faith from such visual aids as religious monuments, images, reliquaries, and paintings. With their own eyes they could see before them the depictions of saints, of Mary the Mother of God, and of Christ, the very Son of God himself. Bible stories and saints' legends explaining the images and relics must have been in oral circulation. Sometimes the central incident of a story or legend was painted on the church wall before the illiterate laymen. In homes above the very poorest, painted cloths hung in many a room to serve as constant reminders of the favorite stories of medieval Christianity.

(i) Upon special occasions those very stories would be enacted before the people in village mystery plays. These dramatic presentations of religious history and traditions were irresistible in their power through entertainment to enlighten the laity. Estimating the importance of the mystery play for popular religious education in medieval England, Cardinal Gasquet writes:

> The inventories of parish churches and the churchwardens' accounts which have survived show how very common a feature these religious plays formed in the parish life of the fifteenth century, and the words of the various dramas, of which we still possess copies, show how powerful a medium of teaching they would have been among the simple and unlettered villages of Catholic England, and even to the crowds which at times thronged great cities like Coventry and Chester, to be present at the more elaborate plays acted in these traditional centres of the religious drama.[27]

(j) A final means of popular religious education in pre-Reformation England was song. In this respect, the carol was perhaps even more important than the church hymn. The carol was at the height of its popularity in the fifteenth century, and it had by no means disappeared in the sixteenth. Reformers found it necessary to disapprove of carols; Puritans, to denounce them. They were rooted in the life of the people. Beginning in the dim past as accompaniments to ring dances, carols had developed into rousing songs to be sung either at a dance or around the table or fireside. Many of them were far from religious in theme; some of them were very profane. But others carried a religious burden and gave voice to a kind of religious exultation. In describing the nature and typical contents of the medieval carol, H. Maynard Smith says:

> Carols should be distinguished from hymns. The primary object of a hymn is praise and, after that, aspiration. Carols on the other hand

relate a past event as a reason for present rejoicing. Hymns are addressed to God; carols to men.

> Nowell, nowell, nowell, nowell,
> Tidings glad I think to tell.

expresses the purpose of a carol-singer and his spirit of hilarity. He intended to be noisy, for *nowell* in English was equivalent to *hurrah*, as *noël* in France was used for *vivat*. . . .

Most of the carols have a great similarity. They insist on the virginity of Mary; they speak of Bethlehem that fair city, of the crib between the ox and the ass, of the shepherds and the angels' song, of the star which the wise men followed and of the offerings which they brought. They insist on the theological truths *Verbum caro factum est* and that the child was *Redemptor mundi*. . . . The carols of the Passion are inspired by the . . . sentiment [of a mother's love]; they are almost exclusively concerned with the sorrow of the Mother on the death of her Son.[28]

To just how many of these agencies of popular religious education John Shakespeare and Mary Arden were exposed and in just what ways these agencies were effective in their case it is impossible to say. But that in the early life of both John and Mary some of these instruments of religious education operated effectively it seems unreasonable to deny. Both John and Mary had their share of native intelligence; they spent their youth in parishes which could not be called wholly backward or remote from the main stream of religious life; they were reared in homes of the better sort in their own neighborhood. They must have received a religious training which informed them of a considerable body of Catholic doctrine and habituated them in the performance of many Catholic practices.

(2) A second permissible generalization with respect to the Catholic home of the early and middle sixteenth century is that Catholic parents of that period were aware of their responsibility to train their children in religious matters and could be expected to exert themselves in that direction.

If John and Mary Shakespeare, now the parents of a family of children, were themselves informed Catholics, they could not rest easy in conscience unless they sought earnestly to make their children informed Catholics also.

. . . in Wynkyn de Worde's *Exornatorium Curatorum*, printed to enable those having the cure of souls to perform the duties of instruction laid down by Archbishop Peckham's Provincial Constitution, whilst setting forth a form of examination of conscience under the head of deadly sins, the author bids the curate teach his people to ask themselves: "Whether you have been slothful in God's service. . . . Furthermore, whether you have been negligent to learn your *Pater Noster*, your *Ave Maria*, or your Creed, or whether you have been negligent to teach the same to your own children or to your godchildren. Examine yourself also whether you have taught your children good manners, and guarded them from danger and bad company."[29]

Virtually the same admonitions are made to parents in Richard Whitford's *A werke for Housholders, or for them that have the guyding or governance of any company*, printed by Wynkyn de Worde in 1534, and again by Robert Redman in 1537. Whitford enjoins those who can read to

get their neighbours together on holidays, . . . especially the young and teach them the daily exercise, and in particular the "things they are bound to know or can say: that is the *Paternoster*, the *Ave*, and the *Creed*." . . . Parents, above all things, he urges to look well after their children and to take care of the company they keep. "At every meal, dinner or supper, I have advised, and do now counsel, that one person should with loud voice say thus, 'Paternoster,' with every petition paraphrased and explained, and the Hail Mary and Creed likewise. . . ."

. . . . In the same place our author urges parents to correct their children early for any use of oaths and strong expressions. "Teach your children," he says, "to make their additions under this form: 'yea, father,' 'nay, father,' 'yea, mother,' 'nay, mother,' and ever to avoid such things as 'by cock and pye,' and 'by my hood of green,' and such other."

Finally, . . . Whitford says: "Teach your children to ask a blessing every night, kneeling, before they go to rest, under this form: 'Father, I beseech you a blessing for charity.' " If the child is too stubborn to do this, he says let it "be well whisked." If too old to be corrected in this way, let it be set out in the middle of the dining-room and made to feed by itself, and let it be treated as one would treat one who did not deserve to consort with its fellows. Also teach the young "to ask a blessing for every bishop, abbot, and priest, and of their godfathers and godmothers also."[30]

(a) A good idea of what the daily religious routine of a Catholic layman in the time of John and Mary Shakespeare was supposed to be like and of what habits the Shakespeares might seek to establish in their children is given by the set of directions found in the English Prymer printed at Rouen in 1538:

"First rise up at six o'clock in the morning at all seasons, and in rising do as follows: Thank our Lord who has brought you to the beginning of the day. Commend yourself to God, to Our Lady Saint Mary, and to the saint whose feast is kept that day, and to all the saints in heaven. When you have arrayed yourself say in your chamber or lodging, Matins, Prime, and Hours, if you may. Then go to the church before you do any worldly works if you have no needful business, and abide in the church the space of low mass time, where you shall think on God and thank Him for His benefits. Think awhile on the goodness of God, on His divine might and virtue. . . . If you cannot be so long in the church on account of necessary business, take some time in the day in your house in which to think of these things." . . . Take your meal "reasonably without excess or overmuch forbearing of your meat, for there is as much danger in too little as too much. If you fast once in a week it is enough, besides Vigils and Embers days out of Lent." After dinner rest "an hour or half-an-hour, praying God that in that rest He will accept your health to the end, that after it you may serve Him the more devoutly."

" . . . . As touching your service, say up to *Tierce* before dinner, and make an end of all before supper. And when you are able say the *Dirge* and *Commendations* for all Christian souls, at least on holy days, and if you have leisure say them on other days, at least with three lessons. Shrive yourself every week to your curate, except you have some great hindrance. And beware that you do not pass a fortnight unless you have a very great hindrance. If you have the means refuse not your alms to the first poor body that asketh it of you that day. Take care to hear and keep the Word of God. Confess you every day to God without fail of such sins you know you have done that day." Think often of our Lord's Passion, and at night when you wake turn your thoughts to what our Lord was doing at that hour in His Passion. In your life look for a faithful friend to whom you may open "your secrets," and when found follow his advice.[31]

It is not to be concluded, of course, that the routine daily life of any of the members of the Shakespeare household from 1564–82 followed this pattern. But it can be inferred that John and Mary Shakespeare, taking a serious view of their religious obligations, attempted some approximation of the ideal. The parents must have tried in many ways to foster in

young William and his brothers and sisters the sweet temper of the prayer
to the Guardian Angel which was highly recommended in *Dives et Pauper*
and which Gasquet says was taught by generations of pre-Reformation
Catholic mothers to their children:

> O angel who my guardian art,
>   Through God's paternal love,
> Defend, and shield and rule the charge
>   Assigned thee from above.
>
> From vice's stain preserve my soul,
>   O gentle angel bright,
> In all my life be thou my stay,
>   To all my steps the light.[32]

(b) Apart from the nurture of their children in purely religious matters,
the Shakespeares would do what they could to train their children in the
elementary phases of a secular education. In this training, the religious
aspect would not disappear, but become secondary.

(i) If the Stratford Grammar School required entering pupils to
be able to read, young William may have been introduced to the
mysteries of the horn-book at home. The typical horn-book was a single
printed page mounted on a piece of wood and covered with a thin piece
of transparent horn. On the page were printed the alphabet in large and
small letters, a list of monosyllables combining vowels and consonants,
the exorcism "In the name of the Father, and of the Son, and of the Holy
Ghost, Amen" (placed there, says George A. Plimpton, "to be learned
because every boy was supposed to be more or less full of the devil"[33]),
and finally the Lord's Prayer. Not every horn-book had the same parts,
but those listed above were most common.

At the beginning of the top row of the alphabet was a cross, giving
that row the name of "Christ Cross row." Shakespeare refers to the
"cross-row" in *Richard III* (I, i, 55) as the row from which King Richard
"plucks the letter G" and thinks that George Clarence, since his name
begins with "G," is the one by whom "his issue disinherited should be."
Shakespeare's other allusion to a horn-book, in *Love's Labour's Lost*
(V, i, 50)

> Yes, yes; he teaches boys the horn-book.
> What is a, b, spelt backward, with the horn on his head?

(words spoken by Moth in reference to Holofernes) is taken by some[34] to prove that William himself was taught to read the horn-book by a schoolmaster, hence not at home.*

(ii) Shakespeare's allusion to "an absey-book," as in the Bastard's speech in *King John* (I, i, 196) and in Speed's simile in *The Two Gentlemen of Verona* (II, i, 23–24), suggests his familiarity with another elementary book first knowledge of which he may have gained at home.

The ABC book was an elementary reader to which the Catechism was often added. There must have been many thousands of copies printed during the reign of Queen Elizabeth. An exclusive license for printing the *ABC with the Cathechism* had been given to Richard Day, his heirs and assigns, by King Edward VI in 1553, and that license had been renewed by Queen Elizabeth. But of all the Elizabethan ABC books only a single fragment of four imperfect leaves remains to us today. It is in the library of Worcester College, Oxford, and has survived by the accident of being used as binding material for a Latin work by Jac. Ludovicus Strebaeus when it was printed in Cologne in 1582. Its title page, with omissions supplied by H. C. Anders, reads as follows:

> Th[e] AB[C] with the Catec[hisme] that is to saie the [in]struction of the [Christian] faith, to be learne[d by eve]rie Childe befor[e he be] brough to be [con]firmed of t[he bishop]. Newlie [im]print[ed by the] *assign[s] of John D[aie]*—to be sold at the . . . Starre in [Pater]noster Ro[w]. Forbidding all oth[ers to print] this Catech[ism].[35]

Of course, a Protestant ABC book would not be acceptable in a strict Catholic home. That does not mean, however, that there could have been no ABC book in the Shakespeare home, for there were Catholic editions of the book in circulation. Anders notes three editions, any one of which might have served the Shakespeares. The first dates about 1553–58 and is known to us only from a title page in the Bagford collection. That title page reads:

An ABC, with the Pater noster, Ave Maria, the Crede; & ten com-

---

* W. J. Rolfe (*Shakespeare the Boy* [New York, 1896], p. 99) thinks William learned to read his horn-book at home. So, too, does Oliver Baker (*in Shakespeare's Warwickshire* [London, 1937], pp. 170–71), who says, ". . . we can take it for granted that . . . William . . . would be one of such scholars and children who were 'set' for the Grammar School, and that he was, at least, ready to enter into his accidence and grammar. . . ." Baker explains Andrew W. Tuer's inability, while preparing his *History of the Hornbook*, "to find any trace of horn-books in any cathedral libraries, or public schools of old foundation" and his amazement at the discovery that "the word horn-book does not once occur" in the dozen histories of English public schools by the fact that "most grammar schools did not teach their pupils until after they had done with any such elementary aids as horn-books." It still remains true, however, that William Shakespeare may have learned his horn-book in a petty school, of which more later.

maundements with certaine instructions that Scholemasters ought to bring vp children in. Imprinted at London, by Thomas Hacket.[36]

The second edition is of about 1555. A copy exists today in Queen's College, Oxford. Its confident title page makes claims which sound very much like modern advertisements of home-study English courses:

> An ABC for chyldren. Here is an ABC devysed with syllables with the Pater noster, the Ave Maria and the Crede, both in Latin and Englishe. —And by this Booke, a man that hath good capacitie and can no letter on the boke, may learn to reade in the space of vi wekes, both Latin and Englysch, yf he gave therto good diligence, as it hath been divers times proved. Also ye mai lern therbi to write English truly and to knowe the true Ortography of the Englishe tongue.[37]

The fact that the author spells "English" three different ways in the space of a few lines makes it obvious that his notions of "true Ortography" were highly flexible. The colophon shows the work to have been "Imprynted at London in Poules Churchyarde by Jhon Kyng, in the signe of the Swane." The book contains twelve pages of reading exercises, an invocation of the Trinity, the *Gloria tibi . . . virgo sancta et beata intercede pro nobis . . .* , the Lord's Prayer in Latin and English, *Ave Maria . . .* Hail Mary, the Creed in Latin and English, the Ten Commandments, and "Preceptes of good lyvynge."[38]

The third Catholic edition mentioned by Anders is a later version of the second. A copy exists today in the Library of Trinity College, Dublin. Its colophon shows it to have been "Imprinted at London for Abraham Veale, dwelling in Paules Churchyard at the sign of the Lamb." Noteworthy differences in content from the earlier edition are the omission of the *Ave Maria* and the inclusion of two graces: (1) "O Merciful Father, the which nourishest all creatures feed us with thy gifts, that we misuse them not, but . . . may live virtuously and godlily," and (2) "We thank thee . . . for thy manifold benefits, and we beseech thee further . . . thou wilt also fatherly maintain our souls always in the true faith."[39]

(iii) Other books which careful Elizabethan parents had in their homes are the "Books of Nurture." These were manuals of behavior for boys at home, at school, at church, and elsewhere. To make them relatively palatable and easier to remember, they were often written in doggerel verse. The well-known *The Schoole of Vertue, and booke of good Nourture for Chyldren and youth to learne their dutie by*, written by Francis Seager, was probably published too late to serve in the training of William Shakespeare, since it did not appear until 1577, but *The Boke of Nurture, or*

Schoole of good maners for men, servants, and children, compiled by Hugh Rhodes, which went through five editions between 1554 and 1577, was in the field early enough to be available if the Shakespeares wanted it.[40]

(c) The problem of whether young William was taught to read the Bible at home need not detain us here, for it will be discussed later. It may be said that from 1564 to 1582 no faithful Catholic household could have had an English Bible in it, for no Catholic translation had yet been made. Existing translations would be either too expensive and unwieldy, as in the case of the Great Bible or the Bishops' Bible, or too strongly Protestant, as in the case of the Geneva. If it could be proved that William Shakespeare's use of the Bible in his writings reveals that sort of familiarity which comes only from regular and extensive reading and memorizing during childhood, the case for the Catholicity of the Shakespeare household would be considerably weakened.

(d) A final possible religious influence exerted in the Shakespeare home upon the boy William is that of painted cloths. That there were painted cloths in the Henley Street house is almost a foregone conclusion:

> In the absence of an inventory of his effects, we cannot tell with great exactness what there was of furniture or domestic implements in John Shakespeare's house, but we can be quite sure that he had painted cloths, and also we can make some likely guesses at their subjects.
> . . . Cloths, sometimes stained but generally painted, were cheap; and in Stratford the houses being built of "half-timber" needed them to counteract the draughts that would have found their way through the chinks in the walls.[41]

Shakespeare himself testifies to the influence of painted cloths as teachers of conventional morals when in *The Rape of Lucrece* he has Tarquin encourage himself in the contemplation of his evil design by saying:

> Who fears a sentence or an old man's saw,
> Shall by a painted cloth be kept in awe.[42]

The same function of the painted cloth is much more dramatically pointed out in Pandarus' last speech in *Troilus and Cressida*. Pandarus enters just as Troilus is leaving. He calls to the young prince, only to have Troilus scorn him and call down upon him a curse of "ignominy and shame." The rebuff throws Pandarus into a mood of satirical moral reflection, and he exclaims:

A goodly medicine for my aching bones! O world! world! world! thus is the poor agent despised. O traitors and bawds, how earnestly are you set a-work, and how ill requited! why should our endeavor be so loved, and the performance so loathed? what verse for it? what instance for it?—Let me see!—

> Full merrily the humble-bee doth sing,
> Till he hath lost his honey and his sting;
> And being once subdu'd in armed tail,
> Sweet honey and sweet notes together fail.

Good traders in the flesh, *set this in you, painted cloths.*[43]

A hint of the didactic stodginess of the painted cloth is given by Shakespeare in *As You Like It.* Orlando and Jacques meet in the forest of Arden and make cutting remarks to each other. Jacques asks questions about Rosalind, which Orlando answers evasively and testily. Jacques remarks:

> You are full of pretty answers. Have you not been acquainted with goldsmiths' wives, and conn'd them out of rings?

To which Orlando replies:

> Not so; but I answer you right painted cloth, from whence you have studied your questions.[44]

To Falstaff we are indebted for a hint as to what subjects were common in the painted cloths which Shakespeare may have seen. When Mistress Quickly complains that she will have to pawn her plate and the tapestry of her dining-chambers if, instead of bringing Falstaff to justice for his failure to pay old debts, she grant him a new loan of ten pounds, the ever-ready roisterer shouts:

> Glasses, glasses, is the only drinking: and for thy walls a pretty slight drollery, or the story of the Prodigal, or the German hunting in water-work, is worth a thousand of these bed-hangings and these fly-bitten tapestries.[45]

"A pretty slight drollery" would be some "sort of fanciful design with groups of grotesque figures which more or less grew out of foliage, or sometimes of animal forms."[46] It would have no religious or moral significance. "The story of the Prodigal" would be the very popular Bible story of the Prodigal Son, with its several moral lessons to teach. "The German hunting in water-work" would be a forest scene profuse with hounds, game and quarry. The adjective "German" applies to the painter and his style, rather than to the scene. As an example of a "German hunting," Baker describes a series of engravings called *Fox and Hare Hunting*, done in 1576 by a Flemish artist, Joannes van der Straet, who is known to have designed many sporting subjects for wall hangings.[47]

If the Falstaff of *The Merry Wives of Windsor* were the same Sir John of the two parts of *King Henry IV*, there would be a peculiar appropriateness to the decoration of his room in the Garter Inn in *The Merry Wives*, either as proof of the sincerity of Sir John's preference for the subject of the Prodigal or as a just punishment for his self-interested advice to Dame Quickly, for that room is described by the Host as "painted about with the story of the Prodigal, fresh and new."[48]

Finally we are indebted to Falstaff for the hint that the Parable of Lazarus and the Rich Man was a favorite subject of painted cloths and one familiar to Shakespeare, for the redoubtable captain describes the men he has pressed into military service as

ancients, corporals, lieutenants, gentlemen of companies, slaves as ragged as Lazarus in the painted cloth, where the glutton's dogs licked his sores.[49]

Another informant with respect to subjects of paintings familiar to Shakespeare is Borache in *Much Ado about Nothing*. Speaking on fashion, Borache says to Conrade:

Seest thou not, I say, what a deformed thief this fashion is? how giddily he turns about all the hot bloods between fourteen and five-and-thirty? sometime fashioning them like Pharaoh's soldiers in the reechy painting; sometime like god Bel's priests in the old church-window; sometime like the shaven Hercules in the smirched worm-eaten tapestry, where his cod-piece seems as massy as his club?[50]

Though painted walls were not likely to have been part of William Shakespeare's home environment, there were undoubtedly wall paintings which he saw during his youth and which contributed in some small way to the formation of his religious conceptions.

Fripp points to one example "which dates from Shakespeare's birth" and which "was doubtless seen by him fresh and new in a house by the 'Mere-side' in Rother Market, a tavern, the property of the Perrotts."

The painting . . . gives scenes from the story of Tobias and the Angel in the Apocrypha. . . . A frieze-text in black-letter tells the story, the scenes of which are interspersed with bold designs of flowers and fruit. In the first (of the three preserved) Tobit and Anna, outside their house in Nineveh, in out-door garments, take farewell of their son, Tobias, and his companion, the disguised Raphael. Tobit wears a long black gown edged with gold, with a high collar, Anna a black gown over a dress of gold brocade. They have low-brimmed hats, she a coif and pleated ruff. Tobias is gay in yellow doublet with red sleeves, orange pantaloons, light hose, and yellow-pointed low-heeled shoes, black cape and greenish cloak. Neither wears his hat. They have short-cut hair and beards, and long moustaches. In such garb might the story have been staged in the year of Sir Robert Dudley's portrait, painted on his being made a Knight of the Garter in 1559. Tobias, indeed, in feature and dress, bears considerable resemblance to Sir Robert in that portrait, and Raphael might be his godly brother, Lord Ambrose Dudley. . . .[51]

The other two scenes, as well as the first, are reproduced in black and white by Fripp.[52] They are less striking than the first.

The second scene is half obliterated. It shows Tobias and Raphael starting out on their journey to Ragae in Media to get the money which Gabael, of that place, held for Tobit. The third scene is well preserved and shows Tobias stooping down to wash in the river Tigris and the fish jumping out of the river to swallow him. The river flows between a medieval walled city with towers and battlements in the background and a wooded rolling country in the foreground.

Whether or not the boy William saw any paintings in the Stratford Guild Chapel, we cannot say. In 1807 the whitewash and paint covering the Chapel murals were removed to reveal that depictions of St. George and the Dragon and of the murder of Thomas à Becket had once adorned the wall in the nave, that the Day of Judgment had been painted above the chancel-arch, and that St. Helena's finding of the True Cross had been depicted in the chancel. But these paintings must have been defaced in 1563.[53] Leland, writing in 1542, said that about "the body" or nave of the Guild Chapel was "curiously painted *The Dance of Death*."[54] Fripp suggests that since this "satirical conception" of mortality "was solemnly regarded by the Reformers," the painting of it in the Stratford Guild Chapel may have survived the defacement and may have been familiar to young William, though all trace of the picture has since disappeared.[55]

In an effort to evaluate the importance of painted cloths as an influence upon the growing Shakespeare, wherever he may have seen them, Baker asks:

How much did they mean to him, these storied hangings and their admonitory inscriptions? When in the long winter nights the flickering flames rose and fell on his father's hearth, and the bright flashes chased one another across the walls, what visions might he not have espied, what shapes would start into life? These gods and devils, heroes and beggars, revels of prodigals, sieges of cities, forests and leafy glades. What fantastic dreams, what thick-coming fancies would an imaginative child indulge? "Such tricks hath strong imagination!"

And as he grew in years and grammar school learning and visited the homes of his uncles and aunts, who can tell how much the Classical Mythology of these old hangings, the Bible incidents, the sage proverbs, wise saws and mottoes which surrounded him may have meant for him? Can we hope to measure the influence they may have had on the poet and the works he has left us?[56]

The same attitude of suggestive questioning in which Baker views the matter of painted cloths must characterize anyone who attempts to summarize the religious home training of William Shakespeare. It seems right to say that the Shakespeares were parents who had ample opportunity to inform themselves of the major tenets of Catholicism, who became somewhat imbued with its spirit, who practiced the simple customs of Catholic devotion in their home, who understood their duty to train their children in the things of the faith, and who had means at their disposal to help them in this duty.

2. The School

(1) Whatever the influences of the home may have been, they would soon be modified by the influences of the school. Although no documentary evidence is known to exist to prove that William Shakespeare attended the Stratford Grammar School, the assumption is so natural that few deny it.[57] The writings of the poet reveal such an intimate familiarity with the curriculum and textbooks of the grammar schools of his day as to suggest irresistibly that the poet himself had gone through a grammar school training.

The school at Stratford-upon-Avon had been established in 1553 by the Stratford Corporation Charter as the direct successor of the ancient Guild School and was flourishing during William's youth. John Shakespeare had risen to the eminence of the chief aldermanship by the time William was of school age. In consideration of his place in the community the father would scarcely have kept his eldest son from the benefits of a free education in the local institution.

(2) The exact age at which young William began his schooling is conjectural. Foster Watson writes that for grammar schools "the entrance age was usually seven years, though sometimes six and sometimes eight

was prescribed," and he quotes John Brinsley as saying, "Six is very young."[58] The reason why "six" seemed "very young" to Brinsley is that entrance requirements to many grammar schools included an ability to read and write. Some schools even went so far as to require an ability to read Latin.[59] Stowe points out, however, that

> not a few schools were burdened with the task of furnishing the elementary education as well as the higher. Thus the school at Burford was to consist of "grammarian scholars" and "petties," "so that every man in the town and parish, minding to set his child to school, being mere children having no infirmity or sickness, should be taught his A. B. C., his Catechism, primer, and to read and write until he should be able to be preferred to the grammar school," while in Burford, Ringwood, Wellingborough, and Worcester, reading and writing were to be taught.[60]

In such schools as had an elementary department or "petty school," six years would not be a "very young" entering age. Speaking of the usual entering age for elementary schools, Charles Hoole, in his *A New Discovery of the Old Art of Teaching School, The Petty School*, writes:

> It is usual in cities and greater towns to put children to school about four or five years of age, and in country villages, because of further distance, not till about six or seven.[61]

The reason of distance could not apply in William Shakespeare's case, for it was a matter of a few minutes' walk from the Henley Street home to the Guild Hall in Church Street.* If there was a petty school at Stratford, William may have started school at an age as early as five.

(3) Opinions vary as to whether or not a petty school was kept at Stratford. Fripp says:

---

* On the basis of an entry in the Stratford Town Council records under date of February 14, 1596, to the effect that "School was not to be kept in the Chapel," it has been widely assumed that William Shakespeare went to school in the Guild Chapel. But earlier entries, notably those of the year of John Shakespeare's bailiwick, 1568, recording expenditures for "repairing the school," "dressing and sweeping the school-house," and "ground-selling the old school, and taking down the sollar over the school," are strong indications that classes in William's day were held in a schoolroom in the Guild Hall. The entry of 1596 merely marked the completion of repairs undertaken at that time. See J. Q. Adams, *op. cit.*, p. 49, footnote 1.

With respect to the comparison in *Twelfth Night* (III, ii, 82) of Malvolio to "a pedant that keeps a school i' the church," Sir John Edwin Sandys (*Shakespeare's England*, I, 227), though he says that "from 1568 to 1595 the [Stratford] school was held in the adjoining chapel," and though he repeats the suggestion that in *Twelfth Night* "the poet is . . . recalling the chapel in which the school was held in the days of his own boyhood," nevertheless concedes that "it is at least as likely that he was thinking of the school in St. Olave's, Southwark (near his theatre), or that of St. Michael's, Cornhill."

There was an elementary school in Stratford, such as was kept in later years by Thomas Parker, a teacher licensed by the Bishop. He taught small boys to read, while his wife instructed girls in needlework. From such a master Shakespeare learned his 'horn-book', also known as the 'ABC book'. . . .[62]

Fripp's statement seems to mean that William was sent to a small private school, rather than to a branch of the grammar school proper. There were such schools, and Fripp points to one "at Henley-in-Arden endowed by George Whately of Stratford in 1586."[63] The advantage of attending a private petty school was questionable, for a school of this sort was likely to be a dame school taught by some poor woman almost as ignorant as her pupils and impelled, as Hoole complains, to undertake teaching "as a mere shelter from beggary."[64]

Rolfe, Lee, and Sandys, in writing of Shakespeare's education, have young William enter grammar school directly, at the age of seven.[65] Thus they presuppose that William either attended a private petty school or learned his horn-book and ABC book at home.

There are those, however, who assume that William attended a petty school connected with the Stratford Grammar School. Thus, Thomas Spencer Baynes, in his essay "What Shakespeare Learnt at School," in pointing out that "children were often sent to the petty school, or English side of the grammar school, about the age of five, and after remaining there two years entered the grammar school proper, and began the study of Latin at seven,"[66] implies that William attended the public petty school. Arthur F. Leach, in his *Victoria County Histories: Warwickshire*, speaks of William's "being initiated into the first elements among the 'petties.'"[67]

Perhaps the strongest evidence for the existence of a public petty school at Stratford is the circumstantial fact that Stratford school masters were well paid and had assistants. The Charter of 1553, in establishing "the King's New School of Stratford-upon-Avon," provided that the "Master of the Free School of Stratford-upon-Avon" should have

> a certain annual revenue, pension, or annuity of twenty pounds per year with a clause of distriction for the security of those said payments, as also certain other lands, tenements, possessions, and inheritances from any persons or any person, besides the stated annuity, revenue, or pension of twenty pounds, provided that they shall not exceed the yearly value of twenty pounds a year.[68]

This meant a possible maximum of forty pounds a year, a sum attractive to the best grammar school teachers of the day and putting the incumbent in a position to pay for an assistant to teach the petty school and lower forms of the grammar school. The overlapping of dates in the terms of office of some of the masters suggests that two teachers were serving at the same time, one as the assistant of the other. Walter Roche is credited with serving as master until 1572, but Simon Hunt was licensed to teach in Stratford school in October, 1571, so that it appears as if Hunt began his teaching in a subordinate capacity under Roche. Lewis calls Hunt "Roche's assistant."[69]

The arrangement would be quite regular. As Stowe remarks:

Where the staff consisted of two, the master and the usher, the latter was generally given the elementary work. Thus, in Ipswich, the usher was elected to teach "to write, Cipher, and Cast accompt, chiefly suche as are to learn ye Grammer;" in Aldenham the usher was to "train up young beginners in A.B.C., Primer, Catechism, and other English books." In Leicester the usher was to teach the "petits" while the master taught the "upper grammar scholars." In Wellingborough "English, writing, and casting accompts" were to be taught by the undermaster, while in Saint Bees the usher was to teach "the children to read and write English, and to say by heart the Catechism in English . . . ;" when the scholars were able to "learn construction" they were to be admitted into the master's school.[70]

And Hunt's succession to the mastership after the resignation of Roche would also be regular. Stowe writes:

In the case of the absence of one [master or usher], the duties of both were to be performed by the other, and so when a vacancy occurred caused by death, dismissal, or leaving of either master or usher, the other was to perform the duties of both until the vacancy was filled, while in some such cases the usher if qualified for the position of master was to be preferred.[71]

The significance of all this for the purpose in hand is that if William was sent to a petty school, either a private one or the public one, some of the training considered earlier in this chapter as having been received in his parents' home would have been received in school, and the modifying influences of outside religious contacts would have begun sooner than was earlier implied. If it was the *public* petty school to which William was sent, then the personal influence of his schoolmasters was first brought to bear at a more tender age and was extended over a period two years longer than if William entered grammar school directly at the age of seven. Since we know something about his schoolmasters, this is a significant consideration.

(4) (a) If William started school immediately after his fifth birthday, that is, late in April or early in May, 1569, he may have had John Acton for his first schoolmaster. Fripp says that John Acton left Stratford at Christmas, 1569, and infers that his departure was a direct and punitive result of his sympathy with, if not participation in, the Northern Rebellion.[72] In that case, Acton would have been Catholic in his religious views, and going to school under him would have meant for little William no disruptive break with the religious atmosphere of his home. A. R. Bayley, in giving the dates of Walter Roche's mastership as 1570-72,[73] infers that the five-year-old William would have come under the care of Acton, whom Roche succeeded.

(b) Entering school at any time between Christmas, 1569, and early 1572, William would have had Walter Roche for his first teacher. There is good reason to believe that Roche was rather strongly Protestant. In the first place, he was chosen to succeed Acton, and if Acton lost his position through support of the Northern Rebellion, his successor must have been c'.osen with regard to his political and religious views. In the second place, Roche's education suggests more than indifference in religious matters. A Walter Roche was admitted a scholar of Corpus Christi College, Oxford, on February 16, 1554, from Lancaster. He was a Devon Probationary Fellow of the same College in 1558 and received the B. A. degree on June 1, 1559.[74] Bayley elsewhere points out that "as he appears to be identical with one of the two Corpus Christi College Choristers of 1552, he would probably have attended Magdalen College School in the early part of his career, in accordance with the provisions of his founder, Bishop Foxe, as expressed in the Corpus Statutes."[75] Magdalen College was puritanic in tendencies. Its president, Laurence Humphrey, a returned exile, "made a determined protest against the reading of Ovid and other authors 'in whom they [the students] study strange tongues to the decay of godliness.' "[76] Magdalen College School must have been likewise strongly Protestant. In the third place, the later career of Roche suggests his Protestantism. He was presented to the rectory of Droitwich in 1569, and he held that living all during his schoolmastership at Stratford. Perhaps in exchange for the living at Droitwich, he was appointed to the rectory of Clifford Chambers by the Queen on November 4, 1574. His political and religious qualifications, therefore, must have been satisfactory to Protestants. He resigned the rectory of Clifford Chambers on January 20, 1577/8, but continued to live in Stratford, devoting himself to the profession of law. The chamberlains' accounts for 1582 refer to "a tenement in the tenure" of Mr. Walter Roche in Chapel Street,* and thus prove the ex-master's residence in Stratford at that time. As late as 1604 he was living at No. 20 Corn Street, only "three doors above New Place."[77] He had married and reared a family, for the Parish Register records that "Mary daughter to Mr. Walter Roche, minister, was baptized 11th of Sept., 1575."[78]

Accepting, then, the rather pronounced Protestantism of Walter Roche, we may conclude that young William, in coming under the instruction of Roche at an age no older than seven, was exposed to the personal influence of a Protestant schoolmaster. The boy must have sensed a difference in spirit between the Catholic Shakespeare home and the Protestant school. An awareness of this difference may have disturbed the tranquillity of his awakening religious nature. It is not necessary to assume precocity on the part of William to say that Roche's personal influence could be disturbing. If not precocious, Shakespeare was superbly intelligent. A highly intelligent child like him would feel the subtle differences between Catholicism and Protestantism, even in the early stages of differentiation.

(c) This same subtle difference of spirit would be apparent to young William during his earliest associations with his next schoolmaster, Simon Hunt. If, as Lewis says and Adams conjectures, Hunt was "appointed to assist [Roche], and . . . had charge of the beginners,"[79] he may have been Shakespeare's first schoolteacher. There is no doubt that Hunt taught Shakespeare longest and, therefore, gave him most of his school training.

It is only recently that Hunt has been accurately identified. Entries in the Stratford chamberlains' accounts to record the payment of schoolmasters' wages do not mention Hunt's Christian name. There were many Hunts in Warwickshire and a few in Stratford, and from among these Halliwell-Phillipps chose "Thomas" Hunt, later curate of Luddington (from which charge he was suspended for contumacy in 1584) as Shakespeare's schoolmaster.[80] Sir Sidney Lee accepted this identification in the early editions of his *Life of Shakespeare*, but corrected himself in editions since 1915. Others also adopted Halliwell-Phillipps' conjecture.

Another identification was made by A. F. Leach in the *Victoria County Histories*.[81] Leach believed Hunt to be "George" Hunt, a Merchant-Taylor schoolboy, who took his degree from Magdalen College, Oxford,

---

* In connection with Roche's Chapel Street house, Sir Sidney Lee makes a comment which is interesting from the standpoint of the roofing preferences of Stratford real estate owners. He writes: "Tiled roofs were characteristic of such buildings ['the better houses'], but at times an owner of conservative tendencies would insist on the superiority of thatch, like Walter Roche, who moved into a house in Chapel Street in 1582, and replaced the tiles with thatch." *Stratford-on-Avon*, p. 131.

in 1573, and who might have put in a term of teaching at Stratford before he returned as Fellow of his College in 1575.

The question was settled in 1905 when Joseph W. Gray discovered, in the episcopal register at Worcester, Hunt's license to teach. The license gives Hunt's Christian name and the date of his coming to Stratford. The entry appears under "October, 1571," and runs as follows:

> XXIX DIE eiusdem mensis & anno predicto emanavit licencia Simoni Hunt in artibus bacch. docendi literas, instruendi pueros in schola grammaticali in villa de Stratford-super-Avon.[82]

There can now be no doubt, therefore, that Shakespeare's teacher was *Simon* Hunt and that he wielded the ferule at Stratford for a period beginning in the fall of 1571.

Neither can there be any doubt that at the beginning of his mastership (he succeeded Roche late in 1571 or early in 1572) Hunt was a Protestant. Boases's *Oxford University Register* reports Simon Hunt as supplicating for the B. A. on March 30, 1568, as being admitted on April 5 of the same year, and as being determined by a disputation in 1569.[83] Before being awarded a University degree, Hunt would have had to take the Oath of Supremacy, and while the Oath was not an infallible indication of a sincere Protestantism, it was a stumbling block to Catholics and a means adopted by the government to rid Oxford of Catholics. The connivance of friendly proctors sometimes made it possible for Catholics of sensitive conscience to escape taking the Oath, but for most Catholics the Oath was a barrier to academic distinction. It is not likely that Hunt hesitated to take it in 1568, for only two years later he received a license to teach at Stratford, issued by Bishop Nicholas Bullingham of Worcester, "an almost unquestionable proof of Protestantism."[84]

Thus it is that whether Walter Roche or Simon Hunt was Shakespeare's first teacher, the boy's earliest school experience (a remotely possible contact with John Acton being excepted) would have been colored by the personality of a Protestant master, and the observant youth would have marked a difference between the spirit of his parents and the spirit of his teacher.

But from what we know of the later life of Simon Hunt, it is apparent that as William continued to go to school under Hunt, he found his master more and more sympathetic with the Old Faith. For Hunt became first a Catholic, then a Douay seminary student, and finally a Jesuit.

A convenient presentation of the documentary evidence to prove this conversion is given by J. H. Pollen in his article "A Shakespeare Discovery, His School-Master afterwards a Jesuit," published in two parts

in *The Month*, October and November, 1917.[85] The first bit of evidence
is an entry in the *Douay Diaries* of a list of Englishmen who matriculated
in the University of Douay before 1612 containing the name of "M.
Simon Hunt, major."[86] The list of *Angli pauperes* in which Hunt's name
occurs is without date, and Pollen, by a study of the names and terms
of office of successive Rectors of the University, concludes that the date
is "not later than 1575." This date is the same as that given by Fripp[87]
and Leach[88] as the date terminating Hunt's mastership at the Stratford
Grammar School. The Stratford chamberlains' accounts rendered March
14, 1575/6, report 3*s*. "paid to the serjeantes for a schole master that
came from Warwick,"[89] so that it appears as if Hunt's successor had by
that time been chosen, or at least was being interviewed by the appointing authorities. Pollen believes that the "M" in the entry stands for
"Magister" and the "major" for "past the usual age for admission."

The next two documentary traces of Hunt are in the *Douay Diary* also
and are related to each other. Father Knox presents the first as follows:

> 17 September, 1576, D. Hunt and D. Viccareus of Marchiennes
> College, undertook the voyage to Rome. But as the pest was raging,
> they were forced to desist from their journey.[90]

The second and related trace is an entry in the *Diary* under March 6,
1577:

> About this time we heard that not only Mr. Holt and Standish, but
> also Mr. Madder, Mr. Hunt and others, who left us here last summer
> or afterwards for Rome, had reached there safely.[91]

All that we know of what happened to Hunt after he reached Rome
we learn from a single entry in the *Catalogus Primorum Patrum vel
Fratrum Societatis Jesu ex Anglia*, "written at Rome in 1640 from the
materials then in General's Archives, by Father Nathaniel Southwell
(*vere* Bacon)," whose autograph "is now at Stonyhurst." The entry is
as follows:

> No. 56. SIMON HUNTUS admissus Romae in domo probationis,
> 20 Aprilis 1578. *Liber Procuratoris*. Videtur ibidem studia perfecisse,
> nam Poenitentiarius postea fuit ad S. Petri eoque in munere diem
> obiit, 11 Junii 1585. *Catalogus Defunctorum*.[92]

It is clear, then, that Hunt entered the English College at Rome,
completed his studies, and was ordained a priest. The date of Hunt's
priesthood is not known, but Pollen believes it "to have been not later
than 1579." This is interesting, for it means, as Pollen suggests, that

Hunt was probably ordained by "Thomas Goldwell, the venerable old Bishop of St. Asaph, of the Order of Theatines and Warden of the English Hospice," who "as Vicegerent (then called suffragan) of the Cardinal Vicar of Rome (Jacomo Savelli) . . . was a sort of vicar-general of Rome *in Pontificalibus*" upon whom "devolved in ordinary course the great labor of pontificating in the vast ceremonies of consecrating priests at St. John Lateran's."[93] Since, as we have pointed out in Part II of this work, Bishop Goldwell was the head of the English mission of 1580 (though he never reached England), there is a point of personal contact, through Hunt, between the English mission and Stratford and the Shakespeares. That personal contact may have had a double aspect, for "as English Penitentiary at the Basilica of St. Peter's, Hunt succeeded Robert Persons." Persons did get to England, and perhaps to Stratford.

Under what circumstances and at exactly what time Hunt became more Catholic than Protestant in his sympathies we cannot know. Fripp believes Hunt's conversion came early in his mastership. He says that "the lot of the English Romanists" after the Northern Rebellion and the St. Bartholomew massacre "was pitiable, and to Hunt's credit his sympathy was with the persecuted. His opinions changed at the moment when it was all to his advantage that they should coincide with those of the powers in being."[94] But the meaning of the evidence which Fripp cites as proof of this early change of heart is not clear. The evidence is the entry in the chamberlains' accounts from Michaelmas, 1572, to Michaelmas, 1573, reading:

> Received of Master Hunt towardes the repayringe of the Schole wyndowes 7*s*. 11*d*.

Fripp concludes that "a little before Christmas 1572 or Easter 1573 . . . , 'Chapel' was the scene of an exceptional rag between master and boys, or at least some of the boys, in which 'evil opinion' and 'mislike' found vent in the smashing of glass and damage to wood-work."[95] But the entry (the only one related to Hunt's teaching term at Stratford yet found) does not necessarily prove hostility on the part of the students, nor that the hostility, if any existed, was a reaction to the schoolmaster's religious convictions. Arthur F. Leach points out that items for the repair of school windows appear frequently in school accounts of the Elizabethan period, and that boys seem to have broken school windows systematically at the "barring out" of the master upon leaving for the holidays.[96]

Lewis makes the "barring-out" not the consequence of Hunt's stand for Catholicism, but rather the very occasion for declaring himself. He says, "Stratford Puritanism was not to his liking, for, consequent upon a barring-out by his pupils in 1573, he turned staunch Roman Catholic."[97]

As plausible an assumption as any with regard to Hunt's change of heart is that of Pollen, to the effect "that the first seeds of Hunt's conversion were sown during his stay at Oxford; for the old faith had always had her favourers there."[98] Such an assumption would mean that Hunt, though formally approved by the Earl of Warwick, Bishop Bullingham, and the Stratford Corporation, was already leaning toward Catholicism when he became William Shakespeare's teacher in 1571 and that the "conversion" was merely a gradual clarification of Hunt's views in his own mind during the next four years. In any event, it is safe to say that Hunt's personal influence upon his young pupil was in the main Catholic.

The extent of that influence would depend, of course, upon Shakespeare's respect for Hunt, and the question becomes pertinent: Did Shakespeare later ridicule Simon Hunt in the character of Holofernes? Leach is quite certain "that poor Mr. Hunt was the original of Holofernes" and asks, "Is not his very name suggested when Holofernes enters talking of a hunt, 'very reverend sport, truly'?"[99]

It is hard to determine whether Shakespeare drew his picture of Holofernes from his own experience with schoolmasters during his youth or from his observation of them during his adult years. Of the schoolmasters Shakespeare knew from having sat under their ferule, he knew Simon Hunt best. But Shakespeare must also have known very well the rather pedantic Master Alexander Aspinall who came to Stratford in 1582 and stayed for forty years. In Aspinall, Fripp sees "the prototype of Holofernes,"[100] and, indeed, his case is not a weak one.

> He was a dominating, able, pompous person, an Oxford scholar (he took his M. A. from Brasenose in 1578), vastly respected for his learning and judgment, and ready to play many parts in borough matters— principal burgess, Chamberlain, bum-bailiff on occasion, alderman, Deputy Town Clerk. He was exact and exemplary, and facetiously known among his colleagues as 'Great Philip Macedon.'[101]

The receipt for his salary which Aspinall made out on November 6, 1585, is as Fripp says, "a model of fussy long-windedness."[102] The resolution which he drew up in his own handwriting upon the occasion of his being 'amoved' from his aldermanship to "first place amongst the Chief Burgesses" in 1614 is an amusing piece of self-emulation:

> Master Aspinall, with most worthy commendations of his continual and faithful service, secrecy, fidelity and diligence, with exceeding and hearty thanks by this Company to him for his very many and great

pains taken in the affairs and for the good of this borough, is, at his earnest request, discharged from the office of an alderman; and he is now by common consent of courtesy (in regard he is an ancient Master of Art, and a man learned, and Schoolmaster of the King's Free School) placed in the first place amongst the Chief Burgesses.[103]

Even if it were certain that Shakespeare had Hunt in mind when he drew the picture of Holofernes, it is not apparent that Shakespeare was manifesting a disrespectful attitude toward Hunt. It is true that the pedant Holofernes overflows with Latin words and English synonyms to the point of making himself ludicrous. His "extemporal epitaph on the death of the deer" does "something affect the letter," as Holofernes said it would, and does show his "rare talent" to be a gift "simple, simple; a foolish extravagant spirit, full of forms, figures, shapes, objects, ideas, apprehensions, motions, revolutions."[104] But all this does not indicate an attitude on Shakespeare's part which proves a childhood antagonism toward Hunt and a resistance to his personal influence. Rather is there something in Shakespeare's picture of the schoolmaster which suggests nostalgia and amused, good-natured reminiscence. The characterization leads Sir Sidney Lee to say that "in the pedantic Holofernes . . . , Shakespeare has carefully portrayed the *best* type of the rural school-master. . . ."[105]

If the date of Hunt's matriculation in Douay is later than 1575 (as it may well have been, since Pollen establishes the date upon the circumstantial evidence of the names and terms of office of Douai rectors), and thus if Hunt continued to teach at Stratford until as late as 1577, as Adams[106] and others think, the Catholic influence of the master upon young William would have been that much more considerable and, in the years 1575–77, more significant.

(d) However, if Hunt left Stratford in 1575, he was succeeded by a schoolmaster whose name we do not know, but who nevertheless taught William for three years, until Thomas Jenkins assumed the mastership in 1578. Though it is not true, as Lamborn and Harrison suggest, that the unknown master "stayed longest,"[107] it is true, on the basis of the entry in the chamberlains' accounts rendered on March 14, 1575/6 and already mentioned, that "he came from Warwick Grammar School, which was then one of the best in England."[108] In view of the fact that William Shakespeare grew from eleven years to fourteen years old and thus spent the most important period of his adolescence from the standpoint of religious psychology under the direction of the schoolmaster from Warwick, the anonymity of that schoolmaster is particularly annoying. Warwick records leave us completely in the dark as to who was the head

of the school in 1575, and Stratford records give us no positive information about Stratford teachers from 1575 until 1578.

(e) It is, of course, possible, as Fripp assumes, that the Warwick
schoolmaster who sought to better himself by going to Stratford in 1575
was Thomas Jenkins.[109] In support of the early incumbency of Jenkins
is the Parish Register entry to the effect that "Thomas, son to Mr.
Thomas Jenkins was baptized 19th January, 1577."[110] If Jenkins came
as early as 1575, he would have been Shakespeare's teacher for a period
as long as Hunt, perhaps longer, and his influence upon William would
have been profounder than biographers of Shakespeare have hitherto
recognized.

Rather against the theory of an early incumbency is what we know of
Jenkins' departure from Stratford. A receipt, formerly in the possession
of Robert Wheler, shows "that on July 9, 1579, Thomas Jenkins departed
from this school 'on receiving 6^1 from John Cottom of London, by whom
he was succeeded in the mastership.' "[111] The supposition is that Jenkins
was unpopular, if not unsatisfactory, and that he was bought off by
Cottom (Cottam) before the expiration of a term. If Jenkins was incom-
petent, or even unpopular, it is not likely that he would have remained
in office as long as four years. It is probable that he came to Stratford
as late as "Lady Day, 1578"[112] and that he was bought off within the
next twelvemonth.

But whether Jenkins' influence upon William was exerted for one year
or four, that influence was Protestant, if Fripp's account of the man is
correct. Fripp writes that Jenkins was the

> . . . son of an old apprentice to Sir Thomas White, the founder of
> St. John's College, Oxford. From St. John's, Thomas Jenkins suppli-
> cated for his B. A. in 1566 and determined in 1567. He took orders, and
> was granted, on the application of the founder, two years' absence for
> schoolteaching, with enjoyment of his fellowship on his return to col-
> lege. . . . Where Jenkins spent his two years teaching we are not
> informed. He took his M. A. in 1570, and became master of Warwick
> School. . . . He may have been a kinsman of Thomas Jenkins (Jenks)
> of Warwick, who was bailiff there in 1572-3, ... [In 1579] Jenkins
> was actively loyal in the musters and was paid 10*s.* for carriage of the
> soldiers' implements to Warwick on 8 June. He probably accepted a
> chaplaincy to the forces. . . .[113]

The scene in *The Merry Wives of Windsor*[114] in which Sir Hugh Evans
asks young William Page "some questions in his accidence" is most likely
a humorous recollection of a similar interrogation of young William
Shakespeare by "Sir" Thomas Jenkins, and the character of Sir Hugh

throughout the play is probably based upon the Stratford master. Sir Hugh is represented as a less lovable character than Holofernes, but the characterization is still good-natured. In fact Shakespeare's only downright condemnatory characterization of a schoolmaster is in Pinch in *The Comedy of Errors*, the prototype of which, if there was one, we cannot guess. Evidently Shakespeare forgave Master Hunt his pedantry and Master Jenkins his Welsh brogue and his making "fritters of English," but the smooth hypocrisy of some other schoolmaster he could not condone.

(f) It is possible that William left school during the mastership of Jenkins and never had John Cottam for a teacher. If Shakespeare did come under the tutelage of Cottam, he experienced still another swing of the pendulum in religious influence, for Cottam was probably Catholic in sympathy. He may have been a fellow student of Hunt at Oxford, for he graduated from that University in the same year as Hunt. Fripp thinks Cottam may have been "an older brother of Thomas Cottam, a Lancashire man, who took his B. A. from Brasenose in 1569 and was executed as a seminary priest in May 1582."[115] John Cottam served as Stratford schoolmaster until the autumn of 1582, when he was succeeded by Alexander Aspinall, master until 1624. By the time Aspinall appeared on the scene, William was well past the schoolboy age and point of view. It was in the year that Aspinall came that William Shakespeare and Anne Hathaway were married.

The foregoing account of Shakespeare's schoolmasters should serve to exhibit one thing: namely, that in his school experience, William was subjected to a regular alternation of Protestant and Catholic religious influence. Assuming Shakespeare to have had the longest possible public school experience, from 1569–80, the youngster went from a Catholic home to a Catholic Acton, to a Protestant Roche, to a Catholic Hunt, to a Protestant Jenkins, to a Catholic Cottam. And if the shortest probable schooling was his experience, William went from a Catholic home to a Protestant Roche, to a Catholic Hunt, and to a Protestant Jenkins. Such an alternation might mean a growing doubt in the boy's mind of the finality of either faith. The final result of the personal influence of Shakespeare's schoolmasters must have been the liberalization of the mind and spirit of the growing dramatist.

(5) The personal influence of a petty or grammar school teacher would be exerted in many intangible ways. Whatever our impression of the sixteenth-century teacher as to his severity and pedagogical aloofness, it is inconceivable that, as a human being, he could keep from making deep and lasting impressions upon his charges. More tangibly, the teacher could exert a personal influence upon his pupils through his control over

the selection and use of textbook materials and over the conduct of the class program.

It is true, however, that whatever the religious sympathies of an Elizabethan grammar school teacher, he could hardly avoid a show of compliance with state requirements concerning religious instruction. As Stowe remarks, "The attitude of the State towards this [the religious] phase of education was very definite."[116] The State required licensing of schoolmasters, and so made certain that "they should be men who 'professed the true religion.' "[117] It required that schoolmasters in office attend divine service at the appropriate hours on Sundays and holydays. To make definite the duties of schoolmasters with regard to religious instruction, the Injunctions of Elizabeth (1559) stipulated:

XLI. Item. That all teachers of children shall stir and move them to live and do reverence to god's true religion now truely set forth by public authority.

XLII. Item. That they shall accustom their scholars reverently to learn such sentences or scriptures as shall be most expedient to induce them to all godliness.[118]

(a) The most widely used educational tool for meeting these state requirements and for expounding religious truth to the school children was the Catechism.

Emphasis upon the catechetical method of religious instruction and the publication of a series of Catechisms were Protestant developments. The question-and-answer method of instruction in doctrine had fallen somewhat into disuse in the early part of the sixteenth century, but the value of the method was apparent to early Reformation church leaders, and they sought to utilize it for their purposes. In a set of injunctions issued by Cranmer in 1536 there is a clear indication of an attempt to revive the practice of catechizing, for "the clergy were to take care that children should be taught the Creed, the Lord's Prayer, and the Ten Commandments in their mother-tongue."[119]

Eleven years later the Protectorate followed the lead of Cranmer and Henry VIII. A set of injunctions issued in 1547, the first year of Edward VI, directed:

That every holy-day throughout the year, when they (deans, archdeacons, parsons, vicars and other ecclesiastical persons) have no sermon, they shall immediately after the gospel, openly and plainly recite to their parishioners in the pulpit, the *Paternoster*, the *Credo*, and the ten commandments in English, to the intent the people may learn the same by heart: exhorting all parents and householders to

teach their children and servants the same, as they are bound by the
law of God, and in conscience to do.[120]

To follow up the method and to insure results, the same injunctions
required that these ecclesiastical persons

> shall in confessions every Lent, examine every person that cometh to
> confession to them, whether they can recite the articles of their faith,
> the 'Paternoster' and the ten commandments in English, and hear
> them say the same particularly; wherein if they be not perfect, they
> shall declare then, that every Christian person ought to know the said
> things before they should receive the blessed sacrament of the altar,
> and monish them to learn the said necessary things more perfectly, or
> else they ought not to presume to come to God's board without a
> perfect knowledge, and will to observe the same. . . .[121]

The earliest catechisms were compiled to help the priests and their
parishioners to meet the requirements of these injunctions. In 1549, the
makers of the English Prayer Book included a Catechism in the Confirmation Service to help candidates for church membership prepare for
their reception. Who wrote the Catechism is not certain; it has been attributed to Alexander Nowell,* to John Poynet, Bishop of Rochester and
Winchester, and to Thomas Goodrich, Bishop of Ely. Arguments sum-
marized by William Hunt in his article on Nowell in *The Dictionary of
National Biography*[122] make plausible Nowell's authorship of the Catechism in the Prayer Book of 1549 and distinguish between that Catechism and another which appeared in the Prayer Book of 1553, the
authorship of which, though ascribed to Nowell by Strype in his *Memo-
rials* (II.i.590, ii.25), "should be ascribed to John Poynet. . . ."[123]

That two distinct Catechisms existed in 1556 and that Nowell's Catechism was looked upon as somewhat different from that appearing in the
latest authorized Prayer Book (1553) seems to be indicated by the following injunction which occurs in the Statutes of Rivington School in
1556:

> On Saturdays and Holy Day eves, the Usher shall exercise his younger
> sort in learning their short Catechism in English in the Common Book,
> and the same days to all sorts the Master shall read Mr. Nowell's or
> Calvin's Catechism, taught in Calvin's Institutions, willing the elder
> sort both to learn it by heart, and examine them briefly the next day
> after, when they come to School again, before they go to other things,

---

*Alexander Nowell (1507?–1602) was master of Winchester School from 1543–60 and
Dean of St. Paul's from 1560–1602.

how they can say it, and shall commend them that have done well, and encourage others to do the like.[124]

Nowell is credited with writing three later Catechisms: the "Large Catechism," the "Middle Catechism," and the "Small Catechism." The "Large Catechism," written "at the request of some great persons in the church," was intended to be not only a means of religious instruction, but "a fixed standard of doctrine in order to silence those who asserted that 'the Protestants had no principles.' "[125] The manuscript, in Latin, was sent to Cecil in 1563. It was first published on the 16th of June, 1570, in a quarto edition by Reginald Wolf, under the title *Catechismus sive prima Institutio Disciplinaque Pietatis Christianae*. An English translation by Thomas Norton, bearing the title *A Catechisme or first Instruction and Learning of Christian Religion, by T. Norton*, appeared in the same year in the form of a quarto volume bearing the imprint of John Day. In preparing the original text, Nowell drew upon the "Short Catechism" of the 1553 Prayer Book and upon John Calvin's Catechism.

The "Middle Catechism" is an abridgment of the "Large Catechism." Nowell published it in 1570 under the title *Christianae Pietatis prima Institutio ad usum Scholarum*. An English translation, also by Norton, appeared in 1572 under the title *A Catechisme or Institution of Christian Religion to be learned of all youth next after the little catechisme appoynted in the Booke of Common Prayer*. As a duodecimo volume, in this first edition by John Day, the English translation was certainly more useful as a textbook than its Latin original, which had first appeared as a quarto. The "Middle Catechism" was also translated into Greek in 1575 by Nowell's nephew, William Whitaker, who had previously translated both the "Large Catechism" and the "Small Catechism" into Greek.

The "Small Catechism" appeared in 1572 as a Latin text bearing the title *Catechismus parvus pueris primum Latine qui ediscatur, proponendus in scholis*. It, too, was translated into Greek by Whitaker by 1574 and into English by Norton no later than 1577. It is upon the basis of a comparison of the contents of Nowell's "Small Catechism" and of the Prayer Book Catechism that Hunt affirms Nowell's authorship of the Catechism of 1549.[126]

If young William Shakespeare was sent to school before his seventh birthday, that is, before the spring of 1571, he must have been taught the Catechism in English, and the English Catechism available at that time would have been the Prayer Book Catechism, either Nowell's of 1549 or Poynet's of 1553. If he was not sent to school until after his seventh birthday, he probably would have been required already to know his

Catechism in English and would have begun to study the Catechism in Latin at once.

Just where William could have learned his English Catechism, if not in the petty school, is problematical. He would have to be taught it either at a dame school or at home, and in either case the text would have to be that of the Prayer Book. It was not until some time after 1572 that Nowell's "Small Catechism" was translated into English by Norton.

The Latin Catechism which young William would have had to learn in the lower forms of the Grammar School would most likely be the Prayer Book Catechism *before* 1572, or Nowell's "Small Catechism" *after* 1572. The Book of Canons of August, 1571, required that "Schoolmasters shall teach no other Latin Catechism than that which was set forth in the year 1570,"[127] that is, Nowell's.

From the standpoint of religious influence, it would not matter much which Catechism young William studied, either in English or in Latin. All the Catechisms available were Protestant. The boy Shakespeare must have been conscious of the marked doctrinal emphasis of any Catechism which he studied and of the difference between its polemic spirit and the more serene and mystical spirit of his Catholic home.

(b) Not all the religious instruction given in Elizabethan grammar schools proceeded from the Catechism, however. There were other sources. For example, in the list of books authorized by statute in 1583 to be used in the Free Grammar School of St. Bees in Cumberland, besides "The Catechism in English, set forth by public authority" and "The Small Catechism in Latin, publicly authorised," there appear "The Psalter and Book of Common Prayer" and "The New Testament," both in English.[128]

With respect to the situation in Stratford Grammar School, it can hardly be doubted that the Psalter and the Book of Common Prayer, one book, was used as a basis of religious instruction. We have already remarked about the catechetical portion of the Prayer Book. H. R. D. Anders, in his *Shakespeare's Books*,[129] gives instances of Shakespeare's reference to the Litany, the form for administering baptism, the Ten Commandments, the Paternoster, the form for the solemnization of matrimony, the form for the burial of the dead, and the Psalms of the Psalter to prove Shakespeare's familiarity with the Elizabethan Prayer Book, but proof is hardly necessary. The influence of the Prayer Book was inescapable for any Elizabethan who had eyes to read or ears to hear. Shakespeare had both. He grew familiar with the contents and style of the Prayer Book through his use of it not only in school, but also in church. That familiarity must have deepened with the years, for there is no reason for doubting that Shakespeare attended the services of the

Church at Stratford and at London with more or less regularity through-out his life. The parts of the Prayer Book most likely to be learned in school are the Catechism already mentioned and the Psalms.

Anders cites no fewer than twenty-two parallelisms[130] between passages from Shakespeare and passages from the Psalms in the Book of Common Prayer to show that Shakespeare was thoroughly conversant with the Psalter. He attributes that marked familiarity to attendance upon church services and, parenthetically, to the fact that "perhaps [Shakespeare] had belonged to the choir of Trinity Church at Stratford, when a boy."[131] Richmond Noble, however, in his *Shakespeare's Biblical Knowledge and Use of the Book of Common Prayer*, while he finds Anders' suggestion attractive in that it helps account for Shakespeare's "acquaintance with some of the elements of vocal music," prefers to give more credit to the school. He writes:

> It is more likely . . . that Shakespeare knew certain of the Psalms in the Prayer Book thoroughly from having learnt them by heart at school. The Psalter in the school was no innovation at the Reformation; traditionally pupils had been taught several of the Psalms. . . . It is not at all improbable that some exercise of the sort was a part of the curriculum at Stratford Grammar School.[132]

(c) In addition to pointing out Shakespeare's acquaintance with the Psalms of the Prayer Book Psalter, Anders also cites a number of expressions used by the playwright to indicate his familiarity with the metrical Psalms.[133] He refers to Sir Hugh Evans' distorted line in the *Merry Wives of Windsor*:

When as I sat in Pabylon[134]

as being a quotation of William Whittingham's metrical version of Psalm 137, and to Mrs. Ford's statement in the same play,[135] that Falstaff's disposition and words "do no more adhere and keep place together than the Hundredth Psalm to the tune of 'Green Sleeves,' " as being an unmistakable allusion to the famous Old Hundredth. Besides these references, Fripp also finds Shakespeare quoting or paraphrasing the metrical version of the 19th Psalm in *3 Henry VI* (II, 1, 22–4), the 24th Psalm in *2 Henry VI* (IV, ix, 11), the 30th Psalm in *Richard II* (V, i, 14), and the 49th Psalm in the *Merry Wives* (I, iii, 95 and II, i, 117 f).[136]

Shakespeare may have become familiar with these Psalms, and others, while attending school. It was customary to dismiss school, if not also to open it, with devotional services which included the singing of a Psalm.[137] At Ashby, devotions at the opening and closing of the school included "two staves of a psalm," and "stress was laid on . . . the training of each boy in turn to start the tune."[138] If the example of the Ashby school was followed at Stratford, Shakespeare's "acquaintance with some of the elements of vocal music" is sufficiently explained without making him a member of the church choir.

The metrical Psalms which William learned in school, if he learned them there, must have been those contained in *The Whole Booke of Psalmes: collected into English Meeter, by Thomas Sternhold, John Hopkins, and others, conferred with the Hebrew; with apt Notes to sing them withall.* . . . It was a product of Protestantism, and more particularly of Calvinism. It drew its inspiration from the metrical Psalms of Clement Marot, secretary of Francis I, and of Theodore Beza. Its initiator was Thomas Sternhold, Groom of the Robes of Henry VIII and later of Edward VI, who published versions of nineteen Psalms in 1549 and died soon afterwards, leaving eighteen more Psalms to be published in a second edition in 1551. To this second edition of thirty-seven Sternhold Psalms, John Hopkins, a Suffolk clergyman, added seven of his own. The accession of Catholic Queen Mary did not stop the growth of the work, for it was carried on by English refugees at Geneva. Chief among these, as contributors to the Psalter, were William Whittingham, brother-in-law of John Calvin and successor to John Knox as the minister of the English congregation at Geneva, and William Kethe, or Keith, a Scotchman. A Genevan edition appeared in 1556 containing fifty-one English metrical Psalms. Later editions increased the number to eighty-seven. When Queen Elizabeth succeeded Mary, this Genevan Psalmody was introduced into England by the returning refugees, first in London and then in other cities. In 1562 the first edition of the complete Psalter, now known as the "Old Version," appeared. Of the 150 Psalms in this complete edition, Sternhold is the author of forty, Hopkins of sixty, and Thomas Norton, Whittingham, and Kethe of forty-seven of the remaining fifty. This Psalter was annexed to the Book of Common Prayer and adopted under Queen Elizabeth as the Metrical Version to be used in the Church of England.[139]

The Protestant inspiration of the metrical Psalms is hence indisputable. Psalm-singing came to be a mark of the advanced Protestant, and later of the Puritan. It may not be too much to say that the relatively few references to the metrical Psalms and the somewhat derogatory allusions to psalm-singers and psalm-singing which Shakespeare makes in his plays show Shakespeare to have reacted rather unfavorably to the Genevan Psalmody, whether he first came in contact with it at school or not. It is not hard to understand, however, that a poet of esthetic sensibilities should be offended by the metrical Psalms for artistic, rather than religious reasons, so that it is unsafe to conclude much from Shakespeare's use of the metrical Psalms and from his treatment of psalm-singers.

(d) The use of the Bible, or particularly the New Testament, as a *textbook* in Stratford School at the time of William's attendance is improbable. Although in his study of *English Grammar Schools to 1660* Foster Watson points out that as early as 1547 the Injunctions of the Commissioners to Winchester College required daily Bible reading, "both at Dinner and Supper,"[140] and though he quotes school statutes at East Retford for 1552, at Hartlebury for 1565, and at Rivington for 1566 requiring some form of Bible reading or Bible teaching in the schools,[141] he concludes:

> It may safely be asserted that the Statutes of Schools much more frequently include the teaching of the Catechism, Primer and A B C than they explicitly name the "Bible." The most important consideration was that the child should know the articles of faith.[142]

"The Bible," Watson says, ". . . was not definitely and officially fixed as a school subject till the Canons of 1604."[143]

Dealing with the same problem of whether or not the Bible was used as a *textbook* at Stratford, Richmond Noble writes:

> There is good reason for believing that the English Bible was not taught at schools like Stratford during Shakespeare's youth and adolescence. There were practical difficulties in the way of any such general instruction. For the purpose, an ample supply of Bibles of handy size and small cost would have been requisite. . . . Before 1575 no great efforts were made to push the Genevan Bible, whose handy size and small cost would have made it the version most convenient for school use. In fact, it was not until 1587, when the Tomson New Testament began to supersede the ordinary Genevan Testament, that large quantities of Bibles began to appear on the market, and it was not until the nineties that those quantities were such as to prove a considerable school demand.[144]

But if the Bible was not used as a textbook at Stratford, it was almost certainly read by the master in the conduct of devotions. School prayers and religious observances were required by school statutes generally, and Foster Watson quotes a number of these statutes over a period from 1440 to 1585, with others following, to establish the point.[145] The size of the Bible and its cost would not be matters of great practical difficulty in this connection, and the master could use any of the several Protestant Bibles in print. The selection of passages to be read would naturally rest with the master, and pedagogical theory and teaching experience probably impelled the master to choose narrative historical passages to interest his boys.

The foregoing pages do not pretend to exhaust the subject of Shakespeare's schoolbooks. That effort has been made too well in other places to be repeated here. The present purpose is merely to single out such textbooks as could be expected to exert a religious influence upon Shakespeare as a schoolboy and to make some estimate of that influence. The one statement that can safely be made is that every religious textbook with which Shakespeare came in contact during his school years was Protestant in contents and tone and would therefore be a force counteracting the Catholic influence of his home. Even the personal influence of a Catholic schoolmaster like Simon Hunt could not offset the gradual and irresistible Protestantizing effect of these textbooks. Shakespeare's total school experience must have led to a divergence between the religious outlook of the growing young man and that of his parents. John and Mary Shakespeare continued to look toward Rome and to walk the Old Road, but their son began to look away from Rome and to set his feet on the New Road of the Reformation, whithersoever it might lead. That change in outlook was encouraged and widened by the ministrations of the Stratford Parish Church. To consider the influence of the church upon the boy Shakespeare is the next and last undertaking of this chapter.

3. The Church

William Shakespeare could hardly have known the Rev. John Bretchgirdle, M.A., the vicar of the Stratford Parish Church who baptized him, for the vicar died soon after in 1565, most likely as the result of the plague. Neither could he have known much of Bretchgirdle's successor, the Rev. William Butcher, M.A. and B.D., "late President of Corpus Christi College, Oxford, who because of his Catholicism was deprived at the time of the Northern Rebellion"[146] in 1569. Such association as William, a child under six, could have had with a parish priest while Butcher was vicar would have meant merely an extension of the Catholicism of his parents' home.

With Butcher's successor, the Rev. Henry Heycroft, M.A., of Cambridge, came a new spirit, that of Protestantism. Heycroft's influence lasted throughout the whole period of Shakespeare's youth and early manhood. It was Heycroft who, in 1583, baptized Susanna, the first child of William Shakespeare and Anne Hathaway.

(1) There can be no doubt that the boy William sat under the preaching of the Rev. Mr. Heycroft and that he had to pay attention to his

sermons.* One of the things upon which Elizabethan school statutes generally agree is that the boys of the grammar schools should attend church in a body, at least on Sundays. At East Retford, masters were "to command and compel their scholars to come and hear divine service in the Parish church every Sunday and Holyday."[147] At Dronfield the scholars "upon every Sunday and Holyday in the morning" were to "resort orderly to the school," and thence were to go to the church "two and two in rank" carrying their service book with them.[148] At most places masters were held responsible for the attendance and conduct of their pupils. The scholars "were usually seated apart from the rest of the congregation," often in the chancel or choir, a side chapel or transept, or special gallery.

The boys were expected to take notes on the minister's sermon and to report the results to the master at school on Monday morning. So general did this custom of sermon note-taking become that it is thought modern systems of shorthand were developed from the practice.[149] That some sort of shorthand would be necessary can be gathered from the advice which Brinsley gives schoolmasters with respect to what should be required of their pupils:

> The very lowest can bring some notes, at least three or four. . . . Those who have been longer practised (1) to set down the text, or part of it, (2) To mark as near as they can, and set down, every doctrine, and what proofs they can, the reasons, and the uses of them, (3) In the highest forms, cause them to set down all the sermons: as text, division, exposition or meaning, doctrines, and how the several doctrines were gathered, all the proofs, reasons, uses, applications. . . . You may, if you think good, cause them the next morning to translate it into a good Latin style, instead of their exercise the next day.[150]

Although we know nothing of those sermons which the Rev. Mr. Heycroft composed in his own study, we do know much about those sermons which, by the appointment of Queen Elizabeth, he, along with every other vicar in England, would have to preach at stated times. The text of these sermons is before us to read in the Book of Homilies.

There are thirty-three of them in all. Twelve had been made during the reign of Edward VI and published in 1547. Of the remaining twenty-one, twenty were prepared by the bishops and first published in 1562. The twenty-first (thirty-third in the whole collection) was added in 1569.[151]

* The dialogue between Olivia and Viola in *Twelfth Night*, I, v, 236 ff., is a commentary on textual preaching.

The Preface of the 1562 edition is quite explicit with regard to the way the homilies were to be used, and leaves no doubt as to their typically Protestant biblical and polemical emphasis. The opening sentences of the first homily, "A Fruitful Exhortation to the Reading and Knowledge of holy Scripture," set the doctrinal tone of the collection:

> Unto a Christian man there can be nothing either more necessary or profitable, than the knowledge of holy Scripture, forasmuch as in it is contained God's true word, sitting forth his glory, and also man's duty. And there is no truth nor doctrine necessary for our justification and everlasting salvation, but that is, or may be, drawn out of that fountain and well of truth. Therefore as many as be desirous to enter into the right and perfect way unto God, must apply their minds to know holy Scripture; without the which, they can neither sufficiently know God and his will, neither their office and duty.[152]

This first Edwardian homily is followed by eleven others on these subjects:

2. Of the Misery of all Mankind
3. Of the Salvation of all Mankind
4. Of the true and lively Faith
5. Of Good Works
6. Of Christian Love and Charity
7. Against Swearing and Perjury
8. Of the Declining from God
9. An Exhortation against the Fear of Death
10. An Exhortation to Obedience
11. Against Whoredom and Adultery
12. Against Strife and Contention

The Elizabethan additions are entitled:

1. Of the Right Use of the Church
2. Against Peril of Idolatry
3. For repairing and keeping clean the Church
4. Of good Works; and first of Fasting
5. Against Gluttony and Drunkenness
6. Against Excess of Apparel
7. An Homily of Prayer
8. Of the Place and Time of Prayer
9. Of Common Prayer and Sacraments
10. An Information of them which take Offence at certain Places of holy Scripture

11. Of Alms-deeds
12. Of the Nativity
13. Of the Passion, for Good-Friday
14. Of the Resurrection, for Easter-day
15. Of the worthy Receiving of the Sacrament
16. An Homily concerning the coming down of the Holy Ghost, for Whitsunday
17. An Homily for Rogation-Week
18. Of the State of Matrimony
19. Against Idleness
20. Of Repentance, and true Reconciliation unto God
21. An Homily against Disobedience and wilful Rebellion

Our only hint of Shakespeare's personal reaction to the homilies which he heard as a boy and which he continued to hear throughout his lifetime is given in *As You Like It*, when Rosalind, hearing Celia read Orlando's poetical effusion in praise of herself, stops Celia with the words:

O most gentle pulpiter! what tedious homily of love have you wearied your parishioners withal, and never cried, 'Have patience, good people!'[153]

(2) A church ceremony which was linked with the Grammar School and which must have made a vivid impression on every school boy was that celebrated during Rogation week. Six weeks after Easter it was the custom for "the clergy, the magistrates and public officers, and the inhabitants, including the boys of the Grammar School"[154] to assemble at a starting point for "the perambulation of the boundaries" of the parish.

They marched in procession, with waving banners and poles crowned with garlands, over the entire circuit of the parish limits. Under each "gospel-tree," as at the first boundary elm, a passage from Scripture was read, a collect recited, and a psalm sung.[155]

It was the duty of the curate to "admonish the people to give thanks to God in the beholding of God's benefits" and to denounce those who removed their neighbor's landmarks. To help the curate in the performance of these duties a form of devotion for the Rogation days of procession was prescribed in 1575. Before 1575, the curate had the help of the Book of Homilies, for the seventeenth homily among the Elizabethan additions is "An Homily for the Days of Rogation-Week." The homily has three parts. The first part dwells upon the thought "that all good Things come from God" and extols the Creator. The second part considers the distribution of worldly gifts according to the wisdom of the

Creator and recommends patience and contentment. The third part declares the fact "that all spiritual gifts and graces come specially from God." At the end of the homily is "An Exhortation, To be spoken to such Parishes where they use their Perambulation in Rogation Week, for the oversight of the Bounds and Limits of their Town." Its theme is

> to consider the old ancient bounds and limits belonging to our own township, and to other neighbours bordering about us, to the intent that we should be content with our own, and not contentiously strive for others, to the breach of charity, by any incroaching one upon another, for claiming one of the other, further than that in ancient right and custom our forefathers have peaceably laid out unto us for our commodity and comfort.[156]

In spite of its fundamentally serious nature, the Rogation week procession was much like a community field-day and picnic. It was the sort of affair that would appeal strongly to youngsters, and probably the schoolmaster had little difficulty in getting his pupils to take part. The ceremony was rooted in pre-Reformation tradition and would appeal to Catholics as "one good custom" which had survived the iconoclasm of reformers.

(3) The parish church would likewise supplement the school in connection with catechetical instruction. The Injunctions of Elizabeth, 1559, imposed the duty of such instruction upon the parson, vicar, or curate. Article XLIII reads:

> Every parson, vicar, and curate shall upon every holyday and every second Sunday in the year hear and instruct the youth of the parish for half an hour at the least before evening prayer in the ten commandments, the Articles of the Belief, and the Lords Prayer, and diligently examine them and teach the Catechism set forth in the book of public prayer.[157]

In consideration of the fact that Heycroft was named to succeed a Catholic sympathizer (Butcher) and that he held his vicarate until as late as 1584, it is not likely that he neglected his duty to catechise "all the children, apprentices and servants of both the sexes that be of convenient age" in his parish, or to seek out such fathers, mothers, masters, and dames of the parish as did not send their young people, "being above six years and under twenty," to be catechised.[158]

How regularly the boy Shakespeare attended the services of Holy Trinity Church we cannot know. That his father grew to be very irregular in church attendance is proved by the recusancy returns. But the well-known tendency of parents to send their children to church when they themselves do not go may have induced John and Mary Shakespeare to send their children to the Stratford Parish Church, though they themselves stayed away. If the Shakespeares wanted their children to enjoy the benefits of public worship, they would have to send their children to Holy Trinity, for there was no other church in the community in which approved services could be held.

(4) At the regular services of the church, the boy Shakespeare would receive the full impact of the Elizabethan Prayer Book. From its Litany, its Collects, its forms of worship must have come a stream of words, phrases, and sentences bearing religious ideas to penetrate the mind of the youth and to lie there until years later when he sought to express himself in an artistic vein. So it is that, as Fripp writes:

> We catch echoes of Cranmer's matchless phrasing or selection, 'absolution' and 'remission', 'world without end', 'Lord, have mercy upon us', 'the imagination of their hearts', 'Good Lord, deliver us', 'love, honour and obey', 'depart in peace', 'grant us Thy peace', 'graffed inwardly in our hearts', 'everlasting damnation', 'picking and stealing', 'know any impediment', 'consummation', and so forth.[159]

(5) In church, too, the Bible would come into its own as a religious influence. A part of every service of public worship was the Bible Lesson. How comprehensive the scope of that Bible reading was is emphasized in Noble's summary of the lectionary:

> The Elizabethan lectionary of 1559 (slightly corrected in 1561) provided for the reading at Morning and Evening Prayer in the course of the year of all such parts of the Old Testament (except the Psalms), as were considered 'edifying'; of portions of the Apocrypha; and for the Second Lesson all of the New Testament (with the exception of Revelation) three times in the year—at Matins, the Gospels, and Acts, and at Evensong, the Pastoral and Catholic Epistles. There were Proper Lessons appointed—namely, for each Sunday and Holy Day a particular portion of the Old Testament or Apocrypha was appointed for each of the two services, but Proper Lessons of the New Testament were only appointed for the Holy Days and a few special Sundays, so that, with the exception of Revelation, there was little interference with the reading of the New Testament.[160]

The version of the Bible supposed to be read in the churches was the Bishops', a revision of the Great Bible. It had appeared first in 1568 and had been reissued in 1569 and 1572. If the Stratford church had not supplied itself with a copy of the Bishops' Bible when Heycroft, the new vicar, came in 1569, Heycroft may have read from the Great Bible of Cranmer's days. Or, since he probably had ardent Protestant sympathies, he may have preferred the Genevan Bible, a version which had appeared in 1560 and which eventually found its way into Puritan pulpits.

(6) In church, too, the growing Shakespeare could exercise himself fully in the singing of the metrical Psalms annexed to the Prayer Book. In church, too, young William could see such wall paintings as may have escaped the whitewashing of Puritan churchwardens. If the sermon was dull, the embryonic dramatist could allow his imagination to play over the depiction of the Last Judgment, of incidents in the lives of Old Testament patriarchs and New Testament saints, or, perhaps, of the Seven Deadly Sins.

(7) The influence of the church was one which continued throughout Shakespeare's life. While living in London, Shakespeare probably attended Matins and Holy Communion on Sunday mornings.* Sunday afternoon was a usual time for giving performances in the theatre, but there may have been Sunday afternoons when Shakespeare was free from the demands of the theatre and when he attended Evensong at church. If he spent a great deal of time in Stratford-upon-Avon after he had established himself as a dramatist in London, the influence of Holy Trinity Church would have been almost unbroken.† At Stratford the vicar after Heycroft, the Rev. Richard Barton, was a Puritan from Coventry. He baptized the Shakespeare twins, Hamnet and Judith, in 1585. His successor was John Rushton, who served during the year 1589. Next came John Bramhall, who served from 1589 to 1596—years when William Shakespeare was very busy in London. After Bramhall came Richard Bifield, a Professor of Sacred Theology, who supervised the copying of early Parish Church Register entries. In 1605 John Rogers became vicar. Rogers had been a sympathizer of Cartwright at the time of the latter's troubles with Whitgift.[161] He remained vicar at Stratford until after Shakespeare's death. Describing Rogers, Fripp writes:

> There were presbyterians *and* presbyterians, and Master Rogers seems to have been of the liberal wing. He had 'faults and failings' which exposed him to censure.[162]

To attempt to state what part of church influence belongs to boyhood years and what part to adult years is futile. Both in London and in Strat-

---

* In connection with Shakespeare's church attendance in London, James J. Walsh, in "Was Shakespeare a Catholic?" *The Catholic Mind*, XIII (April 22. 1915), 209, makes the interesting point that one of the advantages of Shakespeare's living with the Huguenot Montjoy family was that Shakespeare could with impunity avoid attending services of the Anglican church.

† The deed to New Place carried with it the right to a pew in the parish church.

ford the influence of the church would have become more and more Protestant. By the time Shakespeare had reached the point at which he made independent religious decisions, the influence of his Catholic home would have been largely dissipated. Nevertheless, there must have been occasions when out of the deep well of the subconscious there arose reminiscences of the Old Faith—thoughts and feelings of an almost nostalgic sort which, in becoming vivid to the artist, would take him back to the house on Henley Street. Once more he would hear the voice of his mother at prayer. In her he would see a faint reflection of Mary, the Virgin Mother of God. The very name would strengthen the association. Often, throughout the busy writings years, bits of Catholic imagery, Catholic sentiment, Catholic tradition, slipping unawares along the channels of the imagination, would enter the main stream of the poet's creative effort and give to that stream slight shifts of direction and touches of color discernible today in the poet's poems and plays.

To present typical traces of Catholicism in the writings of Shakespeare will be the last undertaking of this discussion of the Shakespeares and the Old Faith.

PART FOUR

CATHOLICISM IN THE WRITINGS OF WILLIAM SHAKESPEARE

*A*T THE outset of this final chapter, the reader should understand that the author, by the evidence to be presented, does not intend to prove that William Shakespeare was a Catholic. The aim of the chapter is merely to show that in Shakespeare's writings there are signs that the dramatist held a greater respect for the Catholic faith than is sometimes supposed. In the presentation of material the author makes no attempt to be exhaustive. The treatment is suggestive; the evidence is typical.

1. Shakespeare's Use of the Bible

Shakespeare's use of the Bible will be considered first. Of all Elizabethan dramatists, Shakespeare quoted Scripture most frequently. Indeed, the number of biblical allusions in his works is legion. Though it may be extreme to believe with William Burgess

> . . . that Shakspeare drank so deeply from the wells of Scripture that one may say, without any straining of the evidence, without the Bible Shakspeare could not be,[1]

it is not extreme to believe that a study of Shakespeare's usage of the Bible will reveal something of the dramatist's religious disposition. Several such studies have been made.[2] They are painstakingly complete and leave little for one to do in the way of collating material. From them and other sources we shall use such evidence as seems pertinent to our discussion.

(1) The first question to be asked is: Did Shakespeare ever use the Catholic version of the Bible? Such evidence as exists is of the most tenuous sort. There is, for example, the evidence presented by the Countess de Chambrun as follows:

> A small circumstance, but one of singular interest, indicates that when William Shakespeare made use of the parable of the sowers from the

Gospel of St. Matthew, he had the Reims translation in mind and not either the so-called "Breeches" or "Bishops'" Bible. Though verbal, the evidence is striking. Down to the present day all Protestant Bibles employ the word *tares* in speaking of ill weeds sown among the wheat whereas the Catholic texts use *cockle*.

Now, in the whole course of Shakespeare's works the word *tares* is never found, but when he recalls the parable of the sowers the word *cockle* appears in its place as in the Reims translation. . . .

In "Love's Labour's Lost" we find:

> Sowed cockle reaps no corn.

and again in "Coriolanus" the same term appears in similar connection:

> That cockle of Rebellion, Insolence, Sedition,
> Which we ourselves have ploughed for, sowed and scattered.[3]

Aside from the fact that Shakespeare's allusion seems to be more directly to the passage: ". . . . for whatsoever a man soweth, that shall he reap" in Galatians 6:7, the evidence is weakened by the probability that the line in *Love's Labour's Lost* is a popular proverb and not a scriptural allusion at all.

In addition to this, Noble finds two "specks of evidence" in *All's Well that Ends Well* and *The Tempest*. In *All's Well*, the Clown says to Lafeu:

> I am for the house with the narrow gate, which I take to be too little for pomp to enter: some that humble themselves may; but the many will be too chill and tender, and they'll be for the flowery way that leads to the broad gate and the great fire.[4]

These words allude to Matthew 7:13. In Protestant versions this verse reads:

> Enter yee in at the *straite* gate, for *wide* is the gate, and broad is the way that leadeth to destruction, and many there be which goe in thereat.[5]

The Rheims translation has: "Enter ye by the *narrow* gate: because *brode* is the gate . . . ."[6] Shakespeare is therefore closer to the Rheims version in this passage.

In *The Tempest* when Prospero asks Ariel whether the King of Naples and his company are all safe after suffering shipwreck in the tempest, Ariel answers:

> Not a hair perish'd.[7]

Since the occasion is that of a shipwreck, it seems likely that Ariel's answer is an echo of Acts 27:34 in the Rheims version, where St. Paul assures the Centurion shortly before the wrecking of the ship on which the company is proceeding to Rome, that "there shal not an heare of the head perish of any of you." The Bishops' Bible and the Genevan Bible here read: ". . . there shall not an heare *fall* from the head of any of you."[8] There remains the possibility that the echo is not from Acts 27:34, but from Luke 21:18, where Jesus assures his disciples that during the troublous last days, though they be hated for his name's sake, ". . . a hair of your head shall not perish." In this verse, however, all three versions—the Rheims, the Bishops' and the Genevan—use the word "perish."

In introducing his discussion of these two "specks of evidence," Noble observes that "the Rheims in a good many places adopted readings to be found in its English precursors, with the result that in numbers of instances it might be taken with the others to rank as a source for Shakespeare."[9]

The tenuousness of this evidence does not detract from its value as much as may at first appear. Shakespeare's opportunity to use a Catholic version would be slight indeed. The Rheims New Testament, first of Catholic translations, was not published until 1582. It was, of course, proscribed in England, and its circulation must have been small. Knowledge of the text would have been spread somewhat through the publication in 1589 of William Fulke's *The Text of the New Testament of Jesus Christ, translated out of the Vulgar Latine by the Papists of the traiterous Seminarie at Rhemes*, to which was added, for purposes of comparison, the text of the New Testament from the Bishops' Bible. The Douai Bible, which included the Rheims New Testament drastically revised, was not published until 1609–10. It is not likely that many copies of this Bible were circulated in England before Shakespeare stopped writing. Noble believes Shakespeare never saw the Douai Bible.[10] If Shakespeare was to gain any extensive biblical knowledge, he would have to gain it from versions other than Catholic.

(2) If it could be shown convincingly that Shakespeare used only the Genevan version, produced as it was by Calvinists and favored by Puritans, the conclusion that Shakespeare had no Catholic sympathies whatever would be difficult to escape. There are those who believe that Shakespeare showed a special preference for the Genevan version and that therefore he was himself a Puritan. This is the thesis of Carter's *Shakespeare and Holy Scripture*.

No one has attempted to deny that Shakespeare was familiar with the Genevan Bible and that his indebtedness to that version is clear in his writings. But the evidence can be overestimated. There is, for example, the bit of dialogue in *King Richard II* between the King and Mowbray, the Duke of Norfolk. When Mowbray resists the efforts of the king to make peace between him and Bolingbroke, King Richard says:

> Rage must be withstood:
> Give me his gage: lions make leopards tame.
> *Mowbray.* Yea, but not change his spots. . . .[11]

Carter accepts these lines as a reference to Jeremiah 13:23, rendered by the Genevan Bible: "Can the blacke Moore change his skin? or the leopard his spots?" He points out that previous versions gave "cat o' mountain."[12] But Noble points out that in *Euphues* occurs the passage: "Can the Aethiope chaunge or alter his skinne? or the leopard his hiew?"

> The phrase about the leopard and his spots, from its occurrence in Euphues, sounds as though it was proverbial and hence gives the impression that it was from popular speech rather than from any Biblical version that Norfolk quoted.[13]

Euphues was written two decades before *King Richard II*. Shakespeare must have read it.

Similarly, the citation of Shylock's speech in the *Merchant of Venice* mentioning the "parti-colour'd lambs"[14] that were to be Jacob's cannot be accepted as indisputable evidence of Shakespeare's use of the Genevan Bible. Though it is true that the Genevan rendering of Genesis 30:39 speaks of the sheep as bringing forth "yong of partie colour," it is also true that the Bishops' Bible of 1585 has the sheep bring forth "lambes ringstraked, spotted, and partie." Moreover, the Bishops' Bible of 1569, in rendering Verse 35 of the same chapter, speaks of "shee goates that were spotted and partie coloured." Other expressions used by Shylock, such as "streaked," "then conceiving," "lambs," and "Iacob" (rather than "Iaakob" as in the Genevan) are closer to expressions in the Bishops' Bible than in the Genevan. There is also to be considered Bayne's suggestion that the term "partie-colour'd" may have occurred in the pre-Shakespearean play, no longer extant.[15]

Again, the phrase "amendment of life," used by Prince Henry in speaking to Falstaff in *1 King Henry IV*,[16] though it occurs only in the Genevan New Testament,[17] may have come to Shakespeare's mind from his recollection of the Exhortation in the Communion Service, or the Homily on Repentance, in both of which the phrase occurs. The phrase "amend your lives" and similar phrases also occur in the Prayer Book.

Also in the Prayer-book, in the rendering of John 19:17 as part of the Gospel appointed for Good Friday, is the phrase "place of dead mennes sculles" as descriptive of Golgotha. Therefore, this phrase as spoken by the Bishop of Carlisle in *King Richard II*:

> The field of Golgotha and dead men's skulls[18]

cannot be taken as unquestionable proof of Shakespeare's reliance upon the Genevan Bible at this point, even though the phrase occurs in no other version.[19]

Another bit of evidence for the Genevan version which has been too favorably interpreted appears in Falstaff's description of his ". . . hundred and fifty tattered prodigals, lately come from swine-keeping, from eating draff and husks."[20] Carter points out[21] that the word "huskes" is found in the Genevan rendering of Luke 15:16, but not in the other Protestant versions. He ignores the fact that the word does occur in the Catholic Rheims rendering.

Sidney Lee seems to make too much of Shylock's phrase: "your prophet the Nazarite"[22] when he says that the term "Nazarite" comes from the Genevan version, because the word is "Nazarene" in "other English versions."[23] The allusion is to Matthew 2:23. Noble says:

> All Tudor versions from Tindale to Rheims translated Matt. ii.23 as: "He shall be called a Nazarite." The authorized was the first to make a distinction and translate "Nazarene" for "man of Nazareth." Shylock used the only term that Bibles of that day gave for Christ in Matt. ii.23.[24]

One instance of Shakespeare's borrowing from the Genevan version seems to satisfy the critics.[25] It is Hamlet's use of the phrase "full of bread," when that distraught prince, reflecting upon the murder of his father by Claudius, laments:

> He took my father grossly, full of bread.[26]

The allusion is probably to Ezekiel 16:49, the Genevan rendering of which is: "Behold, this was the iniquitie of thy sister Sodom, Pride, fulnesse of bread, and abundance of idlenesse was in her, and in her daughters." Other versions have "meate" instead of "bread."[27]

Not only can the evidence for Shakespeare's use of the Genevan version be overestimated; the interpretation of that evidence can be strained. The Genevan Bible was a remarkably popular book. About two hundred editions of it were printed in the first half-century after its appearance in 1560. It was readable and handy. The text was broken up into verses; pictures and maps enlivened its pages; pithy notes explained difficult passages. To use it did not stamp the reader as a Puritan, nor even as a

Calvinist. Richard Hooker made large use of it in his *Ecclesiastical Polity*, yet Hooker was the outstanding defender of the Prayer Book against Puritan attacks.[28] The truth is that all sorts of men possessed Genevan Bibles.

Moreover, even though it be granted that many of Shakespeare's quotations of the Bible correspond to the Genevan version, one must be cautious in drawing the conclusion that therefore Shakespeare depended upon that version. The influence of the Genevan Bible in the England of Shakespeare's day was widely diffused. One could read that Bible in private; one could hear it read in some churches; one could hear it quoted in sermons; one could come upon it in secular reading; one could absorb its phrases from the conversation of others. To say which characteristically Genevan phrase Shakespeare borrowed from the Bible and which he learned in any of the other ways is difficult indeed.

(3) For the purpose of this discussion, it is not so much the frequency of Shakespeare's reference to the Genevan Bible that matters as the extent and character of the biblical knowledge which such references imply. The question becomes: Did Shakespeare have an exceptional knowledge of the Bible? Did he have the kind of knowledge which could be gained only through persistent home training in the reading of the Bible and in the memorization of texts?

Those interested in proving Shakespeare a Puritan answer both questions in the affirmative. Others, like Bishop Wordsworth,[29] interested in deriving Shakespeare's genius from the inspiration of revealed truth and in making Shakespeare himself a revealer of divine truth, also answer in the affirmative.

How extensive was Shakespeare's knowledge? In the course of his study, Noble finds that

. . . Shakespeare definitely made identifiable quotations from or allusions to at least 42 books of the Bible (18 each from the Old and New Testaments and 6 from the Apocrypha)—Genesis, Exodus, Numbers, Joshua, Judges, 1 and 2 Samuel, 1 and 2 Kings, Job, Psalms, Proverbs, Ecclesiastes, Song of Solomon, Isaiah, Jeremiah, Ezekiel, Daniel; Tobit, Judith, Wisdom, Ecclesiasticus, Bel, Susanna; the Four Gospels, Acts, Romans, 1 and 2 Corinthians, Ephesians, Philippians, Colossians, 1 Thessalonians, 1 Timothy, Hebrews, James, 1 and 2 Peter, and Revelation.[30]

Certainly an impressive list, especially when one remembers that there are many biblical allusions not "identifiable" as to exact source. But certain restrictions must be made with respect to the list. With another end in view, Fripp calls attention to the fact that Shakespeare is peculiarly partial to the beginnings of Testaments and books.

Of his one hundred and seventy and odd references, direct and indirect, to Genesis nearly one hundred and thirty are to chapters i-iv. . . . It is the same with the New Testament. The Poet's allusions to chapters i-vii of St. Matthew far outnumber those to the rest of the gospel. He reveals, moreover, a much closer knowledge of Genesis than of any other book in the Old Testament, and of St. Matthew than of any other in the New.[31]

Of other Old Testament books, Noble finds Shakespeare partial to the Psalms, Job, Proverbs, Ecclesiasticus, and Isaiah.[32] It appears then that Shakespeare's biblical knowledge was not as general as some suppose, and that in his preferences for biblical material he did not follow the lead of the Puritan movement with its emphasis on such books as Galatians and Romans, or the other Pauline epistles.

If Shakespeare's knowledge was, with certain qualifications, extensive, how intensive was it? Was it the knowledge of an acute Bible student? Sidney Lee makes a guarded, almost self-contradictory, answer:

> References to scriptural characters and incidents are not conspicuous in Shakespeare's plays, but such as they are, they are drawn from all parts of the Bible, and indicate a general acquaintance with the narrative of both Old and New Testament. Shakespeare quotes or adapts biblical phrases with far greater frequency than he makes allusion to episodes in biblical history. Elizabethan English was saturated with scriptural expressions. Many enjoyed colloquial currency, and others, which were more recondite, were liberally scattered through Holinshed's 'Chronicles' and secular works whence the dramatist drew his plots. Yet there is a savour of early study about his normal use of scriptural phraseology, as of scriptural history. His scriptural reminiscences bear trace of the assimilative or receptive tendency of an alert youthful mind. It is futile to urge that his knowledge of the Bible was mainly the fruit of close and continual application in adult life.[33]

An interesting biblical allusion cited to prove Shakespeare's especially keen understanding of the Bible is that found in the last words of Othello in the First Folio edition of *Othello*. The remorseful Moor implores Ludovico in his "letters" to speak

> Of one that lov'd not wisely, but too well,
> Of one not easily jealous, but being wrought
> Perplexed in the extreme; of one, whose hand
> (Like the base Judean) threw a Pearle away
> Richer than all his tribe.[34]

Though the Quarto reading of 1622, substituting "Indian" for "Judean," has been widely adopted, the adjective "base" and the dying words of Othello:

> I kiss'd thee ere I kill'd thee; no way but this,
> Killing myself to die upon a kiss,[35]

impel an association of Othello's murderous act with the treachery of Judas Iscariot. Shakespeare's extraordinary knowledge is supposed to be revealed by the fact that he knew Judas and Jesus were both Judeans. All the other disciples were Galileans. Shakespeare is supposed to have learned that Judas was a Judean from reading Beza's note at Matthew 10:4 in the Genevan-Tomson Bible, informing the reader that "Iscariot" meant "man of Kerioth" and that Kerioth was in Judea. The note does not appear in the ordinary Genevan, the Bishop's or the Rheims New Testament. The Genevan-Tomson New Testament was issued in 1576, when William Shakespeare was twelve years old. However, the knowledge that "Iscariot" meant "man of Kerioth" and that Kerioth was in Judea could have come to Shakespeare in other ways than through Bible reading; for example, through hearing a sermon on the text.

Again, when Shakespeare, in *3 Henry VI*, makes Clarence say to Warwick:

> To keep that oath were more impiety
> Than Jephthah's when he sacrific'd his daughter,[36]

he is supposed to reveal extraordinary insight, because the Genevan and Bishops' Bible, in rendering Judges 11:31: "That thing that commeth out of the doores of mine house against me, when I come home in peace from the children of Ammon, shal be the Lorde's, and I will offer it for a burnt-offering," do not make plain that Jephthah meant the vow to include his daughter and that the vow was therefore one of human sacrifice. But no special insight was necessary on Shakespeare's part, for the "Homily against Swearing and Perjury" speaks of Jephthah's promising "to offer for a sacrifice unto him that person which of his own house should first meet with him after his return home."[37]

A third instance cited to prove Shakespeare's biblical acumen is his understanding of the words of Jesus quoted in *King Richard II*:

> It is as hard to come as for a camel
> To thread the postern of a needle's eye.[38]

The biblical source is Matthew 19:24; Mark 10:25 or Luke 18:25. In preferring the interpretation of "camel" as a "large animal" rather than as a "rope," and of "a needle's eye" as a "needle" literally rather than as a "small gate," Shakespeare is thought to have shown an uncanny understanding of the lines as they were meant to be understood in a national proverb among the Hebrews. But Noble correctly points out that any uncritical reader not misled by a commentary would take the words literally, just as Shakespeare took them.[39]

Although a stronger case for the exceptional quality of Shakespeare's biblical knowledge might be made in a study of *The Merchant of Venice* than in the cases cited, in that the portrayal of Shylock reveals on Shakespeare's part a remarkable assimilation of the Hebrew character and outlook as revealed in the Bible, it is nevertheless the aptness of the application rather than the quality of Shakespeare's biblical knowledge which is exceptional.[40]

In Shakespeare's application of his biblical knowledge there is sometimes a certain irreverence. This point is remarked upon by Carter, who, somewhat to the detriment of his own theory, points out that Shakespeare, using "Scripture on any and every occasion," is "often unmindful of the meaning or association of the words, and becomes so daring and indiscriminate in his use that he shocks the sensitive mind."[41] Among instances that shock are the jest of Chiron in *Titus Andronicus* (IV, ii, 43),[42] the Prince's questionable remark in *2 Henry IV* (II, ii, 26–28)[43] about the chances of Poin's illegitimate children inheriting God's kingdom, the theological quips of the drunken Cassio in *Othello* (II, iii, 105–17), the slur on "faith" made by the "half-drunk" Sir Toby Belch in *Twelfth Night* (I, v, 135–36), and the somewhat sacrilegious conversation between Pandarus and a servant in *Troilus and Cressida* (III, i, 1–16). These instances are enough to lead Noble to conclude that

> had Shakespeare been instructed by his parents to respect the Bible, the influence of that early teaching might have been expected to act as a deterrent and he might have hesitated before presenting certain cherished opinions in a ridiculous light. It is not denied that the opinions thus made ludicrous were those entertained by types who had made themselves very objectionable to theatre folk and that they deserved all they got. . . .
>
> The impression made on my mind by these sallies of Shakespeare is not that he favoured this or that doctrine, or that he was hostile to some other, but that he regarded the contents of the Bible dispassionately. . . . Such an attitude might be regarded as inconsistent with a mind impregnated in youth with Scriptural teaching. It would be reasonable, therefore, to doubt that Shakespeare was grounded in the Bible in his home.[44]

Noble's opinion as to the improbability of Shakespeare's having received Bible training in his home is concurred in by others. Calling attention to the fact that "Shakespeare's works contain many references to Scripture," Richard K. Morton nevertheless concludes that "these are insufficient to enable us to call him in any sense a Bible student. I think that he rather picked up the phrases and ideas from the people."[45] Walter Raleigh's view is similar. After listing a few typical Bible references which Shakespeare makes, Raleigh says:

> . . . it cannot be inferred from this that he was a deep student of the Bible. The phraseology of his age, like that of later ages, was saturated with Biblical reminiscence. The *Essays of Elia* are a tissue of Biblical phrase; and Shakespeare's knowledge of the Bible, which may fairly be likened to Charles Lamb's, was probably acquired in casual and desultory fashion.[46]

(4) Not only do the instances of daring use of the Bible cited above serve to strengthen the conclusion that Shakespeare was not trained in the Bible during his early years at home, but they also serve to lend support to a contention made by some that Shakespeare used the Bible as a Catholic sympathizer could be expected to use it.

The Protestant use of the Bible is authoritarian. The emphasis of the Lutheran Reformation was upon the sufficiency of the Word of God. The Calvinistic Reformation likewise built upon that sufficiency. There was no need for church tradition or for papal dicta. Hence, for the English Puritan the Bible was everything. His reverence for the Infallible Word led him into excesses and exposed him to the ridicule of those who had a less implicit faith in the unique scriptural revelation. A confirmed Protestant would be restrained in his ridicule of Puritan extremes, but a conformist with Catholic sympathies would feel no such restraint. The argument is that Shakespeare does ridicule the extreme Protestant use of the Bible and so reveal Catholic sympathies.

Shakespeare is said to express his antipathy to the Protestant use of the Bible in two ways. First, he makes direct expression of his sentiments in the words of such characters as Antonio, who, reflecting upon Shylock's clever citation of the story of Jacob and Laban, says:

> The devil can cite Scripture for his purpose.
> An evil soul, producing holy witness,
> Is like a villain with a smiling cheek,
> A goodly apple rotten at the heart.
> O, what a goodly outside falsehood hath![47]

and Bassanio, who, philosophizing on the outward show of things, says:

> In religion,
> What damned error, but some sober brow
> Will bless it and approve it with a text,
> Hiding the grossness with fair ornament?[48]

Secondly, laughable characters in the plays quote Scripture or speak in scriptural language with great glibness. Bowden states the point as follows:

> . . . though Shakespeare did not intend to be profane himself, for "reverence," as he says, "is the angel of the world," he did intend the speaker to be so, and to show by his profanity the abuse which must result from "the Bible only" theory, and that "there is no damned error but a sober brow will write a text on," or that "the devil himself can quote Scripture." With this well-known power of irony, could he have chosen a more efficacious method of exposing the abuse of the new "Gospel method," than by making it the favourite weapon of canting fools, knaves, and hypocrites?[49]

The characters whom Shakespeare is thought to have used for this purpose are principally Jack Cade in *2 Henry VI* (IV, ii), Costard and Holofernes in *Love's Labour's Lost* (IV, ii), Bottom in *A Midsummer-Night's Dream* (IV, i, 218–21), Sir Hugh Evans in *The Merry Wives of Windsor* (I, i), Lavache in *All's Well that Ends Well* (I, iii), Launcelot in *The Merchant of Venice* (III, v), Justice Shallow in *2 Henry IV* (III, ii, 40 ff.), Touchstone in *As You Like It* (V, i, 34 ff.), Elbow in *Measure for Measure* (II, i, 81 ff.), Pandarus in *Troilus and Cressida* (III, i, 146 ff.), and, to a special degree, Falstaff in *1* and *2 Henry IV* and *The Merry Wives*. Quotation of lines is not always feasible, for the instances often occur throughout extended passages. There can be no denying the fact, however, that these characters speak in a scriptural vein and that the impression they make is not always conducive to respect for the Bible. It is a curious fact that Falstaff, the most amusing character in Shakespeare, is also the best versed in the Bible and the glibbest in using its phrases. Largely for this is he accused by some of being a backsliding Puritan.

In reply to the argument of Bowden it is not enough to say that dignified and respected characters also quote Scripture. The dignified characters use scriptural truth in a way which integrates that truth with human experience and throws light upon it. This is the way in which Catholics also would quite properly use scriptural truth. The fact remains that Shakespeare does satirize the authoritarian approach to the Bible. Since that approach is so often adopted by Protestants, there is some ground for believing that he is mocking Protestantism generally.

The foregoing discussion of Shakespeare's use of the Bible has been largely negative in results. It has sought to establish the fact that Shakespeare's knowledge of the Bible was not gained through training in a Puritan home, or through the predominant use of the Genevan version; that at times Shakespeare may have used the Catholic version; that his biblical knowledge was not exceptional for the times; and that there are instances in his use of the Bible that suggest a viewpoint sympathetic with Catholicism. We are now in a position to ask whether elsewhere in his works are to be found any indications which support the view that Shakespeare held Catholicism in greater esteem than is sometimes admitted.

2. *Some Positive Indications of Esteem for the Old Faith*

(1) Here and there in the plays one finds positive indications of Shakespeare's esteem for the Old Faith. First, there is the fact that Shakespeare treats the Catholic clergy more respectfully than the Protestant.[50] In sketching Catholic priests like Friar Laurence in *Romeo and Juliet* and Friar Francis in *Much Ado about Nothing*, not to mention lesser figures like the priest in *Twelfth Night*, Shakespeare seems appreciative of their better qualities. Even the priest officiating at Ophelia's funeral in *Hamlet*, though Laertes calls him "churlish," is trying to do his prescribed duty. No priest is presented in a ridiculous light. On the other hand, there is not a Protestant parish priest who is not made to appear a little ludicrous. The examples of Sir Nathaniel in *Love's Labour's Lost*, Sir Hugh Evans in *The Merry Wives of Windsor*, and Sir Oliver Martext in *As You Like It* illustrate this point. Neither is there any Protestant minister who plays an important part, that is, a part advancing the dramatic action.

There is something to be said for the commonly raised objection that Shakespeare treated Catholic priests romantically because he learned about them from his sources, whereas he treated Protestant ministers somewhat satirically because he saw them in the flesh, weak and erring, all around him. But Shakespeare had opportunity to observe Catholic priests in the flesh. In his youth he could have seen country priests serving quietly in protected places. In his early manhood he must have known about the Jesuits and seminary priests, and he may have observed them in their ministrations to faithful Catholics. That is a suggestive detail which Shakespeare introduces in *The Taming of the Shrew* when he has Lucentio presented to Baptista as a "young scholar, that has been long studying at Rheims. . . ."[51] At Rheims was located the English College where seminary priests destined for service in England were trained. To have Lucentio trained at Rheims sounds like a hint of approval of the seminary. Certainly Lucentio's association with Rheims is not intended to damage his character.

The same gentleness of treatment is accorded nuns, such as Isabella and Francisca in *Measure for Measure* and Amelia, the abbess at Ephesus, in *The Comedy of Errors*, though in these cases there can be no contrast with the treatment of the female religious of Protestantism. The words of the Clown in *All's Well that Ends Well* to the effect that his answer will serve all questions "As fit . . . as the nun's lip to the friar's mouth,"[52] often quoted to prove Shakespeare's disparaging attitude toward nunnery, are not part of a dramatic characterization, but are merely the witticism of a comic whose quips are intended to evoke laughter, not portray character. It remains true that when Shakespeare portrays a nun in a dramatic situation, he handles that character with delicacy and deference. In any event, if the Clown's words are taken seriously, they must be weighed against the words of Lucio in *Measure for Measure* (I, iv, 34–37), when, in addressing Isabella, that otherwise irreverent scoundrel says:

> I hold you as a thing ensky'd and sainted;
> By your renouncement an immortal spirit,
> And to be talk'd with in sincerity,
> As with a saint.

As for the depiction of Catholic prelates, something will be said later in connection with Shakespeare's characterization of Pandulph in *King John*. For the present it is enough to say with Charles Knight: "In an age when the prejudices of the multitude were flattered and stimulated by abuse and ridicule of the ancient ecclesiastical character, Shakespeare always exhibits it so as to command respect and affection.[53]

(2) At times Shakespeare employs a terminology so precise as to indicate an intimate knowledge of Catholicism. Two or three instances will serve to illustrate. Julia's line: "I see you have a month's mind to them,"[54] in *The Two Gentlemen of Verona* has been misunderstood by Shakespearean lexicographers like Alexander Schmidt, who failed to recognize a "month's mind" as being "the name first used for the month of remembrance during which daily Masses were offered for the souls of the dead, and now applied to the Mass said for them a month after death. . . ."[55] Juliet's mention of "evening mass"[56] has been thought to reveal an ignorance of Catholic liturgy,* whereas it turns out to be an indication of

---

*Thus the anonymous author of "Was Shakespeare a Roman Catholic?" in *The Edinburgh Review*, CXXIII (January, 1866), p. 181, after quoting the words of Juliet, says: "It seems to us morally impossible that any Roman Catholic could have made so absurd a mistake."

close knowledge. Bowden shows that "evening mass" meant mass said after noon, that in ancient times there was great latitude as to the hour of mass, and that, though Pope Pius V (1566–72) prohibited afternoon and evening mass, the prohibition was slow in taking effect in some places, notably Verona, the very scene of *Romeo and Juliet*, where evening mass was said as late as 1824.[57]

Bowden also cites the lines spoken by Friar Laurence in his cell:

> I must up-fill this osier cage of ours
> With baleful weeds and precious-juiced flowers.[58]

and maintains that the use of *ours* is not to make rhyme (the whole scene is written in couplets), but to recognize the fact that "it is the rule of the Franciscans, who have all property in common, to call whatever article of this property they use 'ours,' not 'mine,' *e. g.* 'I must put on our shoes,' 'I must go to our cell.' "[59]

The words of the ghost of Hamlet's father, describing the unprepared state in which the father had been murdered:

> Cut off even in the blossoms of my sin,
> Unhousel'd, disappointed, unanel'd[60]

are not recondite, but they are "technical terms connected with the old religion," as Bayne points out.[61] "Unanel'd" is a reference to the Sacrament of Extreme Unction.

Another interesting line in *Hamlet* is that occurring in the Queen's description of the death of Ophelia:

> Her clothes spread wide,
> And mermaid-like awhile they bore her up,
> Which time she chanted snatches of old lauds.[62]

The word "lauds" occurs only in the Quarto edition of 1605. In other texts the word is "tunes." J. Dover Wilson explains the word as follows:

> . . . "laudes" means hymns of praise and is apparently a reference to the *laude* or vernacular hymns which were first heard of in Italy at the end of the thirteenth century, were sung by wandering bands or guilds of singers called *laudesi*, and were still very popular at the end of the fifteenth. Whether they were also the fashion in England or how Shakespeare came to know of them is not clear.[63]

As Wilson remarks, ". . . modern editors . . . have sacrificed a beautiful reading." Some of the beauty lies in the reminiscent quality of the word, a quality stirring up memories of the Old Faith.

Another instance of a somewhat obscure verbal expression derived from
Catholicism is that found in the lines which Berowne, in *Love's Labour's
Lost*, speaks to himself when he discovers that Longaville has fallen in
love with Maria and believes himself to be the first to have committed
perjury:

> I could put thee 'n comfort: not by two that I know:
> Thou mak'st the triumviry, the corner-cap of society,
> The shape of love's Tyburn, that hangs up simplicity.[64]

C. H. Herford, in his edition of the works of Shakespeare, remarks that a
"corner-cap" is "the beretta or three-cornered cap of the Catholic priest.
The shape of this suggests the triangle formed by the timbers of a gallows,
—the Tyburn of love, at which the three 'perjurers' have hung up their
innocence."[65]

Finally, there is Hamlet's quotation of the line: "For, O! for, O! the
hobby-horse is forgot,"[66] in his bitter lament over the speed with which
the Queen has forgotten his murdered father. Hamlet is thus comparing
the fate of his revered father with that of the hobby-horse, a favorite
feature of the May-day Morris-dance which had been discouraged after
the Reformation and the omission of which had led to the writing of the
ballad from which Hamlet quotes.[67]

(3) Shakespeare seems to show an appreciative attitude towards vestments, vessels, and other properties of Catholicism. The King in *1 Henry
IV* explains the awe in which he is held by the people by pointing to his
policy of withholding himself from public view except upon very special
occasions:

> Thus did I keep my person fresh and new;
> My presence, like a robe pontifical,
> Ne'er seen but wonder'd at.[68]

The figure is more significant when one recalls that the lines were written
during days when papal vestments were being destroyed.

Though the word "chalice" is used only four times in Shakespeare, and
though two instances of such usage seem to controvert the point to be
made: first, Falstaff's profane use of the term in *The Merry Wives*,[69] and
again, Claudius' blasphemous use in *Hamlet*,[70] two of those instances have
a deeper significance and seem to indicate what Fripp considers a preference for "the holy vessel of the Old Faith."[71] Coming from Fripp, who
advocates a strong strain of Puritanism in the Shakespeares, the testi-
mony is more telling. The two instances are (a) Macbeth's sober reflection that

> this even-handed justice
> Commends the ingredients of our poison'd chalice
> To our own lips[72]

and (b) the reverently beautiful metaphor of "chalic'd flowers" in the song "Hark! hark! the lark" in *Cymbeline*.[73]

That Shakespeare felt something like pain in the presence of ruined abbeys and monasteries is implied by the well-known line in *Sonnet LXXIII*. The picture is one of melancholy:

> That time of year thou mayst in me behold
> When yellow leaves, or none, or few, do hang
> Upon those boughs which shake against the cold,
> Bare ruin'd choirs, where late the sweet birds sang.

The thought of ruined religious houses brings up the detail contained in King Henry V's prayer on behalf of his soldiers. The King reminds God that he has built

> Two chantries, where the sad and solemn priests
> Sing still for Richard's soul.[74]

These two chantries stood on opposite sides of the Thames: one, of the Brigettine nuns of Sion, at Twickenham; the other, of the Carthusians, at Sheen. These had been restored by Queen Mary, but suppressed by Queen Elizabeth.[75]

(4) In ways unnecessary to the plot or the dramatic situation, Shakespeare sometimes seems to pay tribute to the intercessory powers of the Virgin Mary. For example, in *All's Well that Ends Well*, the Countess of Rousillon expresses her displeasure with Bertram's desertion of his wife by exclaiming:

> What angel shall
> Bless this unworthy husband? he cannot thrive,
> Unless her prayers, whom heaven delights to hear,
> And loves to grant, reprieve him from the wrath
> Of greatest justice.[76]

More pointed still is the counsel which Prospero gives Alonso in *The Tempest*. Alonso is inconsolable in the belief that he has lost his son, Ferdinand, whereupon Prospero says:

> I rather think
> You have not sought her help; of whose soft grace,
> From the like loss I have her sovereign aid,
> And rest myself content.[77]

(5) There is something reminiscent of Catholicism in the kind of piety which is said to be true of Sylvia in the song:

> Who is Silvia? what is she?
>   That all our swains commend her?
> Holy, fair, and wise is she;
>   The heaven such grace did lend her,
> That she might admired be.[78]

About this song, Fripp again comments: "Here indeed (and Shakespeare never threw off the Calvinist) is the Protestant doctrine of *grace*; but Silvia's holiness is of the old devout, naïve kind, examples of which might be found in wealthy and cultivated homes in 1590, none the less sincere and winsome because of its brave endurance of persecution."[79] Fripp precedes this comment with an estimate of *The Two Gentlemen of Verona* as a play in which Shakespeare's

> imagination wandered freely and fearlessly into the not long past, before the savage destruction of monasteries and burning of martyrs, when Englishmen were of one Church, and godly 'fathers' heard confession, sang *requiem*, offered prayers for others' sins, and did penance for their own, in lonely cells and forest retreats; when lovers sought their help in trouble and knights took solemn vows of chastity. . . . In a Catholic environment he set his heroine, his first ideal English maiden, a mere sketch, but full of charm. . . .[80]

(6) There are many allusions to prayer in Shakespeare's writings and many eloquent prayers, most of which cannot be taken as revealing anything characteristically Catholic, but the prayer of Prospero in the Epilogue of *The Tempest* deserves special mention as seeming to refer to the Catholic doctrine of Indulgences and as being a plea for prayers on Prospero's behalf after death.

> Now I want
> Spirits to enforce, art to enchant;
> And my ending is despair,
> Unless I be reliev'd by prayer,
> Which pierces so that it assaults
> Mercy itself and frees all faults.
> As you from crimes would pardon'd be,
> Let your indulgence set me free.[81]

The peculiar efficacy of prayers offered by nuns is averred by Isabella in *Measure for Measure* when she explains to Angelo that she will bribe him for the life of her brother Claudio

> . . . with true prayers
> That shall be up at heaven and enter there
> Ere sun-rise: prayers from preserved souls,
> From fasting maids whose minds are dedicate
> To nothing temporal.[82]

The traditional hours of prayer are spiritual trysting times for Cymbeline and Posthumus, for Cymbeline has charged Posthumus, gone to Rome,

> At the sixth hour of morn, at noon, at midnight,
> To encounter me with orisons, for then
> I am in heaven for him. . . .[83]

The Catholic practice of praying with beads upon the prayer book is alluded to by Proteus in *Two Gentlemen of Verona* when he assures the departing Valentine:

> If ever danger do environ thee,
> Commend thy grievance to my holy prayers,
> For I will be thy beadsman, Valentine.
> *Val.* And on a love-book pray for my success?
> *Pro.* Upon some book I love I'll pray for thee.[84]

(7) The Catholic doctrine of the mediation of angels seems to come to spontaneous expression in the startled words of Hamlet upon seeing his father's ghost:

> Angels and ministers of grace defend us![85]

"It is quite fair," says a Catholic writer quoted by George Wilkes,[86] "to ask whether such an exclamation would come more easily into a Catholic poet's head or into that of a Protestant poet? . . . . a Catholic's natural resource in danger is to angels and other ministers of grace."

(8) The ghost of Hamlet's father comes from Purgatory. In conversation with Hamlet the ghost explains that his time is short:

> My hour is almost come,
> When I to sulphurous and tormenting flames
> Must render up myself,

and then, disdaining Hamlet's pity, says:

> I am thy father's spirit;
> Doom'd for a certain term to walk the night,
> And for the day confin'd to fast in fires,
> Till the foul crimes done in my days of nature

> Are burnt and purg'd away. But that I am forbid
> To tell the secrets of my prison-house,
> I could a tale unfold whose lightest word
> Would harrow up thy soul. . . .[87]

This, then, is no folk-lore spirit, such as "Sweet William's Ghost" in the popular ballad, but a soul returned from the realm of Catholic immortality. The bones left "hearsed in death" by that soul had been "canonized."[88]

(9) Shakespeare makes repeated mention of the church in many connections and in both Protestant and Catholic dramatic situations, but only three times does he use the characteristically Catholic expression "holy church."[89] In all three instances the words are spoken by church dignitaries. Quite properly, too, a cardinal of the church speaks of "the church, our holy mother."[90] In general throughout the plays the Catholic Church is treated in a reverential manner.

(10) Of the seven sacraments of the Roman Catholic Church, two—Baptism and the Eucharist—are recognized by Protestantism, so that Shakespeare's reference to these can offer little of value to this study. References to baptism are relatively few.[91] The word "eucharist" does not occur in Shakespeare. Neither does the more characteristically Protestant term "Lord's Supper" or "Lord's Table." References to "mass" are infrequent.* There is, however, something peculiarly Catholic in Rosalind's reply to Celia's quip about the kisses of Orlando being "Judas's own children." Says Rosalind:

> . . . his kissing is as full of sanctity as the touch of holy bread.[92]

The Catholic quality of the line is brought out when one recalls that in the Sacrament of Holy Eucharist, the administering priest carefully places the sacred Species on the tongue of the communicant, whereas in the Protestant Sacrament of Communion, the communicant takes the bread in his hand. The Eucharist is the source of the striking metaphor in Lorenzo's ecstatic speech to Jessica in *The Merchant of Venice*:

> Sit, Jessica: look, how the floor of heaven
> Is thick inlaid with patines of bright gold.[93]

In the eyes of Lorenzo, the stars were bright and holy like the metal plates upon which the bread of the sacrament was customarily placed. The reverent metaphor serves as an appropriate introduction to the sublime lines which follow it.

---

*The only clear reference to the mass as a religious service is Juliet's mention of evening mass already discussed. Most of the uses of the word "mass" occur in the expression "by the mass."

As for the five peculiarly Catholic sacraments, there are several observations to be made. Shakespeare makes no mention of Confirmation. His every use of the word "confirmation" is in the ordinary sense of "corroborating" or "making certain." The Sacrament of Holy Order may be mentioned twice,[94] both times in contexts which warrant no special comment. The references are dubious; they may refer to the Order of St. Francis, rather than to the sacrament. The Sacrament of Extreme Unction is not mentioned by name, but is clearly referred to in *Hamlet*. The Sacrament of Penance seems to come readily to the mind of Shakespeare. He alludes to it many times.[95] The use is sometimes figurative and suggests that the sacrament had a peculiar appeal for Shakespeare. One instance will serve to illustrate. In *The Two Gentlemen of Verona*, Valentine says to Proteus:

> I have done penance for contemning love;
> Whose high imperious thoughts have punish'd me
> With bitter fasts, with penitential groans,
> With nightly tears and daily heart-sore sighs.[96]

References to marriage are most numerous. The religious aspect of marriage is often brought out, but only twice is the word "holy" specifically applied.[97] The sacramental aspect of marriage is well stated by the priest in *Twelfth Night*, who in response to Olivia's plea, reports to the assembled company that between Olivia and Sebastian he has performed:

> A contract of eternal bond of love,
> Confirm'd by mutual joinder of your hands,
> Attested by the holy close of lips,
> Strengthen'd by interchangement of your rings;
> And all the ceremony of this compact
> Seal'd in my function, by my testimony.[98]

With respect to marriage, a comparison of two passages is interesting. They both have to do with the two-fold ceremony: civil contract, allowing cohabitation; and the religious rite, making it possible for a wife to claim her dowry. In *Measure for Measure* Claudio explains his relationship to Julietta:

> Thus stands it with me: upon a true contract
> I got possession of Julietta's bed:
> You know the lady; she is fast my wife,
> Save that we do the denunciation lack
> Of outward order: this we came not to,
> Only for propagation of a dower
> Remaining in the coffer of her friends.[99]

As has been frequently pointed out, this may explain Shakespeare's own early relationship with Anne Hathaway. The custom was an old one. But Protestantism was taking a stand against it, and that Shakespeare came to believe in the superiority of the new and stricter view is indicated by Prospero's warning to Ferdinand:

> If thou dost break her virgin knot before
> All sanctimonious ceremonies may
> With full and holy rite be minister'd,
> No sweet aspersion shall the heavens let fall
> To make this contract grow.[100]

Also of interest with respect to the marriage rite is Oberon's blessing of the marriage-bed.

> To the best bride-bed will we,
> Which by us shall blessed be;
> And the issue there create
> Ever shall be fortunate.
> So shall all the couples three
> Ever true in loving be.[101]

Bowden believes this to be an echo of the *Benedictio Thalami* in the Catholic Ritual, the words of which read: "Bless, O Lord, this bed. May all who dwell in it remain in Thy peace, abide in Thy will, grow to old age, and be multiplied to the length of days, and attain at last to the kingdom of heaven. . . ."[102]

(11) Shakespeare seems closely acquainted with the rubric of the Roman Catholic Church. He seems attracted to the colorfulness, beauty, and mysticism of the ritual. Pertinent passages include descriptions of the vestments of high church dignitaries (*2 Henry IV*, IV, 1, 45–46), allusions to the confessional (*Romeo and Juliet*, III, v, 231–33), to the rite of "blessed sanctuary" (*Richard III*, III, i, 26–43), to the last rites to the dying (*Hamlet*, I, v, 77), to customs of respect to the dead (*Richard III*, I, ii), and to the burial rites (*Romeo and Juliet*, IV, v, 84–90).

A passage of special interest with respect to funeral rites is that describing the obsequies of Ophelia.[103] Because her "death was doubtful," Ophelia was buried with "maimed rites." The Roman Catholic *Codex Juris Canonici* mentions doubtful cases and provides for "maimed rites,"[104] but no such mention or provision is made in the Protestant Prayer Book. The Canon is the "order" overswayed by "great command." Specifically, the priest could not "sing a requiem." Again the Prayer Book makes no provision for a requiem. It is true that in Shakespeare's day custom prescribed the refusal of church benefit to suicides, but that custom grew out of medieval practices. In 1604 a canon (Canon 68) was adopted by the Church of England forbidding a minister to refuse burial to any corpse brought to the churchyard unless it were the body of one who had been "denounced excommunicated majori excommunicatione, for some grievous and notorious crime, and no man able to testify of his repentance."[105] Though suicide is not mentioned, it might be included among "grievous and notorious" crimes. However, the crime could not be doubtful, for the criminal must have been "denounced excommunicated," and such denunciation leaves no room for doubt. It was not until 1662 that the present rubric forbidding church benefit to suicides was added to the Anglican rite.[106]

(12) The inner significance of certain Catholic practices, such as confession, the use of holy water, and fasting, seems to be familiar to Shakespeare, so that these practices suggest themselves to his imagination when he slips into figurative speech. A good example is found in *The Winter's Tale*, when Leontes, speaking to Camillo, says:

> I have trusted thee, Camillo,
> With all the nearest things to my heart, as well
> My chamber-councils, wherein, priest-like, thou
> Hast cleans'd my bosom: I from thee departed
> Thy penitent reform'd.[107]

A second instance occurs in *King Lear* when the Gentleman reports to Kent upon how Cordelia received the news of her father's suffering.

> There she shook
> The holy water from her heavenly eyes,
> And clamour-moisten'd, then away she started
> To deal with grief alone.[108]

And though the words of Othello to Desdemona are insincere, the figure of speech which heightens their deceptiveness is natural enough and seemingly spontaneous to the dramatist who wrote them:

> . . . this hand of yours requires
> A sequester from liberty, fasting and prayer,
> Much castigation, exercise devout;
> For here's a young and sweating devil here,
> That commonly rebels.[109]

(13) Only one passage in Shakespeare has been brought forward as an expression of Shakespeare's reaction to the religious penal laws of Protestantism. It is the passage which concludes *Sonnet CXXIV*. After avow-

ing that the love of the writer was not of the temporal and opportunistic sort, the sonnet declares:

> It fears not policy, that heretic,
> Which works on leases of short number'd hours,
> But all alone stands hugely politic,
> That it nor grows with heat, nor drowns with showers.
> To this I witness call the fools of time,
> Which die for goodness, who have liv'd for crime.

If the view is taken that this sonnet was addressed to the Earl of Southampton, the lines may have bearing on the fortunes of the Earl's father, who suffered unpleasantness for his Catholic faith.

(14) Shakespeare's interpretation of certain historical characters sometimes seems indicative of Catholic sensibilities. King Henry V, who is generally accepted as Shakespeare's ideal king, is portrayed "as a well-nigh perfect type of a Catholic hero."[110] In reply to the objection that Shakespeare only follows Holinshed in the delineation of the King, Bowden observes:

> But the poet not only follows the chronicler in attributing acts of Catholic faith and worship to the king, he further gives his hero a character of such practical wisdom, graceful piety, and enlightened religion, that his Popish proceedings appear like the flowers of true devotion, not the weeds of superstititon, as they might have been represented under the hands of another dramatist.[111]

On the other hand, the depiction of King Henry VIII, founder of English Protestantism, is that of "a cruel, selfish, base hypocrite." The impression made by the characterization upon Catholics is "that this play furnishes the strongest proof of the poet's Catholic sympathies."[112] The impression is strengthened by the favorable delineation of Henry VIII's queen, the Catholic Katherine, to whom the sympathies of the audience are attracted.

Much of the foregoing evidence is piecemeal. No single bit of it taken alone carries much weight. But the total effect is significant. That effect is heightened by the evidence gathered through a study of what Shakespeare accomplished in the revision of a Protestant source play when he wrote *King John*. Of this a detailed account will next be given.

3. Shakespeare's Revision of *The Troublesome Raigne of John*

Because *The Life and Death of King John* provides "the only occasion on which Shakespeare deals directly with the main issue of his age, viz.

the religious question and the conflict between the English monarch and the Papacy," and because it furnishes "an indisputable example of textual revision"[113] which markedly modifies a fierce antagonism to Roman Catholicism, it is a particularly important play for our purpose.

The source of *King John* is a play published under the title of "THE / TROUBLESOME RAIGNE / of *John*, King of *England*, with the *dis-* / *covery of King* Richard Cordelion's / Base sone (vulgarly named, the Ba- / stard Fawconbridge): *also the* / death of King *John* at *Swinstead* / *Abbey.* / *As it was (sundry times) publicly acted by the* / *Queen's Majesty's* *Players, in the ho-* / *nourable City of* / London. Imprinted at London for *Sampson Clarke,* / *and are to be sold at his shop, on the back-* / side of the *Royall Exchange.* / 1591."[114] The play appeared in two parts, the First Part ending at the peak of John's fortunes just before the death of Arthur Plantagenet. The Second Part carries a separate title page.

The author of the play is not known. Some critics believe the play to have been an early effort of Shakespeare himself,[115] and their views receive superficial confirmation from the fact that the title page of a republication in 1611 "by Valentine Simmes for John Helme" inserted the words "Written by W. Sh." (though it omitted the words "publicly . . . in the honourable City of London"). Moreover, the title page of an edition published in 1622 "printed by Aug: Mathewes for Thomas Dewe" contains the full affirmation: "Written by W. Shakespeare."[116] But there are many good reasons for believing that Shakespeare was not the author of *The Troublesome Raigne,* [117] and the superficial support of Shakespeare's name on the title page of later editions falls away when one considers how often an unscrupulous publisher employed such a device to sell his books.

Although it is probable "that what Shakespeare worked upon for his *King John* was not the published text but a prompt-copy of the play which the anonymous author had sold to the Queen's company . . . from which Shakespeare's own company eventually purchased it,"[118] the published text must be enough like the prompt-copy to make it a fair basis of study.

Several excellent studies of Shakespeare's reworking of *The Troublesome Raigne* have been made.[119] They reveal that as an artist Shakespeare modified and reworked this source in much the same way in which he treated other sources from which he drew. He compressed the two parts containing twenty-two scenes into one play of five acts containing sixteen scenes. He reduced the time from ten days with intervals to seven days with intervals. He eliminated unnecessary preliminaries and duplications to keep the main action clear. He developed the main characters into fuller personalities. He completely rewrote the play, intensifying the dialogue and lifting the level of the poetry. He exploited more skillfully the scenes of strong human interest. He improved the stage-business by avoiding lengthy "asides" and by keeping the dialogue between two characters down to reasonable limits. And finally, he deepened the philosophical tone of the play.[120]

But in addition to these characteristic changes, Shakespeare completely transformed the temper of the earlier drama by eliminating its strong anti-Catholic bias and writing a play which by contrast is so mild in its attitude toward Catholicism that some critics regard Shakespeare's revision as proof of his Catholic faith.

More than one critic has been impressed by the striking nature of this change. Johann M. Raich writes:

> Shakespeare hat aber jeden einzelnen Baustein sorgfältig geprüft und die anti-katholischen sammt und sonders verworfen. Kein Katholik hätte die Aufgabe, das ältere Stuck von seiner katholikenfeindlichen Tendenz zu purificiren, besser und gewissenhafter lösen können, als Shakespeare gethan.[121]

J. Dover Wilson remarks:

> To an ardent Protestant, who might have found much to delight him in Bale's *King Johan* and in *The Troublesome Reign*, *King John* would have seemed Laodicean. Nothing is more remarkable than the evident pains taken by Shakespeare to rid the play of the anti-catholic bias of his predecessors.[122]

Liebermann writes:

> Deutlich verfolgt Sh. bei der Bearbeitung Tendenzen, die ausserhalb der Rücksichts aufs Theater oder auf die dicterische Schönheit seines Werkes liegen. Einer 'systematischen Zensur' unterzieht er nämlich zunächst die zahllosen, dem Katholizismus feindlichen Stellen in *TR*.[123]

And Edward Rose is so conscious of the extraordinary nature of the revision that he confesses that "the omission from the play of the constant attacks on Popery . . . destroys to a certain extent its *raison d'être*, the spirit that helped to animate its old straggling mass, and . . . the motive of its *dénoûment*."[124]

(1) The means by which Shakespeare effected this radical change in the religious atmosphere of *King John* are not far to seek. First of all by recasting the character of John he altered the motivation of the play. The purpose of *The Troublesome Raigne* was to present King John as the forerunner of the English Reformation—to make of him an admirable Protestant hero. The author declares his intention in the prologue to the First Part, addressed "To the Gentlemen Readers":

You that with friendly grace of smoothed brow
Have entertained the Scythian *Tamburlaine*,
And given applause unto an Infidel,
Vouchsafe to welcome, with like courtesy,
A warlike Christian and your countryman.
For Christ's true faith endur'd he many a storm,
And set himself against the Man of Rome,
Until base treason (by a damnèd wight)
Did all his former triumphs put to flight.
Accept of it, sweet Gentles, in good sort,
And think it was prepar'd for your disport.

John himself is conscious of his high calling and twice during the play speaks prophetically. Once, when the fortunes of war and politics have turned against him so that he sees no way to retain the crown "but finely to dissemble with the Pope," John consoles himself with the thought of a more worthy successor:

Thy sins are far too great to be the man
T'abolish Pope and popery from thy realm:
But in thy seat, if I may guess at all,
A king shall reign that shall surpass them all.[125]

Again, in his dying speech, when he sums up the meaning of his reign, John says to the Bastard:

My tongue doth falter. *Philip*, I tell thee, man,
Since *John* did yield unto the Priest of *Rome*,
Nor he nor his have prosp'red on the earth:
Curst are his blessings; and his curse is bliss.
But in the spirit I cry unto my God,
As did the kingly prophet *Davvid* cry,
(Whose hands, as mine, with murder were attaint)
I am not he shall build the Lord a house,
Or root these locusts from the face of earth;
But if my dying heart deceive me not,
From out these loins shall spring a kingly branch,
Whose arms shall reach unto the gates of *Rome*,
And with his feet tread down the strumpet's pride
That sits upon the chair of *Babylon*.[126]

This conception of King John as a Protestant hero was in line with dramatic precedent. His character had first taken this Protestant cast in performances given by a company of actors (probably Lord Cromwell's men) "at my lord of Canterbury's" (Cranmer) as early as January 2, 1539. These performances were under the direction of one "Bale," and from them it might be "perceived King John was as noble a prince as ever was in England, and . . . that he was the beginning of the putting down of the Bishop in Rome."[127] The director was probably John Bale (1495–1563), a Catholic monk turned ardent Protestant, and the play was probably his *Kynge Johan.*

Even though the play performed at Canterbury was not *Kynge Johan*, it is certain that John Bale's play of that name was written before his death in 1563. In *Kynge Johan* also the King is pictured as a Reformation hero. At the end of the first part of the play, the Interpreter declares John's mission to be that of an English Moses:

> Thys noble kynge Johan, as a faythfull Moyses
> withstode proude Pharao, for hys poore Israel,
> Myndynge to brynge it, out of the lande of Darkenesse
> But the Egyptyanes, ded agaynst hym so rebell
> That hys poore people, ded styll in the desart dwell
> Tyll that Duke Iosue, whych was our late kynge Henrye
> Clerely brought vs in, to the lande of mylke and honye.[128]

Though there is no way of proving the fact, the author of *The Troublesome Raigne* may have been influenced by Bale's play. True it is that no printed copy of *Kynge Johan* has come down to us from the Elizabethan period, but that misfortune does not prove the play was never printed. The fact that the one extant manuscript of the drama was discovered in 1835 among papers belonging to the Corporation of Ipswich does not prove that the play could not have been known to Elizabethan dramatists. The last twenty-two lines of the manuscript are a prayer to Queen Elizabeth and are accepted by critics as an addition made at a performance in honor of the Queen when she visited Ipswich from August 5th to 11th in 1561. A play performed before the Queen could scarcely have remained unknown in dramatic circles, and its author's characterization of King John could scarcely have gone unnoticed among later Elizabethan dramatists. In other words, it is not wholly improbable that the author of *The Troublesome Raigne* took his cue from Bale.

If the author did not know of Bale's *Kynge Johan*, he certainly read Holinshed's *Chronicles* and was influenced by it. Even there the characterization of John is generally favorable. Holinshed said John

> was comelie of stature, but of looke and countenance displeasant and angrie, somewhat cruell of nature, as by the writers of his time he is noted, and not so hardie as doubtfull in time of perill and danger. But

this seemeth to be an enuious report vttered by thos that were giuen to speake no good of him whome they inwardlie hated. Howbeit some giue this witnesse of him . . . that he was a great and mightie prince, but yet not verie fortunate, much like to Marius the noble Romane, tasting of fortune both waies; bountifull and liberall vnto strangers, but of his owne people (for their dailie treasons practised towards him) a great oppressour, so that he trusted more to forreners than to them, and therefore in the end he was of them vtterlie forsaken. . . . Certeinlie it should seeme the man had a princelie heart in him, and wanted nothing but faithful subjects to haue assisted him in reuenging such wrongs as were doone and offered by the French King and others. Moreouer, the pride and pretended authoritie of the cleargie he could not well abide, when they went about to wrest out of his hands the prerogatiue of his princelie rule and gouernment. True it is, that to mainteine his warres which he was forced to take in hand as well as in France as elsewhere, he was constreined to make all the shift he could deuise to recouer monie and bicause he pinched their purses, they conceiued no small hatred against him, which when he perceiued, and wanted peraduenture discretion to passe it ouer, he discouered now and then in his rage his immoderate displeasure, as one not able to bridle his affections, a thing verie hard in a stout stomach, and thereby missed now and then to compasse that which otherwise he might verie well haue brought to passe.[129]

The point to be made is that whatever the source of the heroic conception of King John in *The Troublesome Raigne*, Shakespeare rejects the interpretation. He omits the declamatory prologue. He omits the prophecies of fulfilment by a more worthy successor. He proceeds to depict John as a royal villain.

(a) To do this Shakespeare first casts strong doubt upon the legality of John's title to the throne—a title left clear and indisputable in *The Troublesome Raigne*. That doubt is expressed through none other than the King's own mother, Queen Elinor. In the mind and conscience of the Queen, John is a usurper. When John attempts to reassure his mother of the strength of their position in the face of threatening French opposition by declaring:

> Our strong possession and our right for us,

Elinor replies:

> Your strong possession much more than your right,
> Or else it must go wrong with you and me:
> So much my conscience whispers in your ear,
> Which none but heaven and you and I shall hear.[130]

What Shakespeare intended the audience to think of John's title is shown by the words of the Bastard as he watches the English nobles bear the body of Prince Arthur off the stage:

> How easy dost thou take all England up!
> From forth this morsel of dead royalty,
> The life, the right and truth of all this realm
> Is fled to heaven; and England now is left
> To tug and scamble and to part by the teeth
> The unow'd interest of proud swelling state.[131]

It appears from this passage that Shakespeare wanted his audience to look upon King John as a usurper.

(b) Then Shakespeare draws King John in a more traitorous light when the treaty between France and England is concluded. In *The Troublesome Raigne*, after the citizen of Angiers proposes the match between Lewes the Dauphin and John's niece Blanche, Queen Elianor urges John to agree to the proposal in order to

> . . . be sure,
> *Arthur* shall have small succour out of *Fraunce*.[132]

John then asks King Philip how he means to deal in the matter. Philip suggests that he is favorable if Blanche has any affection for the Dauphin. Here the Bastard interposes:

> 'Swounds, Madam, take an English Gentleman:
> Slave as I was, I thought to have mov'd the match.
> Grandam, you made me half a promise once,
> That Lady *Blanche* should bring me wealth enough,
> And make me heir of store of English land.[133]

The Bastard's objection is purely personal; his own interest in Blanche is being frustrated. The Queen silences the Bastard with a promise to find a substitute for Blanche and with a reminder that

> We must with policy compound this strife.[134]

The Bastard contents himself with an obscene threat. To John's direct question, Blanche pleads for time to consider, and the Queen tells the two kings to negotiate the terms of the treaty while she herself helps Blanche to decide quickly. Arthur then shows himself in an unfavorable light. To his raging mother he weakly pleads:

> Sweet mother: cease these hasty madding fits
> For my sake, let my grandam have her will.
> O, would she with her hands pull forth my heart,

I could afford it, to appease these broils.
But, mother, let us wisely wink at all,
Lest further harms ensue our hasty speech.[135]

Philip now asks John what dowry he will give to the Dauphin. John reminds Philip that Blanche's dowry out of Spain alone is regal in value,

But, more to mend and amplify the same,
I give in money thirty-thousand marks;
For land, I leave it to thine own demand.[136]

Now Philip utters a demand that must have sounded hateful in the ears of English playgoers:

Then I demand *Volquesson, Torain, Main,*
Poitiers and *Anjou*, these five provinces,
Which thou as King of *England*, holds't in *Fraunce*:
Then shall our peace be soon concluded on.[137]

The Bastard is taken aback at the size of the demand and asks:

No less than five such provinces at once?[138]

King John appeals again to his mother, expressing a reluctance to yield these lands got

With much effusion of our English blood,[139]

and Elinor appeals again to policy:

John, give it him, so shalt thou live in peace,
And keep the residue sans jeopardy.[140]

Thereupon John consents to Philip's demands. As a sop, John gives to Arthur the dukedom of Britaine, the earldom of Richmond, and the "rich city of *Angiers* withal." The principals then go in to prepare the marriage rites.

The foregoing scene cannot by long odds be considered one calculated to please Englishmen, but John's part in it seems less like treachery to England and the Crown than his part in the corresponding scene in Shakespeare. There, after the Citizen announces the proposal, the Bastard makes a resounding speech of consternation, during which he suggests the danger to England inherent in the offer:

Our ears are cudgell'd; not a word of his
But buffets better than a fist of France.[141]

There, too, though Elinor also encourages John to make the match, she begins her appeal with the suggestion that John

> Give with our niece a dowry large enough[142]

and links the reason with John's illegal title by suggesting that

> . . . by this knot thou shalt so surely tie
> Thy now unsur'd assurance to the crown.[143]

She prods John to "urge" the French to consent to the match

> Lest zeal, now melted by the windy breath
> Of soft petitions, pity and remorse,
> Cool and congeal again to what it was.[144]

King Philip then admonishes John to speak first. John's offer of a rich dowry follows immediately. He seems almost precipitate in blurting out:

> For Anjou, and fair Touraine, Maine, Poictiers,
> And all that we upon this side the sea,—
> Except this city now by us besieg'd,—
> Find liable to our crown and dignity,
> Shall gild her bridal bed. . . .[145]

The description of Touraine as "fair" and the almost ludicrous contrast between the offer of "all that we upon this side of sea . . . find liable to our crown" and the reservation of a paltry "city now by us besieged" could not have enhanced the respect of the audience for King John as a faithful English sovereign.

Agreement between the Dauphin and Lady Blanche is quickly reached, whereupon John repeats the smarting proffer of England's French possessions:

> Then do I give Volquessen, Touraine, Maine,
> Poictiers and Anjou, these five provinces,
> With her to thee; and this addition more,
> Full thirty thousand marks of English coin.
> Philip of France, if thou be pleas'd withal,
> Command thy son and daughter to join hands.[146]

It is important to note that in *The Troublesome Raigne* the offer of money is first and the offer of land second and in proportion to French demands, whereas in *King John* the offer of land is first and in proportion to John's willingness to betray his trust. That betrayal is then made even more enormous by the gratuitous surrender of a large sum of good "English coin."

A final subtle touch is added to the depiction of John's treachery when, at the end of the scene, King John placates Prince Arthur with the bestowal of gifts. The same gifts are bestowed upon Arthur as in *The Troublesome Raigne*, but not out of the largesse of a king willing to forgive a troublesome claimant to the throne and to be generous to a weakling. Now the gifts are made at the suggestion of the King of France. Constance, her every hope dashed by the covenant between Lewis and Blanche, has gone "sad and passionate" to Philip's tent. The French King muses upon the distress of Constance and then turns to John:

> Brother of England, how may we content
> This widow lady? In her right we came;
> Which we, God knows, have turn'd another way,
> To our own vantage.[147]

It is then that John, to "heal up all," creates Arthur Duke of Britain and Earl of Richmond and confers upon him the "rich fair town" of Angiers. The contentment of Constance is therefore gained at the expense of England, though it is France that proposes the placation! No wonder the Bastard breaks into the exclamation:

> Mad world! mad kings! mad composition![148]

and continues, to close the scene, with his famous soliloquy on Commodity! Though the soliloquy has as much to do with the fickleness of France as with the perfidy of Albion, it serves to confirm the contention that in Shakespeare's play, King John is not only a usurper but a duplicitous traitor to England.

(c) A third change in Shakespeare's characterization of John is the distinct lessening of his heroic proportions in the one scene in which he has a chance to please an English audience. The scene is that in which he makes his proud stand against the intervention of Pandulph, the papal legate.

In the first place, Shakespeare cuts down the heroic proportions of John by painting the antagonist, Rome and Roman officialdom, in a more favorable light. In *The Troublesome Raigne* the entrance of Pandulph is made in a way bound to stiffen the spine of every English playgoer. The Cardinal bursts unannounced upon the stage and arrogantly shouts:

> Stay, King of *France*, I charge thee, join not hands
> With him that stands accurst of God and men.
> Know, *John*, that I, *Pandulph*, Cardinal of *Millaine*, and Legate from
> the See of *Rome*, demand of thee, in the name of our Holy Father the
> Pope *Innocent*, why thou dost—contrary to the laws of our Holy

Mother, the Church, and our Holy Father, the Pope—disturb the quiet of the Church, and disannul the election of *Stephen Langhton*, whom his Holiness hath elected Archbishop of *Canterbury*: this, in his Holiness' name, I demand of thee?[149]

How much tempered is the scene in Shakespeare! There Pandulph is first seen and announced by King Philip:

> Here comes the holy legate of the pope,

so that an attitude of receptivity is more or less suggested to the audience. Then Pandulph begins his speech with an address of respect to both kings:

> Hail, you anointed deputies of heaven!

and turns to John:

> To thee, King John, my holy errand is.
> I Pandulph, of fair Milan cardinal,
> And from Pope Innocent the legate here,
> Do in his name religiously demand
> Why thou against the church, our holy mother,
> So wilfully dost spurn; and, force perforce,
> Keep Stephen Langton, chosen Archbishop
> Of Canterbury, from that holy see?
> This, in our foresaid holy father's name,
> Pope Innocent, I do demand of thee.[150]

And if Pandulph is less arrogant, so is King John less sensationally defiant. In *The Troublesome Raigne*, Pandulph is temporarily checked by the proud mien and hot words of King John:

> And what hast thou, or the Pope thy master, to do, to demand of me how I employ mine own? Know, Sir Priest, as I honour the Church and holy churchmen, so I scorn to be subject to the greatest Prelate in the world. Tell thy Master so from me; and say, *John* of *England* said it, that never an Italian Priest of them all, shall either have tithe, toll, or polling penny out of *England*; but, as I am King, so will I reign next under God, Supreme Head both over spiritual and temporal. And he that contradicts me in this, I'll make him hop headless.[151]

Then, to King Philip who feebly interrupts with a charge of blasphemy, John continues in the same trumpeting spirit:

> *Philip*, though thou and all the Princes of Christendom suffer themselves to be abus'd by a Prelate's slavery, my mind is not of such base

temper. If the Pope will be King in *England*, let him win it with a sword. I know no other title he can allege to mine inheritance.[152]

In *King John* the words of the King are proud and resolute, but they burn with less heat. The level of defiance to which John rises seems slightly lower. To the Cardinal's religious demand John replies:

> What earthly name to interrogatories
> Can task the free breath of a sacred king?
> Thou canst not, cardinal, devise a name
> So slight, unworthy and ridiculous,
> To charge me to an answer, as the pope.
> Tell him this tale; and from the mouth of England
> Add thus much more: that no Italian priest
> Shall tithe or toll in our dominions;
> But as we under heaven are supreme head,
> So under him that great supremacy,
> Where we do reign, we will alone uphold,
> Without the assistance of a mortal hand:
> So tell the pope; all reverence set apart
> To him, and his usurp'd authority.[153]

So also in John's reply to King Philip's charge of blasphemy there is a difference, for that reply takes a peculiar turn. Instead of stressing the idea of base slavery to the Pope, it centers its attack on deception and argues from the venality of the clergy:

> Though you and all the kings of Christendom
> Are led so grossly by this meddling priest,
> Dreading the curse that money may buy out;
> And, by the merit of vile gold, dross, dust,
> Purchase corrupted pardon of a man,
> Who in that sale sells pardon from himself;
> Though you and all the rest so grossly led
> This juggling witchcraft with revenue cherish;
> Yet I alone, alone do me oppose
> Against the pope, and count his friends my foes.[154]

A comparison of the two scenes thus far shows that Shakespeare has reduced the anti-Catholic bias, has presented Catholic officialdom in a more dignified light, and has limned John in fainter strokes. The same moderation of anti-Catholic animus and the same diminution of John's heroic size are evident in that part of the scene which follows and in which John is excommunicated.

In *The Troublesome Raigne* the Cardinal's words are more arbitrary and spiteful. To John's indication that he has made his answer, the Legate replies:

> Then I, *Pandulph* of *Padua*, Legate of the Apostolic See, do, in the name of Saint *Peter*, and his successor, our Holy Father, Pope *Innocent*, pronounce thee accursed, discharging every of thy subjects of all duty and fealty that they do owe to thee, and pardon and forgiveness of sin to those or them whatsoever which shall carry arms against thee, or murder thee: this I pronounce, and charge all good men to abhor thee as an excommunicate person.[155]

In *King John*, Pandulph says:

> Then, by the lawful power that I have,
> Thou shalt stand curs'd and excommunicate:
> And blessed shall he be that doth revolt
> From his allegiance to a heretic;
> And meritorious shall that hand be call'd,
> Canonized and worshipp'd as a saint,
> That takes away by any secret course
> Thy hateful life.[156]

It is instructive to note, besides the difference in tone between the speeches of the Legate in the two plays, that there is an interesting difference in the rewards promised to anyone who should assassinate King John. In *The Troublesome Raigne* Pandulph promises "pardon and forgiveness of sins." Such a promise would rankle in the breasts of Elizabethan Protestants, for it was the indulgent power of the Pope to pardon and forgive sins which was disputed so vigorously in the Reformation. In *King John* Pandulph promises merit, canonization, and sainthood. The promise of ascription of merit to the hand that killed the king is a promise more in line with orthodox Catholic moral theology[157] and would be recognized by the Elizabethan playgoer as a proper part of the judicial act of a Catholic official. Moreover, Pandulph's use of the word "murder" in *The Troublesome Raigne* is strongly tainted with partisanship and detracts from the judiciality of the deposition of John by the Legate.

On the other hand, the impression of strict officialism which Shakespeare gives is enhanced by Constance's interruptive remark after the pronouncement of the excommunication and deposition. The frustrated and embittered mother of Arthur picks up Pandulph's word "lawful" and cries:

> O! lawful let it be
> That I have room with Rome to curse awhile.
> Good father cardinal, cry thou amen
> To my keen curses; for without my wrong
> There is no tongue hath power to curse him right.

Whereupon the Cardinal declares:

> There's law and warrant, lady, for my curse.[158]

There is something to be learned, too, from a comparison of John's reaction to the fateful measure of the Church of Rome in the two plays. In *The Troublesome Raigne* King John snaps back at the Cardinal with a challenging witticism: "So, Sir, the more the fox is curst, the better 'a fares: if God bless me and my land, let the Pope and his shavelings curse, and spare not."[159] In *King John* it is Constance who exercises the wit, not John.

Then when the Legate begins to apply the excommunication immediately in the case of Philip's league with John by charging Philip to withdraw his support and make war upon England, John's reaction is revealing. In *The Troublesome Raigne*, Pandulph high-handedly turns to Philip:

> Furthermore, I charge thee, *Philip*, King of *Fraunce*, and all the Kings and Princes of Christendom, to make war upon this miscreant. And whereas thou hast made a league with him, and confirm'd it by oath, I do, in the name of our foresaid Father, the Pope, acquit thee of that oath as unlawful, being made with an heretic. How say'st thou, *Philip*, dost thou obey?

Almost tauntingly John repeats the question of the Legate:

> Brother of *Fraunce*, what say you to the Cardinal?

There follows a colloquy between Philip and John in which John shows up well as standing firmly against the intervention of Rome:

> *Philip.* I say I am sorry for your Majesty, requesting you to submit yourself to the Church of *Rome*.
> *John.* And what say you to our league, if I do not submit?
> *Philip.* What should I say? I must obey the Pope.
> *John.* Obey the Pope, and break your oath to God?
> *Philip.* The Legate hath absolv'd me of mine oath: Then yield to *Rome*, or I defy thee here.
> *John.* Why, *Philip*, I defy the Pope and thee,
> False as thou art, and perjur'd, King of *Fraunce*,
> Unworthy man to be accounted King.

Giv'st thou thy sword into a prelate's hands?
Pandulph, where I, of abbots, monks and friars,
Have taken somewhat to maintain my wars,
Now will I take no more but all they have.
I'll rouse the lazy lubbers from their cells,
And in despite I'll send them to the Pope.
Mother, come you with me, and for the rest
That will not follow *John* in this attempt,
Confusion light upon their damned souls.
Come, Lords,
Fight for your King that fighteth for your good?[160]

With these defiant words John and his retinue stalk off the stage.

How different the impression created by Shakespeare! There Pandulph, after Constance's interruption, turns to the King of France:

Philip of France, on peril of a curse,
Let go the hand of that arch-heretic,
And raise the power of France upon his head,
Unless he do submit himself to Rome.[161]

Thus, to the credit of Rome, it is only France, not "all the Kings and Princes of Christendom," who is called upon to oppose John. Also to the credit of Rome there is no unprovoked offer of release from an oath made to Philip. And to the lesser credit of John, it is not he but the two women, Queen Elinor and Constance, and the two men, Austria and the Bastard, who first speak in reaction to the Cardinal's demand. John seems temporarily stunned by the swift turn of fortune. When he recovers the power of speech, his question seems almost fawningly hopeful:

Philip, what sayst thou to the cardinal?

Constance, Lewis, and Blanche all make remarks and offer advice to Philip before John speaks again. Then in a weak observation, he says:

The king is mov'd, and answers not to this.

In the midst of this confusion of advice, to which the taunting of Austria by the Bastard's insinuations about "hanging a calf-skin" adds not a little, Philip confesses himself perplexed and uncertain what to say. When Pandulph then suggests that his perplexity will be greater if he is excommunicated, Philip asks the Legate how to reconcile the double obligation of obedience to the Pope and of his oath of alliance with John, and there follows the Cardinal's rationalization of vows. John stands silently by.

After Philip has finally come to the decision to break with John, it is again Constance and Elinor who react first. Then John, in disappointment, makes the somewhat pointless threat:

> France, thou shalt rue this hour within this hour.

After a series of philosophical reflections by the Bastard and Blanche, John commands the Bastard to "go draw our puissance together," and sputters:

> France, I am burn'd up with inflaming wrath;
> A rage whose heat hath this condition,
> That nothing can allay, nothing but blood,
> The blood, and dearest-valu'd blood of France.

Philip neatly turns the thrust with a metaphor:

> Thy rage shall burn thee up, and thou shalt turn
> To ashes, ere our blood shall quench that fire:
> Look to thyself, thou art in jeopardy.

John grumbles:

> No more than he that threats. . . .

and, calling his men to arms, leaves the stage.[162]

While there were those who responded to John's call to arms, they could not have responded primarily because they were so much impressed with the heroic conduct of their sovereign in the scenes just discussed.

(d) As a matter of fact the followers of John in Shakespeare's play not only had a less noble king to follow, but they had one less reason for following him than in *The Troublesome Raigne*. In Shakespeare, the issues at stake in the plot of the play are reduced from two to one. In both plays the conflict between Rome and England springs from the rejection of Langton, but in *The Troublesome Raigne* the issue thus raised is two-fold: it involves both spiritual and temporal supremacy. In *King John*, however, the issue of spiritual supremacy is obscured, if not eliminated, and the English sovereign stands out as the defender of his temporal sovereignty alone.[163] In his speech to Pandulph King John omits the explicit qualification "both over spiritual and temporal." He makes it an "earthly name" whose right to interrogate a sacred king he calls into question. And he declares that he is ready to uphold alone "that great supremacy where we do reign."

This simplification of the conflict makes John a political figure first of all. Instead of being the champion of both true religion and true patriotism, he becomes the champion of patriotism alone. The zeal of his followers must then be principally the zeal of patriots, not the zeal of defenders of the faith.

(e) As the play goes on, whatever splendor John may have gained in defying Pandulph and Philip is progressively dimmed to the point of extinction. The process starts immediately after the breach of treaty between France and England. John is shown to be somewhat less valorous than in the source play. While in *The Troublesome Raigne*[164] it is John who rescues his mother after she has been captured by the French in the Battle of Angiers, in *King John*[165] it is the Bastard who performs that creditable feat of arms. And throughout Shakespeare's play, John seems weaker. He is more completely at a loss after the death of his mother and after the other reversals of fortune which come thick and fast. It is in this connection that the Bastard serves so strikingly as a foil to John, for the Bastard is a man of steadfastness and decision, able to weather the shifting storms of battle and adversity, and never without his one clear aim— the preservation of England. The contrast between the courage of the two men is never stronger than when the threat of French invasion is greatest. In *The Troublesome Raigne*,[166] though John has need of the comfort which Pandulph and the Bastard give him, nevertheless he does respond to the situation and, crying out:

> But let us hence, to answer *Lewes* pride,

marches off to battle. In *King John*,[167] however, the King fails to rouse to the martial words of the Bastard and weakly throws the responsibility of resisting the invasion upon the Bastard, saying:

> Have thou the ordering of this present time.

It seems almost like abdication.

(f) A sixth factor in the ignoble characterization of John is Shakespeare's presentation of him as a cold-blooded murderer. The difference in the depiction of John's treatment of Arthur in the two plays is noteworthy. In *The Troublesome Raigne*, King John does hold out an offer of reconciliation to Arthur—an act which makes his later treatment of Arthur dastardly enough—but that offer is not as excessive as in Shakespeare's play. In the source play, the King says:

> But if at last, nephew, thou yield thyself
> Into the guardance of thine uncle *John*,
> Thou shalt be used as becomes a Prince.[168]

In Shakespeare the King says:

> Cousin, look not sad:
> Thy grandam loves thee; and thy uncle will
> As dear be to thee as thy father was.[169]

This cousinly promise is followed, within a few lines, in Shakespeare by King John's obvious enticement of Hubert to kill Arthur. Three times the King suggests to Hubert that he has "a thing to say," and he surrounds that thing with a most elaborate aura of secrecy. He leads Hubert into a protestation of love and an avowal of obedience unto death. Then with a brutal cold-bloodedness the King says:

> Good Hubert! Hubert, Hubert, throw thine eye
> On yon young boy: I'll tell thee what, my friend,
> He is a very serpent in my way;
> And wheresoe'er this foot of mine doth tread
> He lies before me: dost thou understand me?
> Thou art his keeper.
> >   *Hubert.*   And I'll keep him so
> That he shall not offend your majesty.
> *K. John.*   Death.
> *Hub.*   My lord?
> *K. John.*   A grave.
> *Hub.*   He shall not live.
> *K. John.*   Enough.
> I could be merry now, Hubert, I love thee. . . .[170]

No such murderous scene occurs in *The Troublesome Raigne*. There, to Elianor's observation that Arthur would soon be taught to forget his presumptions to the throne, John replies:

> Mother, he never will forget his claim;
> I would he liv'd not to remember it,[171]

and then, as part of a series of arrangements for departure for England, he turns to Hubert and charges him to

>   . . . take Arthur here to thee;
> Be he thy prisoner, *Hubert*, keep him safe,
> For on his life doth hang thy Sovereign's crown;
> But in his death consists thy Sovereign's bliss;
> Then *Hubert*, as thou shortly hear'st from me,
> So use the prisoner I have given in charge.[172]

There can be little doubt that in the source play, King John wished Arthur dead, but it does not appear that he planned the death of Arthur through the duping of Hubert. The directions which Hubert later receives with respect to the treatment of Arthur call for the blinding of the Prince, not his murder. Hubert reads the directions aloud in the presence of Arthur; there can be no misunderstanding of their contents.[173] When, shortly afterwards, the King is upset by the prophecy of the Five Moons, he does exclaim:

> The brat shall die that terrifies me thus,[174]

but the exclamation is a spontaneous threat arising from a suddenly intensified fear, not the evidence of a calculated design to commit murder. In Shakespeare, John's murderous calculations are fully exposed. Though it is true that in Act IV, Scene i, Hubert gives directions to "heat me those irons hot," and though Arthur, after reading to himself the paper which Hubert carries, cries out:

> Must you with hot irons burn out both mine eyes?[175]

that such a blinding was intended to be but a preliminary to murder is shown in the colloquy between the King and Hubert after the latter has spared the Prince but while the former thinks Arthur dead. Because Hubert himself has given the King to believe that Arthur is dead, in reporting the popular unrest to John, Hubert pretends that young Arthur's death is common in the mouths of old men and beldams prophesying in the streets. With great irritation, John asks:

> Why urgest thou so oft young Arthur's death?
> Thy hand hath murdered him: I had a mighty cause
> To wish him dead, but thou hadst none to kill him.
>   *Hub.* No had, my lord! why, did you not provoke me?
>   *K. John.* It is the curse of kings to be attended
> By slaves that take their humours for a warrant
> To break within the bloody house of life,
> And on the winking of authority
> To understand a law, to know the meaning
> Of dangerous majesty, when, perchance, it frowns
> More upon humour than advis'd respect.
>   *Hub.* Here is your hand and seal for what I did.
>   *K. John.* O! when the last account 'twixt heaven and earth
> Is to be made, then shall this hand and seal
> Witness against us to damnation.
> How oft the sight of means to do ill deeds
> Makes ill deeds done! Hadst not thou been by,
> A fellow by the hand of nature mark'd,
> Quoted and sign'd to do a deed of shame,
> This murder had not come into my mind. . . .[176]

There seems no room for doubt that at some previous time John had given his "hand and seal" for the murder of Arthur. His cowardly effort, in the lines just quoted and in those which follow, to make Hubert wholly responsible for a crime which seemed to have miscarried detracts even more from the diminishing prestige of the King.

(g) A seventh factor in Shakespeare's greater degradation of John is the treatment of the episode in which John surrenders his crown to Pandulph and receives it back in fief from the Pope. In *The Troublesome Raigne* there is a scene (not in Shakespeare) in which John decides that dissembling is the only way out of his difficulties and in which, after uttering his first prophecy of a more worthy successor, he summons Pandulph and proceeds to dissemble before the audience itself. Pandulph suspects the dissembling, for he declines John's first offer of submission. Undismayed, John, in an aside, renews his resolution to play the hypocrite. He repeats his plea for absolution and creates in the Cardinal the impression of sincerity. The Cardinal then lays down the condition of reconciliation:

> One way is left to reconcile thyself,
> And only one, which I shall show to thee:
> Thou must surrender to the see of *Rome*
> Thy crown and diadem. . . .[177]

This demand is more than John had foreseen. Ruefully he soliloquizes:

> From bad to worse, or I must lose my realm,
> Or give my crown for penance unto *Rome*,
> A misery more piercing than the darts
> That break from burning exhalations' power.[178]

He has already come to the decision to defend his crown against all odds, when a messenger enters to announce the sighting of the French fleet off Kent. John's determination fails him. In desperation and dire need he turns to the Cardinal for advice. Pandulph suggests being reconciled to the Church, and John accepts the advice.

This scene prepares the way adequately for the one that comes later in which Pandulph absolves John from all his sins and frees him from the excommunication. Says the Legate:

> Receive thy crown again, with this proviso,
> That thou remain true liegeman to the Pope,
> And carry arms in right of holy *Rome*.
>   *John.* I hold the same as tenant to the Pope,
> And thank your Holiness for your kindness shown.[179] ·

Thus in the source play John's surrender of his crown is made to seem as if it were forced upon John by the unhappy coincidence of the failure of his scheme to dissemble and the sudden arrival of the French.

In Shakespeare's play, however, John seems to go out of his way to surrender the crown. The transaction seems much more a matter of barter. No antecedent scene makes clear the motivation. The King and Pandulph enter, the latter carrying the crown, and John says:

> Thus have I yielded up into your hand
> The circle of my glory.
>   *Pand.* [*Giving* John *the crown.*] Take again
> From this my hand, as holding of the pope,
> Your sovereign greatness and authority.
>   *K. John.* Now keep your holy word: go meet the French,
> And from his holiness use all your power
> To stop their marches 'fore we are inflam'd.[180]

In the remainder of John's speech, in which he details the troubles of his realm, there is motivation for the surrender of his sovereignty, but there is no hint of demand by the Pope; and for the audience the speech is a lump of sugar scarcely sweet enough to destroy the bitter taste of national humiliation, especially when that bitter taste is revived by the words of John a few lines later. Pandulph happens to mention "Ascension-day." John is startled into recalling the prophecy of Peter of Pomfret that

> . . . before Ascension-day at noon
> My crown I should give off? Even so I have.

He then consoles himself in a most unusual way—a way that must have reddened the faces and swollen the veins of the Elizabethan audience:

> I did suppose it should be on constraint;
> But, heaven be thank'd, it is but voluntary.[181]

(h) An eighth and final factor in the villainous delineation of John by Shakespeare is the treatment of the scene in which the King dies. John's prestige expires completely with his life. In *The Troublesome Raigne*, at his death John is still the active defender of England. Though he has become thoroughly disheartened, he has not been stripped of the last vestiges of heroism. In fact, he dies a martyr to the true faith—poisoned by a monk of Swinstead Abbey. The death of John is elaborately presented in the source play. There is a scene in which the murderous plan to destroy John is shown hatching in the mind of a fanatic monk and in

which the motivation of the scheme is expressly revealed by the words of
the self-appointed tyrannicide:

> Now, if that thou wilt look to merit heaven,
> And be canoniz'd for a holy saint,
> To please the world with a deserving work,
> Be thou the man to set thy country free,
> And murder him that seeks to murder thee.[182]

Official approval is given the plan by the Abbot himself, who absolves the
monk of all his sins, calls the intended deed "meritorious," and sends the
assassin off to actuate his scheme with a promise that the friars of the
abbey will sing a mass every month for his soul.[183]

And there is a scene in which the actual poisoning is portrayed. The
King is the guest of the Abbot. He is in good health and hungry. The
scheming monk is taster to the King. With merry heart he pledges "Was-
sail" to his liege. The King drinks after him. Almost instantly the monk
falls dead. John is doomed. But he lingers long enough to utter some
bitter words against Rome and to prophesy the coming of Henry VIII,
for whom has been reserved the victory over

> the strumpet's pride
> That sits upon the chair of *Babylon*.[184]

In viewing these scenes, the audience must have felt a resurgence of
sympathy for the stricken king and a willingness to forgive his shortcomings in the light of his larger mission. It must have felt, likewise, a
fierce resentment toward Catholicism for the extremity of the means
which it employed to gain its ends. The desire of the audience for speedy
and violent revenge was partly gratified on the instant by the slaying of
the Abbot by the sword of the impetuous Bastard.

All this is presented or implied on a much more ignominious level in
Shakespeare. There, John is no martyr to the true faith, but a whining
old man who complains most about the fact that nobody helps him.
He dies,

> but a clod
> And module of confounded royalty,[185]

without a word of vision or of hope, at the shock of the bad news that the
Dauphin's army is at hand and that the Bastard's troops have been
drowned in the Wash.

The poisoning, if there is a poisoning, is not shown on the stage.
The audience learns of John's dying condition through Hubert, who tells
the Bastard:

> The king, I fear, is poison'd by a monk:
> I left him almost speechless; and broke out
> To acquaint you with this evil. . . .
>   *Bast.* How did he take it? who did taste to him?
>   *Hub.* A monk, I tell you; a resolved villain,
> Whose bowels suddenly burst out: the king
> Yet speaks, and peradventure may recover.[186]

Hubert's report has about it an air of uncertainty. It is qualified by the words "I fear." A monk has died, but the symptoms attendant upon his death prove to be different from those attendant upon John's, which follows. As a matter of fact John's symptoms are not new. When he is brought upon the stage in the actual death scene, he complains of the "hot summer in his bosom," but he had been afflicted with raging fever before he got to Swinstead. On the plain of St. Edmundsbury, during the battle against the French forces, John complains to Hubert:

> This fever, that hath troubled me so long,
> Lies heavy on me: O! my heart is sick.[187]

And ten lines thereafter, having received news of the wreck of the French supply fleet on Goodwin sands, the King laments:

> Ay me! this tyrant fever burns me up,
> And will not let me welcome this good news.
> Set on toward Swinstead: to my litter straight;
> Weakness possesseth me, and I am faint.[188]

Thus it seems as if John's last fever is but an aggravation of a chronic condition. True, Pembroke mentions poison once,[189] and John twice,[190] but neither mentions the monk, and the context makes it possible to understand the word to mean a mortal infection, not a lethal potion administered by a poisoner. In any event, if there is a poisoning in Shakespeare, the poet makes little of the motivation and provides no immediate vengeance, though the Bastard does remark:

> I do but stay behind
> To do the office for thee of revenge,
> And then my soul shall wait on thee to heaven,
> As it on earth hath been thy servant still.[191]

Not only is this depiction of the death of John by Shakespeare less favorable to the King; it is also more favorable to Rome. In *The Troublesome Raigne* the connection between Pandulph's curse and John's assassination is clear and is so emphasized that the Roman Catholic doctrine of justifiable tyrannicide is shown in a detestable light. In *King John* that connection is less clear. The doctrine of tyrannicide is not emphasized to the detriment of the Roman Church. If it was a monk who was responsible for John's death, that monk appears to be much less designedly the instrument of Rome. Shakespeare seems to take pains to prevent the impression that the Church of Rome is the murderer of John.

The alteration of the character of John and of the motivation of the play is an important phase of the change wrought by Shakespeare in the revision of his source, but it is not the only phase. Shakespeare did other things to make *King John* a play much more favorable to Catholicism.

(2) There is, for example, Shakespeare's treatment of the looting of the monasteries. In *The Troublesome Raigne* the business of looting the monasteries plays an important and frequently recurring part. Moreover, the looting is presented with great relish. The program is inaugurated by John's parting speech at the end of the first scene in the first act. War with France is inevitable.

> And toward the main charges of my wars
> I'll seize the lazy abbey-lubbers' lands
> Into my hands, to pay my men of war.
> The Pope and Popelings shall not grease themselves
> With gold and groats that are the soldiers' due.[192]

In Shakespeare the determination of John to loot the abbeys seems more incidental and less pleasurable. After being informed by the Sheriff about the case of the appealing Faulconbridges, John says:

> Let them approach. [*Exit* Sheriff.
> Our abbeys and our priories shall pay
> This expedition's charge.[193]

In the source play John's intention to loot the monasteries to pay for a foreign war is given a deeper and more vindictive motivation after he has been excommunicated. In his final fling of defiance, the King shouts:

> *Pandulph*, where I, of abbots, monks and friars,
> Have taken somewhat to maintain my wars,
> Now will I take no more but all they have.
> I'll rouse the lazy lubbers from their cells,
> And in despite I'll send them to the Pope.[194]

There is nothing of this in Shakespeare.

In the source play, the looting business is taken up again by John as he leaves for England after having been excommunicated and deposed by Pandulph. There is a note of grim satisfaction in his words:

> But leaving this, we will to *England* now,
> And take some order with our popelings there,
> That swell with pride, and fat of laymen's lands.

He then commissions the Bastard to do the job and lays down the *modus operandi*:

> Philip, I make thee chief in this affair.
> Ransack the abbeys, cloisters, priories;
> Convert their coin unto my soldiers' use:

And then to make the pogrom more inclusive, he adds:

> And whatsoe'er he be within my land,
> That goes to *Rome* for justice and for law,
> While he may have his right within the realm,
> Let him be judg'd a traitor to the state,
> And suffer as an enemy to *England*.[195]

The Bastard's acceptance of the commission seems gleefully anticipatory.

> Now wars are done, I long to be at home,
> To dive into the monks' and abbots' bags,
> To make some sport among the smooth-skin nuns,
> And keep some revel with the fausen friars.[196]

Shakespeare retains the kernel of the foregoing passages, but removes all sense of vindictiveness or relish. John commissions the Bastard with the words:

> Cousin, away for England! haste before;
> And, ere our coming, see thou shake the bags
> Of hoarding abbots; set at liberty
> Imprison'd angels: the fat ribs of peace
> Must by the hungry now be fed upon:
> Use our commission in his utmost force.

To which the Bastard replies:

> Bell, book, and candle shall not drive me back
> Where gold and silver becks me to come on.[197]

In the source play, the audience is treated to the spectacle of abbey looting. The scene[198] is so fanatically anti-Catholic that it warrants a brief résumé here.

Philip the Bastard enters, leading a Friar (Thomas) and charging him to show where the Abbot's gold lies. The Friar utters a prayer in doggerel verse, partly Latin and partly English. Even the form of the prayer is irreverent, for it consists of ten lines all ending on the same rhyme:

> *Benedicamus Domini!*
> Was ever such an injury!
> Sweet Saint *Withold*, of thy lenity,
> Defend us from extremity,
> And hear us for Saint *Charity*,
> Oppressed with austerity.
> *In nomine Domini*,
> Make I my homily;
> Gentle gentility,
> Grieve not the clergy. (3–12)

Not to be outdone in verse-making, Philip replies in couplets, threatening to hang the Friar with his own waist-girdle. Again the Friar prays in doggerel:

> Ah, pardon! *O parce!*
> Saint *Fraunces*, for mercy,
> Shall shield thee from night-spells
> And dreaming of devils,
> If thou wilt forgive me,
> And nevermore grieve me:
> With fasting and praying,
> And 'Hail-Mary' saying,
> From black purgatory,
> A penance right sorry,
> Friar *Thomas* will warn you;
> It never shall harm you. (17–28)

The exasperated Philip orders the "losel" hanged, but another Friar (Anthony) pleads for his life and promises to bring Philip "unto the Prior's chest." Philip relents and is led to the chest. Friar Anthony assures Philip that the chest "wanteth not a thousand pound in silver and in gold." Philip accepts the word of the Friar, promising him the "overplus" but threatening to demand his neck if the chest contains less. The chest is broken open. In it is a nun! Friar Anthony exclaims:

> Oh, I am undone!
> Fair *Alice* the nun
> Hath took up her rest
> In the Abbot's chest.
> *Sancte benedicite!*

> Pardon my simplicity.
> Fie, *Alice*! Confession
> Will not salve this transgression.   (44–51)

Philip bursts into a scathing speech against monasticism:

> Is this the nunnery's chastity? Beshrew me, but I think
> They go as oft to venery, as niggards, to their drink.
> Why, paltry friar, and pandar too, ye shameless shaven-crown,
> Is this the chest that held a hoard, at least a thousand pound?
> And is the hoard a holy whore? Well, be the hangman nimble,
> He'll take the pain to pay you home, and teach you to dissemble.
>
> (54–59)

Hereupon the nun pleads for Friar Anthony and promises to buy off Philip with the seven-year savings of another nun.

> . . . and what is ours, so favour now be shown,
> You shall command as commonly as if it were your own.
> *Friar.* Your honour excepted.
> *Nun.* Ay, *Thomas*, I mean so.
> *Philip.* From all, save from friars.
> *Nun.* Good sir, do not think so.
> *Philip.* I think, and see so: why, how cam'st thou here?
> *Friar.* To hide her from laymen.
> *Nun.* 'Tis true, sir, for fear.
> *Philip.* For fear of the laity: a pitiful dread,
> When a nun flies for succour to a fat friar's bed!   (64–74)

The nun's chest is opened to reveal a Friar (Laurence) hiding in it. After Friar Anthony has expressed his consternation, Friar Laurence explains:

> *Amor vincit omnia*, so *Cato* affirmeth;
> And therefore a friar, whose fancy soon burneth,
> Because he is mortal and made of mould,
> He omits what he ought, and doth more than he should.   (91–94)

Philip is filled with disgust and soliloquizes:

> Is this the labour of their lives, to feed and live at ease?
> To revel so lasciviously as often as they please.
> I'll mend the fault, or fault my aim, if I do miss amending;
> 'Tis better burn the cloisters down, than leave them for offending.
>
> (99–102)

In spite of their prayers for mercy, Philip orders the nun and the Friar Laurence hanged, but Friar Laurence makes a plea and offers a ransom:

> *O tempus edax rerum*!
> Give children books, they tear them.
> *O vanitas vanitatis*,
> In this waning *aetatis*,
> At threescore well near,
> To go to this gear,
> To my conscience a clog,
> To die like a dog.
> *Exaudi me, Domine*,
> *Si vis me parcere*
> *Si habeo veniam*.
> To go and fetch it,
> I will despatch it,
> A hundred pound sterling
> For my life's sparing.   (109–123)

Philip accepts the ransom and grants pardon to Friar Laurence and the rest.

Shakespeare eliminates the whole scene. In its place he gives three lines to Pandulph, spoken to Lewis and persuading him to invade England:

> The bastard Faulconbridge
> Is now in England ransacking the church,
> Offending charity. . . .[199]

The omission of the looting scene is a conspicuous omission—"perhaps the most important 'cut' in the play," says Edward Rose.[200] Various reasons for the omission are ascribed by the critics. Rose suggests that "it was probably more [Shakespeare's] hatred of vulgarity and buffoonery than of Protestantism that made him strike out the scene. . . ."[201] Gervinus makes the interesting comment that, though "the old piece offered [Shakespeare] here a scene . . . certainly very amusing to the fresh Protestant feelings of the time," nevertheless

> . . . to our poet's impartial mind the dignity of the clergy, nay even the contemplativeness of cloister-life, was a matter too sacred for him to introduce it in a ridiculous form into the seriousness of history.[202]

Whatever may have been the reason for Shakespeare's cutting the scene, it must be acknowledged that the elimination makes *King John* a play more favorable in its representation of Catholicism than the source play.

The looting is not allowed to slip from the memory of the audience in the case of *The Troublesome Raigne*, either, for when, a scene or two later, the Bastard enters, John's first words are:

> *Philip* what news, how do the Abbots' chests?
> Are friars fatter than the nuns are fair?
> What cheer with churchmen? had they gold, or no?
> Tell me, how hath thy office took effect?
>   *Philip.* My lord, I have perform'd your Highness' charge;
> The ease-bred Abbots and the bare-foot friars,
> The monks, the priors, and holy cloister'd nuns,
> Are all in health, and were, my lord, in wealth,
> Till I had tithed and toll'd their holy hoards.
> I doubt not, when your Highness sees my prize,
> You may proportion all their former pride.
>   *John.* Why so; now sorts it, *Philip*, as it should;
> This small intrusion into Abbey trunks
> Will make the Popelings excommunicate,
> Curse, ban, and breathe out damned orisons
> As thick as hailstones 'fore the spring's approach,
> But yet as harmless and without effect,
> As is the echo of a cannon's crack
> Discharg'd against the battlements of heaven.[203]

The vengeful motive for the sacking is emphasized by the Bastard's play upon tithing and tolling, the very words of John in his speech of defiance to Pandulph, and by the King's use of the words "excommunicate," "curse," and "ban."

In *King John*, the Bastard makes a report, but it is toned down and closely related to the public reaction. In fact, the looting of the monasteries is shown to be a matter of dangerous policy, inciting the people to rebel. John has been jolted by the decision of the nobles to oppose him; he has learned of the landing of the French on English shores; he has heard of his mother's death and of the loss of his possessions in France to the Dauphin. Just then the Bastard enters with Peter of Pomfret. The King quickly asks:

> Now, what says the world
> To your proceedings? do not seek to stuff
> My head with more ill news, for it is full.[204]

There is no gloating satisfaction in the Bastard's reply. The monastery affair is secondary.

How I have sped among the clergymen,
The sums I have collected shall express.
But as I travell'd hither through the land,
I find the people strangely fantasied,
Possess'd with rumours, full of idle dreams,
Not knowing what they fear, but full of fear.[205]

And that is the end of the looting matter in Shakespeare.

Not so in the source play. When King John arrives at Swinstead Abbey and is assured by the Abbot that the food supply is abundant, he takes occasion to express his abhorrence of the cupidity of the monasteries:

Philip, thou never need'st to doubt of cates;
Nor King nor lord is seated half so well
As are the Abbeys throughout all the land.
If any plot of ground do pass another,
The friars fasten on it straight:
But let us in, to taste of their repast,
It goes against my heart to feed with them,
Or be beholden to such Abbey grooms.[206]

And when the King is seated at the table in the poisoning scene, he observes the frown of the Abbot and suggests that the Abbot looks "like an host that knows his guest hath no money to pay the reckoning." The Abbot says his frown is one of concern lest "the cheer [be] too homely to entertain so mighty a guest. . . ." Whereupon the Bastard remarks:

I think rather, my Lord Abbot, you remember my last being here, when I went in progress for pouches: and the rancor of his heart breaks out in his countenance, to show he hath not forgot me.[207]

From what follows, it appears that the Bastard held the truest opinion of the matter.

(3) There is much to be said for the view that in *King John* the Bastard holds the truest opinions on most matters and that, throughout the play, more than any other character, the Bastard represents Shakespeare. The delineation of Faulconbridge may be considered a third major phase of Shakespeare's alteration of his source.

In *The Troublesome Raigne*, the Bastard contributes much to the impression of anti-Catholicism. Besides the sentiments already pointed out in connection with the abbey looting, the Bastard gives utterance to others which show him to be a Protestant bigot. For example, in the conference of noblemen at St. Edmundsbury one of the arguments which

Faulconbridge advances to induce the rebels to be true to the King is the falsity of papal claims:

> And doth a Pope, a priest, a man of pride,
> Give charters for the lives of lawful kings?
> What can he bless, or who regards his curse,
> But such as give to man, and takes from God.
> I speak it in the sight of God above:
> There's not a man that dies in your belief,
> But sells his soul perpetually to pain.[208]

What the Bastard thinks of John's submission to Pandulph is expressed in two lines:

> A proper jest, when kings must stoop to friars,
> Need hath no law, when friars must be kings.[209]

When the King dies at the hands of a poisoner, the Bastard's bitter comment is:

> This is the fruit of Popery, when true kings
> Are slain and shoulder'd out by monks and friars.[210]

And the very last lines of the source play reiterate his strong feeling against Rome as the Bastard points the moral:

> If *England's* peers and people join in one,
> Not Pope, nor *Fraunce*, nor *Spain* can do them wrong.

All this, added to the prominence given Faulconbridge as the active looter of monasteries, makes the Bastard a Protestant zealot in *The Troublesome Raigne.*

But in Shakespeare's play, expanded though the character of Faulconbridge be, the Bastard is single-heartedly a patriot. His bitterness is directed against "fickle France" rather than against Rome.[211] In the excommunication scene he has not a word to say against Pandulph or Rome. He amuses himself by teasing Austria, his personal enemy. Later, when John announces his submission to the Pope, the Bastard's reactions are political:

> O inglorious league!
> Shall we, upon the footing of our land,
> Send fair-play orders and make compromise,
> Insinuation, parley and base truce
> To arms invasive? shall a beardless boy,
> A cocker'd silken wanton, brave our fields,
> And flesh his spirit in a war-like soil,

Mocking the air with colours idly spread,
And find no check? Let us, my liege, to arms:
Perchance the cardinal cannot make your peace;
Or if he do, let it at least be said
They saw we had a purpose of defence.[212]

When Faulconbridge goes to the French camp as an emissary of John, his address toward Pandulph is respectful:

My holy Lord of Milan, from the king
I come, to learn how you have dealt for him;
And, as you answer, I do know the scope
And warrant limited unto my tongue.

And when Pandulph admits that he is having difficulty in making the "too wilful-opposite" Dauphin abandon the invasion of England, the Bastard makes a fiery speech in disdain of the "pigmy" French arms.[213] He has nothing to say about Rome. At the conclusion of the speech, the Dauphin taunts the Bastard by granting "thou canst outscold us" and by calling him a "brabbler." Pandulph, seeing his promised program of pacification running into deep water, asks leave to speak. The Bastard is abrupt in crying out: "No, I will speak,"[214] but it is not disrespect to the Cardinal so much as martial heat that impels him to interrupt. Though the Dauphin declines to hear either of them, the Bastard resumes his military challenge. In the course of it he seems to cast aspersion upon Pandulph. In reply to Lewis' order to beat the drums, the Bastard says:

. . . another shall
As loud as thine rattle the welkin's ear
And mock the deep-mouth'd thunder: for at hand,—
Not trusting to this halting legate here,
Whom he hath us'd rather for sport than need,—
Is warlike John. . . .[215]

But it is not disrespect for the Cardinal so much as impatience with diplomatic methods that moves the Bastard. The Legate is halting in that he resorts to negotiation; Faulconbridge is for direct military action. To keep his challenge strong, the Bastard declares that King John has agreed to the diplomatic mission of the Cardinal, but that he is not dependent upon its success. It does not appear, then, that the Bastard resents papal interference.

His silence with regard to papal interference and the Roman curse continues to the end. As in the source play so in Shakespeare, the Bastard has the last lines, but in them he does not mention the Pope. He breaks forth into the eloquent speech on the self-sufficiency of a unified England:

> O! let us pay the time but needful woe
> Since it hath been beforehand with our griefs.
> This England never did, nor never shall,
> Lie at the proud foot of a conqueror,
> But when it first did help to wound itself.
> Now these her princes are come home again,
> Come the three corners of the world in arms,
> And we shall shock them. Nought shall make us rue,
> If England to itself do rest but true.[216]

(4) The respectful attitude which the Bastard assumes toward Pandulph is part of Shakespeare's careful delineation of that character as the official representative of the Church of Rome—a delineation which is the fourth major phase in Shakespeare's revision of *The Troublesome Raigne*.

At no point in *King John* is this carefulness more evident than in the scene in which Pandulph explains how Philip can be released from the obligation of his oath to John. Philip is in earnest in his protestation of inability to solve the problem of conflicting vows. He is afraid to "make a riot on the gentle brow of true sincerity" and appeals to Pandulph:

> O! holy sir,
> My reverend father, let it not be so!
> Out of your grace, devise, ordain, impose
> Some gentle order, and then we shall be bless'd
> To do your pleasure and continue friends.[217]

The speech on the nature of oaths which Pandulph thereafter makes is not discreditable casuistry, but sound Catholic doctrine. It points the ethical way out for Philip. Greenewald's statement of the case is convincing:

> The Church's doctrine on oaths is nothing else than a logical deduction from the concept of an oath, and a practical application to varying conditions. Nevertheless, it may rightly be called Catholic doctrine, since the Church has been so specific and consistent in the teaching of this doctrine.
>
> The point of interest here is the promissory oath. A promise is a contract by which some one gratuitously obliges himself to give, do or omit something. The obligation arising from a promise is one of fidelity or of justice. When the promise is made under oath, the obligation of religion is added to that of fidelity or of justice.

If a promise, which directly involves the injury of others, or prejudices the commonweal or one's eternal salvation, is confirmed by an oath, the promise does not therefore acquire any justification. From this it is clear that an oath does not change the essence of a promise, but it is rather superadded to it. Consequently, the promissory oath follows the nature of the promise. If then the obligation of the promise should cease, the promissory oath would be meaningless and, therefore, not binding. In consequence, the same conditions under which a promise ceases to bind applies [*sic*] also to the promissory oath.

The obligation imposed by a promissory oath ceases: 1. if it is remitted by him in whose favor the oath is made; 2. if the object promised under the oath has substantially changed, be it that changed circumstances have made it either sinful or entirely indifferent, or be it that it impedes a higher good; 3. if the purpose or condition for which the oath was taken fails; 4. if competent authority annuls, dispenses or commutes the object. The competent authority here referred to is ultimately the Apostolic See. It will become quite evident that it is the second point that Shakespeare uses to show that Philip's oath to King John has ceased.[218]

That Shakespeare should have stated the doctrine of Catholicism so acutely and that he should have taken the trouble to show how Pandulph's advice to repudiate an oath was ethical is illuminating. The scene is in sharp contrast to that in *The Troublesome Raigne*, in which no effort is made to rationalize the repudiation, but in which the Cardinal bluntly declares to Philip that in the name of the Pope he acquits the King of the oath "as unlawful, being made with an heretic."[219]

A second instance of elaboration by Shakespeare resulting in a more favorable representation of Pandulph is the scene in which the Cardinal induces the Dauphin to invade England. In *The Troublesome Raigne* the scene is brief, and the impression given is one of base opportunism. Says the Cardinal to Lewes:

> Now, *Lewes*, thy fortune buds with happy spring;
> Our Holy Father's prayers effecteth this.
> *Arthur* is safe; let *John* alone with him;
> Thy title next is fair'st to *England's* crown.
> Now stir thy father to begin with *John*;
> The Pope says Ay; and so is *Albion* thine.[220]

In *King John* the dialogue is prolonged, and the impression given is one of astute ecclesiastical statesmanship on the part of Pandulph. The Dauphin is discouraged; he feels that with the capture of Arthur all is lost. The wiser Pandulph sees in the apparent threat of fortune the promise of much good. He points out to Lewes that the path to England's throne is open to his foot. Arthur, in the hands of John, is a constant threat to John's sovereignty. It is inevitable that John will do away with him; nothing can save him. With Arthur gone, Lewis, as the husband of Lady Blanche, is next in line for the throne. His chances for overthrowing John, still excommunicate and anathematized, will be measurably improved by the disaffection of the English people themselves, who will recoil at the murder of Arthur. The ransacking of the church by Faulconbridge will add to the antipathy of the people.

> 'Tis wonderful
> What may be wrought out of their discontent
> Now that their souls are topful of offence.[221]

Lewis is convinced and cries out:

> Strong reasons make strong actions.
> Let us go. . . .[222]

The policy of Pandulph is shown, therefore, to be reasonable, astute, and feasible.

That policy is just as reasonable when circumstances call for a sudden shift—the withdrawal of papal support of the Dauphin. Pandulph appears at the French camp at St. Edmundsbury and greets the Dauphin:

> Hail, noble prince of France!
> The next is this: King John hath reconcil'd
> Himself to Rome; his spirit is come in
> That so stood out against the holy church,
> The great metropolis and see of Rome.
> Therefore thy threat'ning colours now wind up,
> And tame the savage spirit of wild war,
> That, like a lion foster'd up at hand,
> It may lie gently at the foot of peace,
> And be no further harmful than in show.[223]

The reason for the shift in policy clearly is the annulment of the excommunication and deposition. As far as Rome is concerned, John is once more the rightful King of England. The appeal is for the peace of Christendom. When, quite naturally, Lewis remonstrates in proud, rebellious tones, the Cardinal is patient and remarks:

> You look but on the outside of this work.[224]

Lewis cannot understand how, under Catholicism, even kings, whether of England or of France, must bend their will to the will of Rome in order that the larger ends of the Church may be served. Whether later he learns that lesson from the misfortunes of battle or from the Prelate of Rome is hard to say, but apparently he does learn it, for at the end of the play, when the Bastard tries to rally the English forces because

> The Dauphin rages at our very heels,

Salisbury says:

> It seems you know not then so much as we.
> The Cardinal Pandulph is within at rest,
> Who half an hour since came from the Dauphin,
> And brings from him such offers of our peace
> As we with honour and respect may take,
> With purpose presently to leave this war.[225]

It seems, then, as if the Cardinal's policy is vindicated.

In *The Troublesome Raigne* the Cardinal seems more capricious in his shift of policy. The tone of the scene is set by the mild rebuke which the Dauphin administers to the Legate upon discovering him in the presence of King John:

> But ill becomes your Grace, Lord Cardinal,
> Thus to converse with *John* that is accurst.[226]

(As if by intentional contrast, Shakespeare has the Dauphin announce the coming of the Cardinal in terms of reverence:

> Look, where the holy legate comes apace,
> To give us warrant from the hand of heaven,
> And on our actions set the name of right
> With holy breath.[227])

Ignoring the Dauphin's rebuke, Pandulph hails the Prince as a victorious conqueror and says:

> Thy forwardness to fight for holy *Rome*
> Shall be remunerated to the full:
> But know, my lord, King *John* is now absolv'd
> The Pope is pleas'd, the land is blest again;
> And thou hast brought each thing to good effect.
> It resteth then that thou withdraw thy powers,
> And quietly return to *Fraunce* again:
> For all is done, the Pope would wish thee do.[228]

In these words the pleasure and wish of the Pope are emphasized, not the nobler end of an harmonious Christendom.

Though the Dauphin remonstrates much more weakly here than in *King John*, Pandulph impatiently threatens him with a curse. It remains for the Bastard, in response to the charge of "insult" against the kings of Christendom, laid not by the Dauphin but by Meloun, to rationalize the Cardinal's shift in policy:

> My lord of *Meloun*, What title had the Prince
> To England and the crown of *Albion*,
> But such a title as the Pope confirm'd?
> The Prelate now lets fall his feigned claim;
> *Lewes* is but the agent for the Pope
> Then must the Dauphin cease, sith he hath ceast.[229]

That the Bastard should have leaped to serve as the ironical advocate of the Legate's policy is not to the Legate's credit. Neither is it to the credit of Pandulph that, upon Salisbury's avowal to follow Lewes "unto the death," the Cardinal echoes the earlier excommunication scene and peremptorily closes the matter:

> Then, in the name of *Innocent*, the Pope,
> I curse the Prince and all that take his part,
> And excommunicate the rebel peers
> As traitors to the King and to the Pope.[230]

The petulance is obvious; the Cardinal is ready to pronounce a curse and excommunication at the slightest crossing of his will.

On such evidence as that discussed in the foregoing pages, Bowden concludes: "The old play makes Pandulph a hypocrite and a Machiavellian simply because he is a Catholic prelate. In Shakespeare he appears as an experienced, far-sighted statesman. . . ."[231] Bowden even feels that Shakespeare represents the Cardinal as a coefficient of the Bastard —a partner in the work of reconstruction.

> His mission is completely successful. England is reconciled to the Church, France and England are friends again, the rebel nobles are pardoned, the rightful heir ascends the English throne, and all this is effected by the offices of the Legate and the action of Faulconbridge, the typical Englishman, of whom the poet is so fond.[232]

While it must be admitted that the Cardinal is a most disturbing force earlier in the play, it does seem as if Shakespeare viewed Pandulph as a dignified, skillful, and successful official of Roman Catholicism to whom the audience should show respect.

In addition to such major changes as the reduction of John to a purely political villain, the toning down of the sacking of the monasteries, the obliteration of anti-papalism in the Bastard, and the favorable representation of Pandulph, Shakespeare makes a number of minor changes in the revision of *The Troublesome Raigne*. These minor matters are not unimportant, for they add to the cumulative effect.

(5) There is, for example, the vision of the Five Moons. In the source play, the five moons are made to appear on the stage. The phenomenon is then described in awed tones by the Bastard. John and the attendant noblemen express their foreboding. Peter of Pomfret is brought in to interpret the vision:

> The sky wherein these moons have residence,
> Presenteth *Rome*, the great Metropolis,
> Where sits the Pope in all his holy pomp,
> Four of the moons present four provinces,
> To wit, *Spain, Denmark, Germany*, and *France*,
> That bear the yoke of proud commanding *Rome*,
> And stand in fear to tempt the Prelate's curse.
> The smallest moon that whirls about the rest,
> Impatient of the place he holds with them,
> Doth figure forth this Island, *Albion*,
> Who 'gins to scorn the See and the State of *Rome*,
> And seeks to shun the edicts of the Pope:
> This shows the heaven; and this, I do aver,
> Is figur'd in these apparitions.
> *John.* Why, then it seems the Heavens smile on us,
> Giving applause for leaving of the Pope,
> But, for they chance in our Meridian,
> Do they effect no private growing ill
> To be inflicted on us in this clime?
> *Peter.* The moons effect no more than what I said.
> But, on some other knowledge that I have
> By my prescience, ere Ascension Day
> Have brought the sun unto his usual height,
> Of crown, estate and royal dignity,
> Thou shalt be clean despoil'd and dispossest.[233]

For the added bit of what later proved to be ambiguous prophecy Peter of Pomfret loses his life.

Shakespeare separates the vision of the Five Moons and the Ascension Day prophecy. He has the Bastard enter with Peter of Pomfret and report the Ascension Day prophecy to John:

And here's a prophet that I brought with me
From forth the streets of Pomfret, whom I found
With many hundreds treading on his heels;
To whom he sung, in rude harsh-sounding rimes,
That, ere the next Ascension-day at noon,
Your highness should deliver up your crown.[234]

Peter says no more than to explain to the King, upon the latter's questioning him, that he acted so

Foreknowing that the truth will fall out so.[235]

It is Hubert who reports the vision of the Five Moons when he enters a little later:

My Lord, they say five moons were seen to-night:
Four fixed, and the fifth did whirl about
The other four in wondrous motion.
K. John. Five moons!
Hub. Old men and beldams in the streets
Do prophesy upon it dangerously: [236]

But instead of continuing with an interpretation, Hubert describes the popular unrest arising from the death of Arthur. There is not the slightest suggestion of Rome or of England's relationship to the Pope. The vision is simply a bit of supernaturalism adapted by Shakespeare to add to the dramatic effect of the situation.

(6) Another minor change is seen in the rebellion of the noblemen against John. In *The Troublesome Raigne* that rebellion is linked with the excommunication. When, after the finding of the dead body of Arthur, the barons discuss what course of action to follow, Essex asks:

How say you, lords, shall we with speed dispatch,
Under our hands, a packet into *Fraunce*,
To bid the Dolphin enter with his force,
To claim the kingdom for his proper right,
His title maketh lawful strength thereto.
Besides, the Pope, on peril of his curse,
Hath barr'd us of obedience unto *John*.
This hateful murder, *Lewes* his true descent,
The holy charge that we receiv'd from *Rome*,
Are weighty reasons, if you like my rede,
To make us all persever in this deed.[237]

The connection is confirmed at the meeting of the barons at St. Edmunds-

bury. There again it is Essex who discusses the grounds of rebellion. He
dwells upon the tyranny of John and gives specific instances and then
concludes:

> Only, I say, that were there nothing else
> To move us, but the Pope's most dreadful curse,
> Whereof we are assured if we fail,
> It were enough to instigate us all,
> With earnestness of sp'rit, to seek a mean
> To dispossess *John* of his regiment.[238]

Penbrooke agrees with what Essex has said and adds his own comment:

> Short tale to make, the See Apostolic
> Hath offer'd dispensation for the fault,
> If any be, as trust me, none I know,
> By planting *Lewes* in the usurper's room.[239]

When the Bastard, who has listened in on the discussion, undertakes to
dissuade the barons from their purpose, he too recognizes the connection
of the rebellion with the papacy and attacks the authority of the Pope
to command the obedience of the noblemen. After the decision has been
reached and announced to Lewes, the Dauphin says:

> Thanks to you all of this religious league,
> A holy knot of Catholic consent,[240]

and proposes that the covenant be sealed by "oath upon the holy altar
sworn." Then, before the eyes of the English audience, the noblemen
swear "upon the altar, and by the holy Army of Saints, homage and
allegiance to the right Christian Prince, *Lewes* of *Fraunce*, as true and
rightful King to *England*. . . ."[241]

Shakespeare limits the connection to political matters. The rebellion
starts when Salisbury and Pembroke storm out of the King's presence
after erroneously deducing the death of Arthur.[242] The Bastard reports
its spread by telling of having

> . . . met Lord Bigot and Lord Salisbury,
> With eyes as red as new-enkindled fire,
> And many more, going to seek the grave
> Of Arthur. . . .[243]

Hubert's account of the unrest of the people is prefaced by the explanation that the rumor of

> Young Arthur's death is common in their mouths.[244]

The barons take their first step toward a league with France just before finding the dead body of Arthur. It is a step taken in response to overtures by the French. Salisbury has received a letter from Pandulph and says:

> Lords, I will meet him at Saint Edmundsbury.
> It is our safety, and we must embrace
> This gentle offer of the perilous time.[245]

After finding the body of Arthur, the barons take their vow. Salisbury speaks for all when he says:

> Kneeling before this ruin of sweet life,
> And breathing to his breathless excellence
> The incense of a vow, a holy vow,
> Never to taste the pleasures of the world,
> Never to be infected with delight,
> Nor conversant with ease and idleness,
> Till I have set a glory to this hand,
> By giving it the worship of revenge.
> *Pembroke* and *Bigot.* Our souls religiously
> confirm thy words.[246]

When Shakespeare introduces the scene of league-making at St. Edmundsbury, Lewis is already present and the oaths of the covenant have already been made. The treaty has been put on paper, and the Dauphin directs:

> My Lord Melun, let this be copied out,
> And keep it safe for our remembrance.
> Return the precedent to these lords again;
> That, having our fair order written down,
> Both they and we, perusing o'er these notes,
> May know wherefore we took the sacrament,
> And keep our faiths firm and inviolable.[247]

After long speeches by Salisbury and Lewis, the Cardinal appears, and it is then that Lewis suggests a religious confirmation of the pact should Pandulph

> . . . give us warrant from the hand of heaven,
> And on our actions set the name of right
> With holy breath.[248]

The audience is not told that the pact was sealed upon the altar at St. Edmundsbury until in the course of the battle between the English and the French, Lord Melun enters to warn the barons of the intended treachery of the Dauphin, telling them that

> . . . if the French be lords of this loud day,
> He means to recompense the pains you take
> By cutting off your heads. Thus hath he sworn,
> And I with him, and many moe with me,
> Upon the altar at Saint Edmundsbury;
> Even on that altar where we swore to you
> Dear amity and everlasting love.[249]

The result of Shakespeare's stressing the political aspect of the rebellion of the barons and of minimizing the religious aspect of the league with France is a less hostile feeling on the part of the audience toward Catholicism.

(7) A final example of minor change is Shakespeare's omission of many irreverent remarks by principal characters and especially the omission of several ascriptions of blame to Rome for the miseries of John's reign. An example is John's scornful speech summarizing the situation upon his return to England:

> Now, warlike followers, resteth aught undone
> That may impeach us of fond oversight?
> . . . .
> The arch-proud titled Priest of *Italy*,
> That calls himself Grand Vicar under God,
> Is busied now with trental obsequies,
> Mass and month's-mind, dirge, and I know not what,
> To ease their souls in painful purgatory,
> That have miscarried in these bloody wars.
> Heard you not, lords, when first his Holiness
> Had tidings of our small account of him,
> How, with a taunt, vaunting upon his toes,
> He urged a reason why the English ass
> Disdain'd the blessed ordinance of Rome?
> The title (reverently might I infer,)
> Became the kings that erst have borne the load,
> The slavish weight of that controlling Priest,
> Who, at his pleasure, temper'd them like wax,
> To carry arms, on danger of his curse,
> Banding their souls with warrants of his hand.
> I grieve to think how kings in ages past
> (Simply devoted to the See of *Rome*),

Have run into a thousand acts of shame.
But now, for confirmation of our state,
Sith we have prun'd the more than needful branch
That did oppress the true well-growing stock,
It resteth, we, throughout our territories,
Be reproclaimed and invested King.[250]

This jeering tirade has no echo in Shakespeare.

How completely the shadow of the Pope darkens the sun of England's happiness is hinted at by the Bastard upon his leaving to confer with the conspirators at Saint Edmundsbury when he says:

I go, my lord,
See how he is distraught,
This is the cursed priest of *Italy*
Hath heapt these mischiefs on this hapless land,[251]

and is stated fully by King John himself just before he submits to Rome:

For life and land, and all, is levell'd at
The Pope of *Rome*, 'tis he that is the cause;
He curseth thee; he sets thy subjects free
From due obedience to their sovereign:
He animates the nobles in their wars;
He gives away the crown to *Philips* son,
And pardons all that seek to murder thee:
And thus blind zeal is still predominant.
Then, *John*, there is no way to keep thy crown,
But finely to dissemble with the Pope:
That hand that gave the wound, must give the salve
To cure the hurt, else quite incurable.[252]

The foregoing study of Shakespeare's manner of revising *The Trouble-some Raigne* exhibits the details which create the general impression of the dramatist's mild treatment of Catholicism. It still remains to ask what that treatment means. If J. Dover Wilson's statement is true, that "nothing is more remarkable than the evident pains taken by Shakespeare to rid the play of the anti-catholic bias of his predecessors,"[253] why did Shakespeare take those pains?

There is something to be said for the suggestion that he took those pains for the sake of the Earl of Southampton.[254] There is an indirect and a direct side to the evidence supporting the suggestion.

Interesting from the indirect side is the indication that Shakespeare was willing to make changes in his revision for the sake of the personal feelings of Lord Essex, Queen Elizabeth's favorite. One of the minor modifications which Shakespeare makes in *King John* is the virtual elimination of the character of Essex. In *The Troublesome Raigne*, Essex is a prominent leader of the barons' revolt. He makes several long speeches and supplies the reasons for making a league with France. But in *King John* he speaks only three insignificant lines[255] to introduce the Faulconbridges, lines spoken by Salisbury in the source play. Thereafter Essex becomes a silent figure. He is not again mentioned in the stage directions. His name is not incorporated in any of the dialogue, so that the audience is left to guess at his identity. It seems as if Shakespeare did not intend to have him in the cast at all.[256] The Essex of history was the forebear of the wife of Queen Elizabeth's favorite, and Shakespeare's reduction of the character to a shadow would please the Elizabethan Essex for obvious political reasons. And if it pleased Essex, it would please Southampton too, for the latter was a close friend and supporter of the former. In 1595 Southampton married a cousin of Essex. Whether the removal of anti-Catholic elements would please Essex is conjectural, but that it would not displease him is indicated by the fact that in his statecraft Essex, though a Protestant, favored tolerance toward Catholicism.

But Southampton himself would be pleased directly by the changes which eliminated an hostility to Catholicism. Southampton's father was a Catholic formerly active in the persecution of Protestants; Southampton's mother was the daughter of the first Viscount Montagu, who in 1554, as an English envoy, approached the Pope about the reconciliation of the English Church with Rome. Southampton himself remained a Catholic sympathizer until the reign of James I. Thus it is that Liebermann concludes:

> Die unverkennbare zarte Rücksicht auf katholische Gefühle im bearbeiteten *John* wird zurückgehen auf Southamptons Gönnerschaft. . . .[257]

But whatever may have been Shakespeare's purpose, whether personal, political, or patriotic, in writing *King John* as he did, the fact seems indisputable that in the play the dramatist presents Catholicism and the Church of Rome in a tolerant and understanding light.

4. Conclusion

This final chapter has sought to show that there is nothing contrary to the Catholic spirit in Shakespeare's use of the Bible, but rather that there are some indications of his using the Bible as an enlightened Catholic would; that in the works of Shakespeare there is positive evidence to suggest the promptings of a Catholic consciousness to the creative imagination of the artist; and that in writing *King John* as the revision of an anti-Catholic source, Shakespeare wrote a play in which Catholicism is treated sympathetically. The evidence reviewed in this chapter and in the preceding chapters does not warrant the conclusion that Shakespeare was himself a Catholic. But it does supply grounds for the opinion that the poet absorbed more of Catholicism in the course of his development than is generally believed and that throughout his mature years he retained a genuine esteem for certain aspects of the Old Faith.

THE END

NOTES

PART ONE

1. Thomas Carter. *Shakespeare: Puritan and Recusant* (Edinburgh, 1897).
2. Edgar Innes Fripp, *Minutes and Accounts of the Corporation of Stratford-upon-Avon and Other Records, 1553–1620* (Oxford and London, 1921, 1924, 1926, 1929); *Shakespeare Studies: Biographical and Literary* (London, 1930); *Shakespeare: Man and Artist* (London, 1938), 2 vols.
3. Cumberland Clark, *Shakespeare and the Supernatural* (London, 1931), based largely on the work of Fripp.
4. Henry S. Bowden, *The Religion of Shakespeare, Chiefly from the Writings of the Late Mr. Richard Simpson, M. A.* (London, 1899).
5. Herbert Thurston, S.J., "The Religion of Shakspere," *The Month* (May, 1882), pp. 1–19.
6. John Pym Yeatman, *The Gentle Shakspere—A Vindication* (London, n.d.).
7. Clara Longworth de Chambrun, *Shakespeare Rediscovered by means of Public Records, Secret Reports and Private Correspondence Newly Set Forth as Evidence on His Life and Work* (New York and London, 1938).
8. J. O. Halliwell-Phillipps, *Outlines of the Life of Shakespeare* (London, 1882; 11th printing, 1907), 2 vols.
9. G. B. Harrison, "The National Background" in *A Companion to Shakespeare Studies* (New York, 1934), edited by Harley Granville-Barker and G. B. Harrison, pp. 163–86.
10. J. Semple Smart, *Shakespeare, Truth and Tradition* (London, 1928).
11. Edmund K. Chambers, *William Shakespeare: A Study of Facts and Problems* (Oxford, 1930), 2 vols.
12. James Walter. *Shakespeare's True Life* (London, 1890).
13. H. C. Beeching, "The Religion of Shakespeare," in *The Works of Shakespeare in Ten Volumes* (Stratford-on-Avon, 1907), X, 335–49.
14. Karl Elze, *William Shakespeare: A Literary Biography* (London, 1888).
15. Charlotte C. Stopes, *Shakespeare's Family, Being a Record of the Ancestors and Descendants of William Shakespeare, with Some Account of the Ardens* (London, 1901).
16. George Brandes, *William Shakespeare* (New York, 1931).
17. Joseph Quincy Adams, *A Life of William Shakespeare* (New York, 1923).
18. Sidney Lee, *A Life of William Shakespeare*, New Edition (London, 1915).
19. William Haller, *The Rise of Puritanism* (New York, 1938), p. 3.
20. *Ibid.*, p. 5.
21. Champlin Burrage, *The Early English Dissenters*, Vol. I (Cambridge, England, 1912), pp. 37, 41.
22. See, for example, H. S. Bowden, *op. cit.*, pp. 59 ff., and J. O. Halliwell-Phillipps, *op. cit.*, I, 37.
23. B. Roland Lewis, *The Shakespeare Documents: Facsimiles, Transliterations, Translations, & Commentary* (Stanford University, California, 1940), I, 22.
24. *Ibid.*, p. 23.
25. Fripp, *Shakespeare: Man and Artist*, I, 32; Lewis, *op. cit.*, I, 20.
26. Lewis, *op. cit.*, I, 19.
27. *Minutes and Accounts*, I, xxxii.
28. *Op. cit.*, I, 51.
29. Fripp, *Shakespeare: Man and Artist*, I, 19–22.
30. Lewis, *op. cit.*, I, 52.
31. *Ibid.*, p. 53.
32. Pp. 59–63.

33. *Op. cit.*, I, 42, footnote. Based, perhaps, on Fripp's classification, *Minutes and Accounts*, I, xxvi.

34. See article "John Dudley" in *The National Dictionary of Biography* (1917), VI, 109–11.

35. Vol. I, xxviii–xxix.

36. Lewis, *op. cit.*, I, 124.

37. *The Works of Mr. William Shakespear* (London, 1714), I, ii.

38. *Shakespeare: Man and Artist*, I, 26, 29, 46; II, 520.

39. Lewis, *op. cit.*, I, 89.

40. *Ibid.*

41. Fripp, *Shakespeare Studies*, p. 84.

42. Fripp, *Minutes and Accounts*, I, xxxiv.

43. See, for example, H. S. Bowden, *op. cit.*, pp. 65–66.

44. Fripp, *Minutes and Accounts*, I, 90.

45. *Op. cit.*, pp. 24 ff., cited by Fripp, *Shakespeare Studies*, p. 82.

46. *Op. cit.*, pp. 65–66.

47. Lewis, *op. cit.*, I, 57.

48. Fripp, *Minutes and Accounts*, I, 120.

49. *Ibid.*, pp. xlix–l.

50. *Op. cit.*, I, 58.

51. Lewis, *op. cit.*, I, 56–57.

52. Fripp, *Minutes and Accounts*, I, 137–41 and 148–52.

53. *Ibid.*, p. 128.

54. *Op. cit.*, pp. 25–27.

55. Fripp, *Minutes and Accounts*, I, 130.

56. Carter, *op. cit.*, p. 27; Fripp, *Minutes and Accounts*, I, lii.

57. Edward P. Cheyney, *A Short History of England* (New York, 1904), p. 311.

58. Fripp, *Shakespeare Studies*, pp. 13–23.

59. Fripp, *Minutes and Accounts*, I, 130.

60. *Op. cit.*, pp. 69–70.

61. *Shakespeare Studies*, pp. 16–17.

62. Lewis, *op. cit.*, I, 125.

63. *Ibid.*

64. *Ibid.*, p. 126.

65. *Ibid.*, p. 127.

66. H. S. Bowden, *op. cit.*, p. 91.

67. Lewis, *op. cit.*, I, 59.

68. Fripp, *Minutes and Accounts*, I, 147.

69. *Ibid.*, II, 13.

70. *Ibid.*, p. 14, footnote 1.

71. Lewis, *op. cit.*, I, 61.

72. *Op. cit.*, p. 179.

73. P. 158.

74. Vol. I, 37.

75. Henry Gee and William John Hardy, *Documents Illustrative of English Church History Compiled from Original Sources* (London, 1896), p. 449.

76. *Op. cit.*, p. 67.

77. *Op. cit.*, p. 179.

78. *Shakespeare Studies*, pp. 86–87; *Minutes and Accounts*, II, xxiii.

79. Fripp, *Shakespeare: Man and Artist*, I, 48.

80. Fripp, *Minutes and Accounts*, II, xxiii.

81. Lewis, *op. cit.*, I, 60.

82. Fripp, *Minutes and Accounts*, II, 5.

83. *Ibid.*, p. 12.

84. *Ibid.*, p. 13.

85. *Ibid.*, p. 31.

86. *Op. cit.*, pp. 19–20.
87. *Op. cit.*, I, 70.
88. *Ibid.*, p. 62.
89. *Minutes and Accounts*, I, xliii, footnote 2. Italics are mine.
90. *Ibid.*, II, xx.
91. *Ibid.*, I, xxxi.
92. *Ibid.*, II, xx.
93. *Ibid.*, p. xxiv, and pp. 40–42.
94. *Ibid.*, p. xxv, footnote 1.
95. *Ibid.*, p. 35.
96. *Ibid*, p. 77.
97. Edmund Malone, *The Plays and Poems of William Shakspeare*, Third Variorum edition (1821), II, 150–52.
98. P. 13, note.
99. *Op. cit.*, p. 96.
100. *Minutes and Accounts*, II, xxxiii.
101. Pp. 47–48.
102. Fripp, *Minutes and Accounts*, II, 52.
103. *Ibid.*, p. 54.
104. *Op. cit.*, pp. 70–71.
105. *Op. cit.*, X, 336.
106. *Shakespeare: Man and Artist*, I, 162, 193, 306.
107. *Ibid.*, I, 450 and II, 812.
108. Fripp, *Minutes and Accounts*, II, 60–61.
109. *Op. cit.*, p. 74.
110. Fripp, *Minutes and Accounts*, III, 170.
111. *Ibid.*, pp. 99–100.
112. *Ibid.*, p. 100, footnote; *Shakespeare: Man and Artist*, I, 199.
113. Fripp, *Minutes and Accounts*, III, 100, footnote.
114. *Op. cit.*, p. 337.
115. *Op. cit.*, pp. 89–94.
116. *Op. cit.*, pp. 71–72.
117. *Op. cit.*, p. 9.
118. *Op. cit.*, I, 63.
119. *Op. cit.*, p 166.
120. Lewis, *op. cit.*, I, 63.
121. *Ibid.*
122. *Ibid.*, p. 67.
123. *Minutes and Accounts*, I, xl.
124. *Op. cit.*, p. 57.
125. *Op. cit.*, I, 67. Lewis's footnote 16 points to the "Rev. Thomas Carter's *Shakespeare Puritan and Recusant*, 1897, pp. 200–203, for a collation of such writs of 'distringi' to which John Shakespeare was a party."
126. Lewis, *op. cit.*, I, 66.
127. Lewis misunderstands the entry. See his *The Shakespeare Documents*, I, 61–62 and 65, where he speaks as if John Shakespeare had to pay nothing.
128. Fripp, *Minutes and Accounts*, III, 31–32.
129. *Ibid.*, p. xxxv.
130. *Ibid.*, p. 32, footnote 1.
131. *Ibid.*, p. 31, footnote 7.
132. Lewis, *op. cit.*, I, 66.
133. *Shakespeare Studies*, p. 92.
134. Fripp, *Shakespeare: Man and Artist*, I, 157.
135. *Op cit.*, I, 65.
136. Fripp, *Minutes and Accounts*, III, 19.
137. Edmund K. Chambers, *op. cit.*, II, 37.

138. Lewis, *op. cit.*, I, 136–40.
139. *Ibid.*, p. 138.
140. *Ibid.*, p. 140. William Shakespeare is not included in this complaint.
141. *Ibid.*, pp. 134–35.
142. *Op. cit.*, II, 37.
143. Lewis, *op. cit.*, I, 142–43.
144. *Ibid.*, p. 144.
145. *Ibid.*, pp. 131–33.
146. *Ibid.*, p. 133.
147. *Ibid.*, p. 132.
148. *Ibid.*, p. 158.
149. *Ibid.* p. 133.
150. *Ibid.*, pp. 149–52.
151. *Ibid.*, pp. 153–54.
152. *Op. cit.*, pp. 89–90. For a transcript of the petition which Elze mentions, see Fripp, *Minutes and Accounts*, IV, 115–16.
153. Lewis, *op. cit.*, I, 112–13.
154. Fripp, *Shakespeare: Man and Artist*, I, 164–65; *Minutes and Accounts*, III, 57.
155. Lewis, *op. cit.*, I, 24–25.
156. *Ibid.*, pp. 54 and 67. The entry is otherwise important in that it identifies John Shakespeare as "glover."
157. *Ibid.*, p. 72, quoting the papal bull *Regnans in excelsis*.
158. Lewis, *op. cit.* I, 72.
159. Edward P. Cheyney, *op. cit.*, p. 347.
160. *Ibid.*
161. Fripp, *Minutes and Accounts*, III, xxxviii; 35.
162. *Ibid.*, II, xlvii. Fripp refers to *Loseley MSS.*, Kempe, p. 226 f.
163. Made to the Privy Council, November 5, 1577. Transcribed from *State Papers, Dom., Elizabeth, Vol. 118, No. 11*, by Fripp in *Minutes and Accounts*, III, 6–7.
164. *Lansdowne MS.* 153 f., 232 (new folio 212), quoted by Fripp, *Shakespeare: Man and Artist*, I, 155–56. Carter, in *Shakespeare: Puritan and Recusant*, pp. 94–95, also refers to the manuscript and summarizes the devices of recusants therein reported.
165. H. S. Bowden, *op. cit.*, pp. 71–72; Fripp, *Shakespeare: Man and Artist*, I, 156.
166. Fripp, *Shakespeare: Man and Artist*, I, 165.
167. Lewis, *op. cit.*, I, 74–76.
168. Fripp, *Shakespeare: Man and Artist*, I, 166, and footnote 2.
169. Lewis, *op. cit.*, I, 74. In *Shakespeare: Man and Artist*, I, 165, Fripp says "one hundred and forty."
170. *Shakespeare Studies*, p. 93.
171. *Shakespeare's Warwickshire Contemporaries* (Stratford-upon-Avon, 1907), p. 31.
172. Elze, *op. cit.* p. 29, footnote; Halliwell-Phillipps, *op. cit.*, II, 137.
173. P. 31, footnote 2.
174. *Shakespeare Studies*, pp. 93–95; *Shakespeare: Man and Artist*, I. 200.
175. *Shakespeare: Man and Artist*, I, 167; *Minutes and Accounts*, III, xlii.
176. Fripp, *Minutes and Accounts*, IV, xvii and xix.
177. John Strype, *Annals of the Reformation* (3rd edition, 1824), IV, 56.
178. *Ibid.*, p. 59.
179. *Ibid.*, pp. 61–62.
180. *Ibid.*, p. 63.
181. *Warwick Castle MSS*, transcribed in Fripp, *Minutes and Accounts*, IV, 140.
182. *Shakespeare's Family*, p. 58.
183. *Ibid.*, footnote 2.
184. *Op. cit.*, p. 32, footnote 1.
185. *Op. cit.* p. 164.
186 Bowden, *op. cit.* pp. 75–76.
187. *Op. cit.*, I, 15.

188. *Minutes and Accounts*, IV, xxxv-xxxvi.
189. *Op. cit.*, p. 83.
190. *Op. cit.*, I. 16.
191. *Op. cit.*, p. 81.
192. *Ibid.* Bowden's reference is to "*S. P. Dom. Eliz. vol. cxvii,* October 24 1577, No. 12." Brackets are mine.
193. *Ibid.*, pp. 81–82.
194. *Shakespeare Studies*, p. 96; *Shakespeare: Man and Artist*, I, 306–7.
195. *Op. cit.*, pp. 164–65.
196. *Shakespeare Studies*, p. 96.
197. Fripp, *Shakespeare: Man and Artist*, I, 306–7.
198. Fripp, *Minutes and Accounts*, IV, xxxiv-xxxv.
199. *Ibid.*, p. 162.
200. *Shakespeare: Man and Artist*, I, 26.
201. Fripp, *Minutes and Accounts*, IV, xxxv.
202. Fripp, *Shakespeare Studies*, p. 96.
203. *Hatfield MSS.* vi., to Sir Robert Cecil, quoted in part by Fripp, *Shakespeare: Man and Artist*, I, 449–50.
204. *Shakespeare Studies*, p. 97.
205. *Blazon of Gentrie* (1586), pp. 58–60, quoted by Lewis, *op. cit.*, I, 209.
206. Lewis, *op. cit.*, I, 212. The words "Towne" in the third line and "that" in the fourth line are crossed out.
207. Lewis, *op. cit.*, I, 209.
208. *Shakespeare: Man and Artist*, I, 76; *Shakespeare Studies*, pp. 88–89; *Minutes and Accounts*, II, xlvi.
209. *Op. cit.*, p. 13, footnote 1.
210. *Op. cit.*, pp. 26–27.
211. *Minutes and Accounts*, II, xliv-xlv.
212. Lewis, *op. cit.*, I, 301.
213. Fripp, *Shakespeare Studies*, p. 98. The reason the revised impalement was never adopted by William Shakespeare, thinks Fripp, is that William was reluctant to offend his Catholic mother by the use of a Protestant impalement.
214. *Shakespeare's Family*, p. 31.
215. Lewis, "Family Pedigree of the Ancient and Noble House of Mary Arden," *op. cit.*, I, 82–83.
216. Robert Glover, *Complete Body of Heraldry*, quoted by Lewis, *op. cit.*, I, 305.

PART TWO

1. An unpublished letter from Jordan to the editor of the *Gentleman's Magazine*, dated at Stratford-on-Avon, June 14, 1784, and transcribed in Halliwell-Phillipps, *Outlines* (1907), II, 399.
2. Samuel Johnson and George Steevens, eds., *The Plays of William Shakspeare in Fifteen Volumes*, 4th edition, revised by Isaac Reed (London, 1793), II, 298–305.
3. Letter from Malone to the Rev. James Davenport, 21 October, 1789, transcribed by Halliwell-Phillipps in his *Outlines* (1907), II, 399–400.
4. Halliwell-Phillipps, *Jordan Correspondence*, p. 8, quoted by Herbert Thurston in "A Controverted Shakespeare Document," *The Dublin Review*, Vol. 173, (Oct.-Dec., 1923), p. 170.
5. Letter from Jordan to Malone, 19 March, 1790, transcribed by Halliwell-Phillipps, *Outlines* (1907), II, 400–402.

6. Letter from Malone to Jordan, 25 March, 1790, transcribed by Halliwell-Phillipps, *Outlines* (1907), II, 402, with additions from H. Thurston, "The Spiritual Testament of John Shakespeare," *The Month* (Nov., 1911), p. 497.

7. Pp. 198–99. Malone's footnote 118 refers to "*Plays and Poems of William Shakspeare*, 1790, Vol. II, P. II, p. 162 and p. 330."

8. *Third Variorum*, II, 516–17. Malone's copy of the spiritual will is omitted from his *An Historical Account of the Rise and Progress of the English Stage* as it appears in the *Third Variorum*.

9. *Ibid.*, p. 517, footnote 2. See also pp. 53–62 for Malone's discussion of his discovery of the shoemaker.

10. Pp. 197–99. Chalmers in note (c) gives a specimen, unfortunately from the first paragraph, which, though Chalmers quoted it from "Mal. Shak. vol. i. pt. 2. p. 330," Malone himself got from John Jordan and not from the original manuscript, once in his possession.

11. *William Shakspere: A Biography* (London, 1842), pp. 36–37.

12. P. xv.

13. *Outlines* (1907), II, 399.

14. Edition of 1888, translated by L. Dora Schmitz, p. 457.

15. Edition of 1898, pp. 365–66; edition of 1915, p. 647.

16. Vol. 236, p. 231.

17. Vol. I, xxi.

18. Edition of 1838, in one volume, p. 8.

19. Pp. 289–94.

20. Pp. 193–97.

21. Pp. 197–201.

22. *Op. cit.*, pp. 86–91.

23. Vol. I, 16.

24. "Appendix F, No. VI," Vol. II, 381–82. For a biography of Jordan and a less assuring estimate of his character by one who knew him personally, see R. B. Wheler's *A Guide to Stratford-upon-Avon* (Stratford-upon-Avon, 1814), pp. 139–43.

25. "The Religion of Shakspere," pp. 1–19.

26. November, 1911, pp. 487–502.

27. "A Controverted Shakespeare Document," *The Dublin Review*, Vol. 173, p. 165. The booklet which Thurston discovered is catalogued as "4404. h 3" under "Charles [Borromeo]" in the *British Museum General Catalogue of Printed Books*, Vol. XXXVI, CHAR-CHIC (London, 1943), 40. It is described as a quarto. The Mexican pamphlet is listed in Vincente de P. Andrade's *Ensayo Bibliográfico Mexicano del Siglo XVII*, Segunda Edicion (Mexico: Imprenta del Museo Nacional, 1899), as "495" on page 319, and in José Toribio Medina's *La Imprenta en México (1539–1821)*, Tomo II (Santiago de Chile, 1909), for the year 1661 under "San Carlos Borromeo" as "890" on page 357. In both entries the title page is identical and is given very much as Thurston gives it, the variations being in spelling and capitalization only.

In Andrade a notation reads: "En 4.° 4 ff. s.n. por todo.—(P. Fischer.)," thus describing the pamphlet, upon the authority of Father Fischer, an earlier bibliographer, as a quarto of four pages, without page numbers throughout. The notation continues: "Sólo tengo otras tres ediciones de este folleto: una del siglo XVII, sin año, é impreso por la dicha Viuda, y dos de 1785 y de 1797"; that is, "I have only three other editions of this pamphlet: one of the 17th century, without the year, was printed by the aforesaid Widow, and two of 1785 and 1797."

Medina also describes the pamphlet as being a quarto of four pages, without page numbers throughout, on the authority of P. Fischer. He also refers to "*Catalogue Andrade*, n. 2703" and to "Andrade, n. 495." He then remarks: "Hay varias ediciones posteriores y una sin fecha del siglo XVII"; that is, "There are various later editions and one without date of the 17th century."

28. The Spanish version in MS. Egerton (f. 68) is listed in the *Catalogue of the Manuscripts in the Spanish Language in the British Museum*, Vol. II (London, 1877), p. 151,

as Number 9 among "papers chiefly relating to the Inquisition and to the clergy in the West Indies," and its title page is given as follows: "Testamento y ultima voluntad del alma hecho en salud par asegurarse el christiano de las tentaciones del Demonio en la hora de la Muerte, ordenado por San Carlos Borromeo, cardenal del titulo de Santa Praxedos y arcobispo de Milan."

29. The Romansch version is catalogued as "885. i. 12." under "Charles [Borromeo]" in the *British Museum General Catalogue of Printed Books*, Vol. XXXVI, CHAR-CHIC (London, 1943), 40. It is described as a 16° booklet of nineteen pages, published at Banaduz in 1741.

30. *The Dublin Review*, Vol. 173, pp. 166–67. Sauli met St. Charles Borromeo in 1557 and served the Cardinal as a kind of spiritual counsellor from 1568 until Borromeo's death in 1584.

31. *Op. cit.*, p. 75.

32. *Op. cit.*, p. 86.

33. *Ibid.*, footnote 1.

34. *The Month* (Nov., 1911), p. 500.

35. *Op. cit.*, II, 382.

36. Lewis, *op. cit.*, I, 5 and footnote 1.

37. *Ibid.*, p. 6.

38. *Ibid.*, p. 7.

39. *Ibid.*

40. *Ibid.* But Lewis himself (I, 316, Document 155) transcribes the Parish Register burial entry of September 8, 1601, as "Mr Johañes Shakspear[e]".

41. Fripp, *Minutes and Accounts*, I, 70.

42. *Ibid.*, pp. 101, 119, 120, 122, 126, 129, 130, *et al.*

43. *Ibid.*, pp. 130, 131, 132, and 134.

44. *Ibid.*, pp. 120, 121, 126, 129.

45. *Ibid.*, pp. 137, 148.

46. *Ibid.*, p. 128.

47. *Ibid.*, II, 13.

48. *Ibid.*, pp. 28, 30.

49. *Ibid.*, p. 88.

50. *Ibid.*, III, 38.

51. *Ibid.*, p. 57.

52. *Ibid.*, p. 93.

53. *Ibid.*, p. 100.

54. *Ibid.*, p. 111.

55. *Ibid.*, p. 120.

56. *Ibid.*, p. 122.

57. *Ibid.*, p. 128.

58. *Ibid.*, pp. 130, 132.

59. *Ibid.*, p. 139.

60. *Ibid.*, p. 170.

61. *Ibid.*, IV, 157.

62. D. H. Lambert, *Cartae Shakespeareanae* (London, 1904), No. 75, p. 41.

63. *The Month* (Nov., 1911), p. 499.

64. Mrs. Margaret Yeo, *Reformer: Saint Charles Borromeo* (Milwaukee, 1938), p. 169.

65. *Ibid.*, pp. 294 and 155.

66. *Ibid.*, pp. 215–29.

67. Richard Simpson, *Edmund Campion: A Biography* (London, 1867), pp. 111–12.

68. *Records of the English Province of the Society of Jesus* (London, 1877–83), edited by H. Foley, S. J., VI, 69–70. Foley's footnote 1 informs us that "the Douay Diary mentions the arrival of the four at Rheims on October 16, 1580. They all proceeded to England on October 29 following, except Gratley."

69. Quoted by John Hungerford Pollen, *Lives of the English Martyrs*, edited by Dom Bede Camm (London, 1914), II, 328. An interesting account of the "hiding holes" pre-

pared for Jesuits and seminary priests in the event of investigation by pursuivants is given in David Mathew's *Catholicism in England* (London, 1936), pp. 46–48.

70. Quoted by Pollen, *Lives of the English Martyrs*, II, 324.

71. Quoted by J. H. Pollen, *Lives of the English Martyrs*, II, 327. Italics are mine.

72. *State Papers, Dom. Eliz.*, June 23, 1581, quoted by Richard Simpson, *Edmund Campion: A Biography*, pp. 208–10. Italics are mine. Simpson gives the *State Papers* reference date as June 30, 1581, in his note No. 231, page 379.

73. P. 145, margin, *et al.*, cited by Hugh Pope, "A Brief History of the English Version of the New Testament First Published at Rheims in 1582, Continued down to the Present Day," *The Library*, 4th Series, XX (March, 1940), 355.

74. Quoted by Alfred W. Pollard, *Records of the English Bible* (London, 1911), p. 34.

75. *Ibid.*, p. 35.

76. *Op. cit.*, p. 357.

77. *Ibid.*, p. 356.

78. *Op. cit.*, p. 357, footnote 1.

79. *Op. cit.*, p. 357.

80. *Lives of the English Martyrs*, II, 323.

81. Fripp, *Minutes and Accounts*, I, 134, footnote 1; *Shakespeare Studies*, p. 86; Lee, *A Life of William Shakespeare*, p. 6; Chambers, *William Shakespeare*, I, 13.

82. Jordan's copy is published in Halliwell-Phillipps' *Original Collections of John Jordan, etc.*, 1864.

83. H. Thurston, *The Dublin Review*, Vol. 173, p. 175.

84. *Ibid.*, p. 176.

85. *Ibid.*, pp. 171–72. Thurston's first footnote * (p. 171) reads: "This clause in square brackets does not occur in the Italian." His second footnote * (p. 172) reads: "The Italian says *twelve* articles."

86. *The Month* (Nov., 1911), pp. 501–2.

87. *Jordan Correspondence*, p. 49, quoted by Thurston, *The Month* (Nov., 1911), p. 502, footnote 1.

88. *Op. cit.*, p. 49.

89. *Outlines*, II, 403–4. Jordan said that Mosely "was taken ill in a decline" "after Michaelmass in 1788" and "died about Christmass following."

90. *Op. cit.*, p. 647.

91. Lewis, *op. cit.*, II, 471, and Jordan's letter to Malone, March 19, 1790.

92. D. H. Lambert, *op. cit.*, No. 145, p. 83.

93. *Op. cit.*, II, 482.

94. Vol. II, 759, footnote.

95. *Ibid.*, pp. 758–59.

96. P. 36.

97. *Op. cit.*, p. 36.

98. *Ibid.*, p. 37.

99. *Op. cit.*, p. 49.

100. *Ibid.*

101. Bowden, *op. cit.*, p. 87.

102. *The Dublin Review*, Vol. 173, pp. 174–75.

103. Sir N. H. Nicolas, *op. cit.*, II, 581. From the standpoint of Thurston's criticism of the list of those invoked in John Shakespeare's will, it is interesting to note that in Wyndham's will "apostells" precede "evangelists" and that "confessoures" are included. "Martyres," however, are not called "holy." Another interesting will, that of John Dalton of Hull, made in 1487, which mentions women patrons appears in *Testamenta Eboracensia* (Surtees Society), IV, 21. It is quoted by F. A. Gasquet, *The Eve of the Reformation* (New York, 1900), pp. 390–92.

104. P. J. Chandlery, "Winefride," *The Catholic Encyclopedia*, XV, 656–57.

105. P. J. Chandlery, "Holywell," *The Catholic Encyclopedia*, VII, 438.

106. R. Simpson, *op. cit.*, pp. 101 and 104.

107. P. 80.

108. Lewis, *op. cit.*, I, 11. Lewis' source is J. W. Ryland, *Records of Wroxall Abbey and Manor* (1903). Elze, *op. cit.*, p. 11, makes the date "1527."
109. Lewis, *op. cit.*, I, 13; Yeatman, *op. cit.*, p. 169.
110. Elze, *op. cit.*, p. 10.
111. *William Shakespeare, His Family and Friends* (New York, 1904), p. 112.
112. *Op. cit.*, I, 17.
113. *Op. cit.*, I, 11.
114. *Shakespeare: Man and Artist*, I, 33.
115. *Ibid.*, p. 176.
116. *Third Variorum* (1821), II, 517, footnote 2.
117. *Ibid.*, pp. 53–62.
118. *Outlines*, II, 137–40.
119. *Minutes and Accounts*, III, 155, footnote 2.
120. *Op. cit.*, II, 3.
121. Halliwell-Phillipps, *Outlines*, II, 137.
122. *Ibid.*, p. 140.
123. Lewis, *op. cit.*, I, 112.
124. Fripp, *Minutes and Accounts*, IV, 96; I, xxxv.
125. Lewis, *op. cit.*, I, 112–13.
126. Fripp, *Minutes and Accounts*, IV, 96.
127. Lewis, *op. cit.*, I, 223.
128. Fripp, *Shakespeare Studies*, p. 68.
129. Lewis, *op. cit.*, I, 222–24. Italics are mine.
130. Sources of the account of the Birthplace are Fripp, *Shakespeare Studies*, pp. 67–69; Lee, *op. cit.*, pp. 8–10; Chambers, *op. cit.*, I, 13; II, App. A, No. iii; and Lewis, *op. cit.*, I, 111–20.
131. Chambers, *op. cit.*, II, 34.
132. *Op. cit.*, I, 118.
133. Mrs. Charlotte C. Stopes, *Shakespeare's Environment* (London, 1914), pp. 343–44.
134. *Outlines*, II, 399.

PART THREE

1. Quoted by Francis A. Gasquet, *The Eve of the Reformation*, p. 280.
2. H. Maynard Smith, *Pre-Reformation England*, p. 125.
3. Christopher Wordsworth and Henry Littlehales, *The Old Service-Books of the English Church* (London, 1904), pp. 285–86. The authors quote Burnet, *History of the Reformation*, "on Book iii, document 57."
4. *Op. cit.*, p. 126.
5. *Ibid.*, p. 99. Smith quotes Appendix V in *Lay Folks Mass Book*, edited by Simmons (E.E.T.S., 1879), p. 148.
6. It is extant in four texts written between 1375 and 1510. These have been edited by Thomas Frederick Simmons for the Early English Text Society (No. 71, 1879).
7. L. F. Salzman, *English Life in the Middle Ages* (London, 1927), p. 114.
8. Smith, *op. cit.*, pp. 133–34. By permission of The Macmillan Company, publishers.
9. Quoted by H. Maynard Smith, *op. cit.*, p. 129.
10. Vol. II, 286–305.
11. *Ibid.*, pp. 300–301.
12. John Myrc, *Instructions for Parish Priests* (E.E.T.S., 1868), pp. 21–24.
13. *Ibid.*, marginal notes throughout the text.
14. F. Procter and W. H. Frere, *A New History of the Book of Common Prayer* (London, 1902), p. 641, text and footnotes 1, 2, and 3.

15. Wordsworth and Littlehales, *op. cit.*, p. 248.

16. *Ibid.*, p. 250.

17. *Ibid.*, p. 249. Smith (*op. cit.*, p. 102) says "28 editions in English, 18 in Latin."

18. H. C. Anders, "The Elizabethan ABC with the Catechism," *The Library*, 4th Series, XVI (June, 1935), 43.

19. Wordsworth and Littlehales, *op. cit.*, pp. 251–52.

20. Henry Littlehales, ed., *The Prymer, or Lay Folks' Prayer Book*, Part II (London, 1897), p. xliv.

21. *Ibid.*, p. xlv.

22. Smith, *op. cit.*, pp. 339–41.

23. "*Dives et Pauper*," *The Library*, 4th Series, XIV (Dec., 1933), 299.

24. E. L. Cutts, *Parish Priests and Their People* (New York, 1898), p. 249.

25. Pfander, *op. cit.*, pp. 302–3.

26. *Op. cit.*, p. 299, footnote 1.

27. *Op. cit.*, p. 316.

28. *Op. cit.*, pp. 152–54. By permission of The Macmillan Company, publishers. In *A Midsummer-Night's Dream* (II, i, 102), Titania, lamenting the unhappy state of affairs resulting from her feud with Oberon, says: "No night is now with hymn or carol blest."

29. F. A. Gasquet, *op. cit.*, p. 286.

30. *Ibid.*, pp. 312–15.

31. *Ibid.*, pp. 286–88. Gasquet's quotations are from *The Prymer of Salisbury Use* (Rouen: Nicholas le Rour), f.b.vij.

32. *Ibid.*, p. 309. Gasquet translates from a Latin version in the tract *Dextra Pars Oculi*, a manual for confessors to assist them in the performance of their priestly duties.

33. *The Education of Shakespeare* (New York, 1933), p. 47.

34. For example, T. W. Baldwin, *William Shakspere's Petty School* (Urbana, Illinois, 1943), pp. 137–58.

35. *Op. cit.*, p. 32.

36. *Ibid.*, p. 46.

37. *Ibid.*

38. *Ibid.*, pp. 46–47.

39. *Ibid.*, p. 47.

40. W. J. Rolfe, *Shakespeare the Boy*, p. 60. In *As You Like It* (V, iv, 94–96) Touchstone says to Jacques: "O sir, we quarrel in print; by the book, as you have books for good manners: I will name you the degrees."

41. Oliver Baker, *In Shakespeare's Warwickshire*, p. 144.

42. Ll. 244–45.

43. Act V, x, 32–47. Italics are mine.

44. Act III, ii, 270–93.

45. *2 Henry IV*, II, i, 159–63.

46. Oliver Baker, *op. cit.*, p. 149.

47. *Ibid.*, pp. 153–54.

48. *Merry Wives*, IV, v, 8–9.

49. *1 King Henry IV*, IV, ii, 26–29.

50. III, iii, 138–46. Still other hints are given. Simple's mention of "a little yellow beard, a cane-coloured beard" (*Merry Wives*, I, iv, 23–24) may be an allusion to a "Cain-coloured" beard on a painted cloth. Rosalind's description of Orlando's hair as "of the dissembling colour," and Celia's rejoinder, "Something browner than Judas's" (*As You Like It*, III, iv, 7–8) may allude to the typical representation of Judas on painted cloths. In *Love's Labour's Lost* (III, i, 21–22) Moth tells Armado to sing with "your hands in your pocket like a man after the old painting." In the same play (V, ii, 575 ff) Costard exclaims to Nathaniel: "O! sir, you have overthrown Alisander the conqueror! You will be scraped out of the painted cloth for this."

51. *Shakespeare: Man and Artist*, I, 136–37.

52. *Ibid.*

53. *Ibid.*, p. 134.

54. *Ibid.*, p. 133.

55. *Ibid.*

56. *Op. cit.*, p. 159.

57. Arthur Gray, in his *A Chapter in the Early Life of Shakespeare: Polesworth in Arden* (Cambridge, 1926), pp. 62–79, proposes that William went to school at Polesworth.

58. *The Old Grammar Schools* (Cambridge, 1916), p. 116. Brinsley's *Ludus Literarius: or, The Grammar Schoole*, published in 1612, is an invaluable source of information about educational theory, curriculum, textbooks, and methods in Elizabethan schools.

59. A. Monroe Stowe, *English Grammar Schools in the Reign of Queen Elizabeth* (New York, 1908), p. 104.

60. *Ibid.*, pp. 105–6.

61. P. 1, quoted by J. Q. Adams in *A Life of William Shakespeare*, pp. 49–50. Although Hoole's book was not written until 1636, nor published until 1660, it was based upon conditions "prevailing in England during the half century before he wrote" and therefore describes school life approximately as it existed in Elizabethan times. Adams, p. 49, footnote 2.

62. *Shakespeare: Man and Artist*, I, 82. Fripp's authority for Thomas Parker is Dugdale Soc. V, xi.

63. *Ibid.*, footnote 1.

64. Quoted by M. St. Clare Byrne, *Elizabethan Life in Town and Country* (London. 1925), p. 182.

65. W. J. Rolfe, *Shakespeare the Boy*, p. 99; Sir Sidney Lee, *Stratford-on-Avon* (London, 1890), pp. 173–74; and Sir John Edwin Sandys, "Education," *Shakespeare's England*, I, 230.

66. *Shakespeare Studies* (London, 1894), p. 150.

67. II, 335.

68. Lewis, *op. cit.*, I, 49.

69. *Op. cit.*, I, 106.

70. A. Monroe Stowe, *op. cit.*, pp. 109–10.

71. *Ibid.*, pp. 102–3.

72. *Shakespeare: Man and Artist*, I, 48.

73. "Shakespeare's School: Some Early Masters," *Notes and Queries*, 10th Series, VIII (October 26, 1907), 323.

74. *Ibid.*

75. "Shakespeare's Schoolmasters," *Notes and Queries*, 12th Series, I (April 22, 1916), 322.

76. Foster Watson, *The Old Grammar Schools*, p. 93.

77. Fripp, *Shakespeare: Man and Artist*, I, 89.

78. Quoted by A. R. Bayley, *Notes and Queries*, 12th Series, I (April 22, 1916), 322.

79. Adams, *op. cit.*, pp. 48–49.

80. *Outlines* (1887), II, 364, note 299.

81. *Warwickshire*, II, 337.

82. J. W. Gray, *Shakespeare's Marriage, His Departure from Stratford and Other Incidents in His Life*, p. 108.

83. Vol. I, 269, quoted by J. H. Pollen, "A Shakespeare Discovery: His School-Master afterwards a Jesuit," Part I, *The Month*, CXXX (Oct., 1917), 320.

84. J. H. Pollen, "A Shakespeare Discovery: His School-Master afterwards a Jesuit," Part II, *The Month*, CXXX (Nov., 1917), 402.

85. Part I, October, pp. 317–323; Part II, November, pp. 401–9.

86. Edition of Father Knox (1878), p. 275. Pollen points out (Part II, p. 401) that Father Knox's list "is an ancient notarial transcript made in 1643 from the registers of the Douay University, which registers have since perished."

87. *Shakespeare: Man and Artist*, I, 89.

88. *Victoria County Histories: Warwickshire*, II, 335.

89. Quoted by Leach, *loc. cit.*

90. P. 110, quoted by Pollen, Part II, 404.

91. Quoted by Pollen, Part II, 405.

92. Quoted by Pollen, Part II, 404.

93. Part II, 406.

94. *Shakespeare: Man and Artist*, I, 89.

95. *Ibid.*

96. *Journal of Education*, March, 1908, quoted by J. H. Pollen, *The Month*, CXXX (Oct., 1917), 321.

97. *Op. cit.*, I, 107. Lewis is self-contradictory in giving the date of the termination of Hunt's mastership at Stratford as 1577 (p. 106) and of his entrance into Douai University as 1575 (p. 107), that is, two years earlier.

98. *The Month*, CXXX (Nov., 1917), 402.

99. *Victoria County Histories: Warwickshire*, II, 336. It was, of course, "George" Hunt, not Simon, that Leach had in mind, but the mistake in identification has no bearing on the argument.

100. *Shakespeare: Man and Artist*, I, 360.

101. *Ibid.* See also II, 642–46; 800–801.

102. *Ibid.*, II, 801, where the receipt is quoted.

103. *Ibid.*

104. *Love's Labour's Lost*, IV, ii.

105. *Stratford-on-Avon*, p. 176. Italics are mine. For an interesting account of Holofernes as Shakespeare's "Abcedarius," see T. W. Baldwin, *William Shakspere's Petty School*, pp. 137–58.

106. *Op. cit.*, p. 49.

107. E. A. G. Lamborn and G. B. Harrison, *Shakespeare: The Man and his Stage* (London, 1923), p. 7.

108. *Ibid.*

109. *Shakespeare: Man and Artist*, I, 91.

110. Mrs. Charlotte C. Stopes, *Shakespeare's Warwickshire Contemporaries*, p. 245.

111. "Stratford-on-Avon Grammar School," Tercentenary Volume (1853), quoted by A. R. Bayley, *Notes and Queries*, 12th Series, I (April 22, 1916), 323.

112. A. R. Bayley, "Shakespeare's Schoolmasters," *Notes and Queries*, 12th Series, I (April 22, 1916), 322.

113. *Shakespeare: Man and Artist*, I, 91–92.

114. Act IV, i.

115. *Shakespeare: Man and Artist*, I, 92.

116. *Op. cit.*, p. 147.

117. *Ibid.*

118. *Ibid.*

119. T. F. Simmons and H. E. Nolloth, *The Lay Folks' Catechism* (London, 1901), xxxvi.

120. *Ibid.*

121. *Ibid.*, pp. xxxvi-xxxvii.

122. Vol. XIV, 694.

123. *Ibid.*, p. 693.

124. Quoted by George A. Plimpton, *The Education of Shakespeare*, p. 61.

125. William Hunt, "Alexander Nowell," *Dictionary of National Biography*, XIV, 693. Hunt quotes Strype's *Life of Parker*, i, 403.

126. *Op. cit.*, p. 694.

127. Quoted by Fripp, *Shakespeare: Man and Artist*, I, 88, footnote 2.

128. T. S. Baynes, "What Shakespeare Learnt in School," *Shakespeare Studies*, pp. 173–74, footnote 1.

129. Pages 204–17.

130. *Op. cit.*, pp. 211–17.

131. *Op. cit.*, p. 211.

132. P. 48.

133. *Op. cit.*, pp. 218–19.
134. III, i, 24.
135. II, i, 62–64.
136. *Shakespeare: Man and Artist*, I, 87.
137. J. Q. Adams, *op. cit.*, p. 50.
138. Fripp, *Minutes and Accounts*, III, xxvii.
139. "Hymns," *Encyclopaedia Britannica* (14th Edition), XII, 17, and Abraham Coles, *A New Rendering of the Hebrew Psalms into English Verse*, xvi-xviii.
140. P. 53.
141. *Ibid.*, p. 58.
142. *Ibid.*, p. 57. Cambridge University Press, England. By permission of The Macmillan Company, publishers, U. S.
143. *Ibid.*
144. *Shakespeare's Biblical Knowledge*, p. 46.
145. *English Grammar Schools to 1660*. Note B, pp. 38–43.
146. Lewis, *op. cit.*, I, 126, footnote 1.
147. J. Howard Brown, *Elizabethan Schooldays* (Oxford, 1933), p. 64.
148. *Ibid.*
149. Alan F. Herr, *The Elizabethan Sermon* (Philadelphia, 1940), pp. 81–84.
150. Quoted by J. Howard Brown, *op. cit.*, p. 66.
151. Alan Herr, *op. cit.*, p. 20. Herr points out that one more homily was composed in 1580 by Bishop Cooper and was ordered to be used in his own diocese of Lincoln before every celebration of the Lord's Supper.
152. Quoted from *Sermons or Homilies Appointed to Be Read in Churches in the Time of Queen Elizabeth of Famous Memory*. In Two Parts. The First American, from the last Oxford Edition (New York: T. and J. Swords, 1815), p. 1.
153. Act III, ii, 164–67. Alfred Hart contends "that Shakespeare borrowed the doctrines of the divine right of kings, passive obedience and the sin of rebellion from the homilies." See his *Shakespeare and the Homilies* (Melbourne, 1934), p. 74.
154. W. J. Rolfe, *Shakespeare the Boy*, p. 174.
155. *Ibid.*
156. *Sermons or Homilies Appointed to Be Read in Churches*, p. 419.
157. Quoted by Stowe, *op. cit.*, p. 148.
158. Grindal's articles of inquiry for the province of York, 1571 as quoted by Bayne, *Shakespeare's England*, I, 63.
159. *Shakespeare: Man and Artist*, I, 86.
160. *Shakespeare's Biblical Knowledge*, pp. 14–15.
161. Fripp, *Shakespeare: Man and Artist*, I, 241.
162. *Ibid*, II, 802.

PART FOUR

1. *The Bible in Shakspeare* (New York, 1918), xiii.
2. Best among these are Charles Wordsworth's *Shakspeare's Knowledge and Use of the Bible*, first published in 1864; William Burgess' *The Bible in Shakspeare* (1903); T. Carter's *Shakespeare and Holy Scripture: With the Version He Used* (1905), and Richmond Noble's *Shakespeare's Biblical Knowledge and Use of the Book of Common Prayer* (1935).
3. *Shakespeare Rediscovered*, p. 79. Quotations are from *Love's Labour's Lost*, IV, iii, 383, and *Coriolanus*, III, i, 69–70. The parable referred to is found in Matthew 13:24–30.
4. IV, v, 54–59.
5. Quoted by Noble, *op. cit.*, p. 199. Italics are mine.

6. *Ibid.* Italics are mine. The 1609 edition of the Douai Bible reads: "Enter ye in at the narrow gate: for *wide* is the gate, and broad is the way that leadeth to destruction. . . . " The use of *wide* in place of *brode* must, therefore, be an emendation introduced during the "drastic revision" of the Rheims New Testament before its appearance in the Douai Bible. See Noble, p. 13.'

7. I, ii, 217.

8. Noble, *op. cit.*, pp. 249, 88.

9. *Op. cit.*, p. 88.

10. *Op. cit.*, p. 14.

11. I, i, 173–75.

12. *Shakespeare and Holy Scripture*, p. 5.

13. Noble, *op. cit.*, p. 61.

14. I, iii, 89.

15. *Shakespeare's England*, I, 75.

16. I, ii, 114.

17. Luke 15:7; Matthew 3:8; Acts 26:20.

18. IV, i, 144.

19. It occurs in the Genevan version at Mark 15:22; Matthew 27:33; John 19:17.

20. *1 Henry IV*, IV, ii, 37–38. See also *As You Like It*, I, i, 40.

21. Carter, *Shakespeare: Puritan and Recusant.* p. 196.

22. *Merchant of Venice*, I, iii, 35.

23. *A Life of William Shakespeare*, p. 23, footnote 1.

24. *Op. cit.*, p. 275.

25. For example, H. C. Beeching, "The Religion of Shakespeare," in *The Works of Shakespeare in Ten Volumes*, X, 341. Also Noble, *op. cit.*, p. 67.

26. *Hamlet*, III, iii, 80.

27. Noble, *op. cit.*, p. 67.

28. Ronald Bayne, *Shakespeare's England*, I, 74.

29. *Op. cit.*, pp. 353; 345.

30. *Op. cit.*, pp. 20–21.

31. *Shakespeare: Man and Artist*, I, 85–86.

32. *Op. cit.*, pp. 41–43.

33. *A Life of William Shakespeare*, pp. 22–23.

34. V, ii, 343–47.

35. V, ii, 357–58.

36. V, i, 90–91.

37. Quoted by Noble, *op. cit.*, p. 94.

38. V, v, 16–17.

39. *Op. cit.*, p. 96.

40. Noble, *op. cit.*, pp. 96–98.

41. *Shakespeare and Holy Scripture*, p. 4.

42. See Romans 13: 9–10.

43. See Matthew 25:34.

44. *Op. cit.*, p. 51.

45. "The Faith of Shakespeare," *Bibliotheca Sacra*, LXXXIX (July, 1932), 296.

46. *Shakespeare* (London, 1907), p. 74. By permission of The Macmillan Company, publishers.

47. *Merchant of Venice*, I, iii, 99–103.

48. *Ibid.*, III, ii, 77–80.

49. *Op. cit.*, p. 48.

50. For a convenient summary of Shakespeare's treatment of clerical characters, see Cumberland Clark, *Shakespeare and the Supernatural*, pp. 307–32.

51. II, i, 79–81.

52. II, ii, 29.

53. *Biography of Shakespeare*, p. 183, quoted by W. S. Lilly, *Studies in Religion and Literature* (London, 1904), pp. 20–21.

54. I, ii, 134.
55. Frank Mathew, *An Image of Shakespeare* (London, 1922), p. 391.
56. *Romeo and Juliet*, IV, i, 38.
57. *Op. cit.*, pp. 271–74.
58. *Romeo and Juliet*, II, iii, 7–8.
59. Bowden, *op. cit.*, p. 274.
60. *Hamlet*, I, v, 76–77.
61. *Shakespeare's England*, I, 54.
62. *Hamlet*, IV, vii, 176–78.
63. *The Manuscript of Shakespeare's Hamlet* (Cambridge, England: Cambridge University Press, 1934), I, 71–72. By permission of The Macmillan Company, publishers, U. S. In a note on page 72, Wilson remarks: "It is possible that Shakespeare had in mind also Psalms cxlviii–cl which are sung at the service of Lauds." The use of the adjective "old" seems inappropriate in this connection, however.
64. IV, iii, 52–54.
65. Vol. I, 64, footnote on line 53.
66. *Hamlet*, III, ii, 145–46.
67. C. H. Herford, *op. cit.*, I, 41, footnote on line 30. Herford's comment here is on the line: "The hobby-horse is forgot," spoken by Moth in *Love's Labour's Lost*, III, i, 30.
68. III, ii, 55–57.
69. III, v, 29.
70. IV, vii, 160.
71. *Shakespeare: Man and Artist*, I, 721.
72. *Macbeth*, I, vii, 10–12.
73. II, iii, 25. The metaphor here is a curious one. The word "chalic'd" is derived from the Latin *calix*, which is also the source of "calyx," a part of a flower. It may appear, then, as if Shakespeare was speaking of flowers with calyxes and that he did not have the sacred vessel in mind at all. But the preceding line of the song suggests that Shakespeare meant cuplike flowers holding the refreshing morning dew. The chalice of the Eucharist was, of course, a source of spiritual refreshment.
74. *Henry V*, IV, i, 321–22.
75. Bowden, *op. cit.*, p. 39.
76. III, iv, 25–29.
77. V, i, 141–44.
78. *The Two Gentlemen of Verona*, IV, ii, 40–44.
79. *Master Richard Quyny*, p. 77.
80. *Ibid.*, pp. 76–77.
81. Epilogue, 13–20.
82. II, ii, 151–55.
83. *Cymbeline*, I, iii, 31–33.
84. I, i, 16–20.
85. *Hamlet*, I, iv, 39.
86. *Shakespeare, From an American Point of View* (New York, 1877), p. 403.
87. *Hamlet*, I, v, 2–4; 9–16.
88. *Ibid.*, iv, 47.
89. *King John*, V, ii, 71; *Henry V*, I, i, 23; *Romeo and Juliet*, II, vi, 37.
90. *King John*, III, i, 141.
91. See *Henry V*, I, ii, 32; *Henry VIII*, V, iii, 161; *Othello*, II, iii, 352; and *Romeo and Juliet*, II, ii, 50.
92. *As You Like It*, III, iv, 9–14.
93. V, i, 58–59.
94. *Measure for Measure*, IV, iii, 156; *Romeo and Juliet*, III, iii, 113.
95. *Two Gentlemen of Verona*, I, ii, 62–63; V, ii, 38; V, iv, 170; *Much Ado about Nothing*, V, i, 286; *Love's Labour's Lost*, I, i, 115; I, ii, 136; V, ii, 716; *Taming of the Shrew*, I, i, 89; *Twelfth Night*, III, iv, 153; *2 Henry VI*, II, iii, 11; II, iv, 20, 76, 106; *Henry VIII*, I, iv, 17, 32; V, iv, 46.

96. II, iv, 130–33.
97. *Romeo and Juliet*, II, iii, 61; *3 Henry VI*, III, iii, 243.
98. V, i, 160–65.
99. I, ii, 155–61.
100. *The Tempest*, IV, i, 15–19. See also *As You Like It*, III, iii, 91–92, and *The Taming of the Shrew*, IV, iv, 94–95.
101. *A Midsummer-Night's Dream*, V, ii, 33–38.
102. *Op. cit.*, pp. 262–63.
103. *Hamlet*, V, i, 240 ff.
104. Canon 1240, par. 2. which reads: Occurrente praedictis in casibus aliquo dubio, consultatur, si tempus sinat, Ordinarius; permanente dubio, cadaver sepulturae ecclesiasticae tradatur, ita tamen ut removeatur scandalum." Quoted by Noble, *op. cit.*, p. 85.
105. Noble, *op. cit.*, p. 84.
106. For an interesting account of Ophelia's funeral see R. S. Guernsey's "Ecclesiastical Law in *Hamlet*:—The Burial of Ophelia," *Papers of the New York Shakespeare Society*, No. 1, 1885.
107. I, ii, 235–39.
108. IV, iii, 31–34.
109. *Othello*, III, iv, 40–44.
110. W. S. Lilly, *Studies in Religion and Literature*, p. 20.
111. *Op. cit.*, p. 169.
112. *Ibid.*, p. 46.
113. J. Dover Wilson, ed., *King John* (Cambridge, 1936), viii.
114. H. H. Furness, ed., *King John* (New Variorum Edition of Shakespeare, Philadelphia, 1919), p. 471. All quotations from and references to *The Troublesome Raigne* will pertain to the text appearing in Furness, "Appendix," pp. 471–537.
115. So Capell, L. Tieck, Ulrici, Schlegel. See Furness, *King John*, pp. 448–50. Pope ascribes the play to W. Shakespeare and W. Rowley (*Works of Shakespeare*, 1723, III, 115 n.); G. Steevens includes the play in his *Twenty of the Plays of Shakespeare*, 1760, though he omits it from later editions of Shakespeare.
116. F. J. Furnivall and John Munro, eds., *'The Troublesome Reign of King John': Being the Original of Shakespeare's 'Life and Death of King John'* (London, 1913), pp. xiv-xv.
117. See Furness, *op. cit.*, pp. 451–53. Also J. Dover Wilson's "Introduction."
118. J. Dover Wilson, *op. cit.*, p. xxxiii. Cambridge University Press, England. By permission of The Macmillan Company, publishers, U. S.
119. Among these are Edward Rose, "Shakespeare as an Adapter," *Macmillan's Magazine*, XXXIX (November, 1878), 69–77; Johann M. Raich, *Shakespeare's Stellung zur Katholischen Religion* (Mainz, 1884), pp. 151–73; Henry S. Bowden, *The Religion of Shakespeare* (London, 1899), pp. 117–35; F. J. Furnivall and John Munro, eds., *op. cit.*, pp. xxix-xl, and Appendices I and II, pp. 155–70; H. H. Furness, *King John*, New Variorum Edition (Philadelphia, 1919), pp. 447–70: Felix Liebermann, "Shakespeare als Bearbeiter des *King John*," *Archiv für das Studium der neueren Sprachen und Literaturen*, 142. Band (December, 1921), pp. 177–202, and 143. Band (April, 1922), pp. 17–46 (August, 1922), pp. 190–203; J. Dover Wilson, *King John* (Cambridge, 1936), pp. vii-lxi; and Gerard M. Greenewald, *Shakespeare's Attitude Towards the Catholic Church in "King John"* (Washington. D. C., 1938).
120. See F. J. Furnivall and John Munro, *op. cit.*, pp. xxx-xl.
121. *Op. cit.*, p. 172.
122. *Op. cit.*, p. lvii Cambridge University Press, England. By permission of The Macmillan Company, publishers, U. S.
123. *Archiv*, 142. Band, p. 186.
124. *Op. cit.*, p. 77.
125. Part II, ii, 170–73. Furnivall and Munro's reading of "suppress" for "surpass" is more pointed than Furness's.
126. Part II, viii, 89–102.

127. J. Dover Wilson, *op. cit.*, p. xii.
128. Bale's *King Johan* (Malone Society Reprints), quoted by J. Dover Wilson, *op. cit.*, p. xiii.
129. *Chronicles*, III, 196 f, quoted by Furness, *op. cit.*, pp. 564–65.
130. *King John*, I, i, 39–43.
131. *Ibid.*, IV, iii, 142–47.
132. Part I, iv, 100–101.
133. *Ibid.*, 120–24.
134. *Ibid.*, 126.
135. *Ibid.*, 145–50.
136. *Ibid.*, 155–57.
137. *Ibid.*, 158–61.
138. *Ibid.*, 162.
139. *Ibid.*, 164.
140. *Ibid.*, 166–67.
141. *King John*, II, i, 464–65.
142. *Ibid.*, 469.
143. *Ibid.*, 470–71.
144. *Ibid.*, 477–79.
145. *Ibid.*, 487–91.
146. *Ibid.*, 527–32.
147. *Ibid.*, 547–50.
148. *Ibid.*, 561.
149. Part I, v, 63–70.
150. *King John*, III, i, 135–46.
151. Part I, v, 71–78.
152. *Ibid.*, 81–85.
153. *King John*, III, i, 147–60.
154. *Ibid.*, 162–71.
155. Part I, v, 88–94.
156. III, i, 172–79.
157. Gerard M. Greenewald, *Shakespeare's Attitude Towards the Catholic Church in 'King John,'* p. 111.
158. *King John*, III, i, 180–84.
159. Part I, v, 95–96.
160. *Ibid.*, 97–123.
161. *King John*, III, i, 191–94.
162. *Ibid.*, 195–347.
163. F. Liebermann, *Archiv*, 143. Band, p. 23, and J. Dover Wilson, *op. cit.*, lviii.
164. Part I, viii. The scene is without words.
165. III. ii, 7–8.
166. Part II, iv, 70–89.
167. V, i, 62–77.
168. Part I, ix, 4–6.
169. III, iii, 2–4.
170. *Ibid.*, 19–67.
171. Part I, ix, 13–14.
172. *Ibid.*, 30–35.
173. Part I, xii, 48–50.
174. Part I. xiii, 201.
175. *King John*, IV, i, 39.
176. IV, ii, 204–23.
177. Part II, ii, 204–7.
178. *Ibid.*, 213–16.
179. Part II, iv, 1–7.
180. V, i, 1–7.

181. *Ibid.*, 26–29.
182. Part II, vi, 94–98.
183. *Ibid.*, 140–44.
184. Part II, viii, 101–2.
185. V, vii, 57–58.
186. V, vi, 23–31.
187. V, iii, 3–4.
188. *Ibid.*, 14–17.
189. V, vii, 9.
190. *Ibid.*, 35, 46.
191. V, vii, 70–73.
192. Part I, i, 304–8.
193. I, i, 48–49.
194. Part I, v, 114–18.
195. Part I, ix, 15–25. John's reference to Roman Church courts is noteworthy.
196. *Ibid.*, 41–44.
197. *King John*, III, iii, 6–12. In connection with the issue of supremacy, Shakespeare's omission of John's reference to Roman Church courts is significant.
198. Part I, xi.
199. III, iv, 171–73.
200. *Op. cit.*, p. 73.
201. *Ibid.*
202. *Commentaries* (1863), p. 354, translated by Bunett, quoted by Furness, *op. cit.*, p. 643.
203. Part I, xiii, 44–62.
204. IV, ii, 132–34.
205. *Ibid.*, 141–46.
206. Part II, vi, 76–83.
207. Part II, viii, 17–23
208. Part II, iii, 121–27.
209. Part II, iv, 8–9.
210. Part II, viii, 108–9.
211. *King John*, II, i, 581 ff. and III, i, 324–25.
212. *Ibid.*, V, i, 65–76.
213. *Ibid.*, V, ii, 120–58.
214. *Ibid.*, 163.
215. *Ibid.*, 171–76.
216. *Ibid.*, vii, 110–18.
217. *King John*, III, i, 248–52.
218. *Op. cit.*, pp. 118–19.
219. Part I, v, 99–101.
220. Part I, x, 36–41.
221. *King John*, III, iv, 178–80.
222. *Ibid.*, 182–83.
223. *Ibid.*, V, ii, 68–77.
224. *Ibid.*, 109.
225. *Ibid.*, V, vii, 80–86.
226. Part II, iv, 22–23.
227. *King John*, V, ii, 65–68.
228. Part II, iv, 26–33.
229. *Ibid.*, 52–57.
230. *Ibid.*, 67–70.
231. *Op. cit.*, p. 127.
232. *Ibid.*, p. 135.
233. Part I, xiii, 163–87.
234. *King John*, IV, ii, 147–52.

235. *Ibid.*, 154.
236. *Ibid.*, 182–86.
237. Part II, i, 81–91.
238. *Ibid.*, iii, 66–71.
239. *Ibid.*, 78–81.
240. *Ibid.*, 197–98.
241. *Ibid.*, 219–21.
242. *King John*, IV, ii, 93–102.
243. *Ibid.*, 162–65.
244. *Ibid.*, 187.
245. *Ibid.*, iii, 11–13.
246. *Ibid.*, 65–73.
247. *Ibid.*, V, ii, 1–7.
248. *Ibid.*, 66–68.
249. *Ibid.*, iv, 14–20.
250. Part I, xiii, 1–31.
251. Part II, ii, 144–47.
252. Part II, ii, 158–69.
253. *King John*, lvii.
254. F. Liebermann, *Archiv*, 143. Band, pp. 202–3.
255. I, i, 44–46.
256. Furnivall and Munro, 'The Troublesome Reign,' p. xxxi.
257. *Op. cit.*, p. 203.

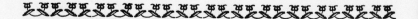

BIBLIOGRAPHY

Adams, Joseph Quincy. A Life of William Shakespeare. Boston: Houghton Mifflin Company, 1923.

Anders, H. "The Elizabethan ABC with the Catechism." *The Library*, 4th Series, XVI (June, 1935), 32–48.

Anders, Henry R. D. Shakespeare's Books. Berlin: Georg Reimer, 1904.

Andrade, Vincente de P. Ensayo Bibliográfico Mexicano del Siglo XVII. Segunda Edicion. Mexico: Imprenta del Museo Nacional, 1899.

Baker, Oliver. In Shakespeare's Warwickshire and the Unknown Years. London: Simpkin Marshall Ltd., 1937.

Baldwin, T. W. William Shakspere's Petty School. Urbana: The University of Illinois Press, 1943.

Barry, William. "The Catholic Strain in Shakespeare." A Book of Homage to Shakespeare. Ed. by Israel Gollancz. London, 1916. pp. 31–34.

Bayley, A. R. "Shakespeare's School: Some Early Masters." *Notes and Queries*, 10th Series, VIII (October 26, 1907), 323–25.

———. "Shakespeare's Schoolmasters." *Notes and Queries*, 12th Series, I (April 22, 1916), 321–23.

Bayne, Ronald. "Religion." Shakespeare's England. Vol. I. Oxford: The Clarendon Press, 1916, pp. 48–78.

Baynes, Thomas Spencer. "What Shakespeare Learnt at School." Shakespeare Studies. London: Longmans, Green & Co., 1894, pp. 147–250.

Beeching, H. C. "The Religion of Shakespeare." The Works of Shakespeare in Ten Volumes. Vol. X. Stratford-on-Avon: The Shakespeare Head Press, 1907, pp. 335–49.

Bowden, Henry Sebastian. The Religion of Shakespeare, Chiefly from the Writings of the Late Mr. Richard Simpson, M. A. London: Burns & Oates, Ltd., 1899.

Brandes, George. William Shakespeare. New York: The Macmillan Company, 1931.

Brinsley, John. Ludus Literarius, or The Grammar Schoole. 1612.

Brown, J. Howard. Elizabethan Schooldays: An Account of the English Grammar Schools in the second half of the Sixteenth Century. Oxford, 1933.

Burgess, William. The Bible in Shakspeare. New York: Fleming H. Revell Company, 1918.

Byrne, M. St. Clare. Elizabethan Life in Town and Country. London: Methuen & Co., 1925.

Carter, C. Sydney. The English Church and the Reformation. 2nd edition. London: Longmans, Green and Co., 1925.

Carter, Thomas. Shakespeare and Holy Scripture. With the Version He Used. London: Hodder and Stoughton, 1905.

————. Shakespeare: Puritan and Recusant. Edinburgh & London: Oliphant Anderson & Ferrier, 1897.

Chalmers, George. An Apology for The Believers in the Shakspeare-Papers, Which Were Exhibited in Norfolk-Street. London, 1797.

Chambers, Sir Edmund K. William Shakespeare: A Study of Facts and Problems. Oxford: The Clarendon Press, 1930. 2 vols.

Chandlery, P. J. "Holywell." The Catholic Encyclopedia, VII, 438–39.

————. "Winefride, Saint." The Catholic Encyclopedia, XV, 656–57.

Cheyney, Edward P. A Short History of England. New York: Ginn & Company, 1904.

Clark, Cumberland. Shakespeare and the Supernatural. London: Williams & Norgate Ltd., 1931.

Colby, Elbridge. "Shakespeare and Catholicism." *The Ecclesiastical Review,* LV (July, 1916), 48–64.

————. "Clerical Characters in Shakespeare." *The Ecclesiastical Review,* LV (August, 1916), 131–45.

Coles, Abraham. A New Rendering of the Hebrew Psalms into English Verse. New York: D. Appleton & Company. 1888.

Craig, W. J., ed. The Oxford Shakespeare. Oxford University Press, n. d. [1902].

Cutts, Edward Lewes. Parish Priests and Their People in the Middle Ages in England. London: Society for Promoting Christian Knowledge, 1898.

de Chambrun, Clara Longworth, Comtesse. "John Shakespeare's Will." *The Commonweal,* XIX (December 15, 1933), 181–83.

————. "John Shakespeare's Will." *The Commonweal,* XIX (February 23, 1934), 468.

————. Shakespeare Rediscovered by means of Public Records, Secret Reports and Private Correspondence Newly Set Forth as Evidence on His Life and Work. New York: Charles Scribner's Sons, 1938.

Dixon, Richard Watson. "Dudley, John, Duke of Northumberland (1502?–1553)." The Dictionary of National Biography, VI (Oxford University Press, since 1917), 109–11.

Drake, Nathan. Shakspeare and His Times. . . . The Two Quarto Volumes Comprised in One. Paris: Baudry's European Library, 1838.

Elton, Charles I. William Shakespeare, His Family and Friends. New York: E. P. Dutton & Company, 1904.

Elze, Karl. William Shakespeare: A Literary Biography. Translated by L. Dora Schmitz. London: George Bell and Sons, 1888.

Foley, Henry. Records of the English Province of the Society of Jesus. Historic Facts illustrative of the Labours and Sufferings of its Members in the Sixteenth and Seventeenth Centuries. London: Burns and Oates, 1877–83. 8 vols.

Frere, Walter Howard. The English Church in the Reigns of Elizabeth and James I (1558–1625). A History of the English Church. Vol. V. Ed. by William Hunt and W. R. W. Stephens. London: Macmillan and Co., 1904.

Fripp, Edgar Innes. Master Richard Quyny, Bailiff of Stratford-upon-Avon and Friend of William Shakespeare. Oxford University Press, 1924.

————, ed. Minutes and Accounts of the Corporation of Stratford-upon-Avon and Other Records, 1553–1620. Oxford: Dugdale Society, 1921, 1924, 1926, 1929. 4 vols.

————. Shakespeare: Man and Artist. London: Oxford University Press, 1938. 2 vols.

————. Shakespeare Studies: Biographical and Literary. London: Oxford University Press, 1930.

Furness, Horace Howard, ed. The Life and Death of King John. New variorum edition. Philadelphia: J. B. Lippincott, 1919.

Furnivall, F. J., and John Munro, eds. 'The Troublesome Reign of King John': Being the Original of Shakespeare's 'Life and Death of King John'. London: Chatto & Windus, 1913. (The Shakespeare Classics, ed. by I. Gollancz.)

Gasquet, Francis Aidan. The Eve of the Reformation: Studies in the Religious Life and Thought of the English People in the Period Preceding the Rejection of the Roman Jurisdiction by Henry VIII. New York: G. P. Putnam's Sons, 1900.

Gee, Henry, and William John Hardy. Documents Illustrative of English Church History Compiled from Original Sources. London: Macmillan and Co., Ltd., 1896.

Gilfillan, George. The Poetical Works of William Shakespeare and the Earl of Surrey. Edinburgh: James Nichol, 1856.

Granville-Barker, Harley, and G. B. Harrison, eds. A Companion to Shakespeare Studies. New York: The Macmillan Company, 1934.

Gray, Arthur. A Chapter in the Early Life of Shakespeare: Polesworth in Arden. Cambridge, England, 1926.

Gray, Joseph William. Shakespeare's Marriage, His Departure from Stratford and Other Incidents in His Life. London, 1905.

Greenewald, Gerard M. Shakespeare's Attitude Towards the Catholic Church in "King John." Washington, D. C.: The Catholic University of America, 1938.

Guernsey, R. S. "Ecclesiastical Law in *Hamlet:*—The Burial of Ophelia." *Papers of the New York Shakespeare Society, No. 1* (1885), pp. 5–50.

Haines, C. R. "Recent Shakespearean Research." *The Quarterly Review*, CCXXXVI (October, 1921), 225–43.

Haller, William. The Rise of Puritanism, or, the Way to the New Jerusalem as Set Forth in Pulpit and Press from Thomas Cartwright to John Lilburne and John Milton, 1570–1643. New York: Columbia University Press, 1938.

Halliwell-Phillipps, James O. Outlines of the Life of Shakespeare. 11th edition. London: Longmans, 1907. 2 vols.

Harney, Martin P. The Jesuits in History: The Society of Jesus Through Four Centuries. New York: The American Press, 1941.

Hart, Alfred. Shakespeare and the Homilies. And Other Pieces of Research into the Elizabethan Drama. Melbourne: Melbourne University Press, 1934, pp. 9–76.

Herford, Charles Harold, ed. The Works of Shakespeare. London: Macmillan and Co., 1899. (The Eversley edition.) 10 vols.

Herr, Alan Fager. The Elizabethan Sermon: A Survey and a Bibliography. Philadelphia: University of Pennsylvania, 1940.

Hoole, Charles. A New Discovery of the Old Art of Teaching School, The Petty School. Ed. by E. T. Campagnac. London: Constable, 1913.

Huhner, Max. "Shakespeare's Conception of the Clergy." *Shakespeare Association Bulletin 11* (1936), 161–70.

Hunt, William. "Nowell, Nowel, or Noel, Alexander (1507?–1602)." The Dictionary of National Biography, XIV (Oxford University Press, since 1917), 688–95.

Hyland, St. George Kieran. A Century of Persecution Under Tudor and Stuart Sovereigns from Contemporary Records. London: Kegan Paul, Trench Trübner & Co., Ltd., 1920.

"Hymns." Encyclopaedia Britannica, 14th edition, XII, 14–19.

Knight, Charles. William Shakspere: A Biography. Books I and II. London: Charles Knight and Co., 1842.

Lambert, D. H. Cartae Shakespeareanae. Shakespeare Documents. A Chronological Catalogue of Extant Evidence Relating to the Life and Works of William Shakespeare. London: George Bell and Sons, 1904.

Lamborn, E. A. G., and G. B. Harrison. Shakespeare: The Man and his Stage. London: Oxford University Press, 1923.

Leach, A. F. "Schools." The Victoria History of the County of Warwick. Vol. II. Ed. by William Page. London: Archibald Constable and Company, 1908, pp. 297–373.

Lee, Sir Sidney. A Life of William Shakespeare. New [7th] edition, rewritten and enlarged. London: Smith, Elder & Co., 1915.

———. Stratford-on-Avon from the Earliest Times to the Death of Shakespeare. New edition. London: Seeley and Co., 1890.

Lewis, B. Roland. The Shakespeare Documents: Facsimiles, Transliterations, Translations, & Commentary. Stanford University, California: Stanford University Press, 1940. 2 vols.

Liebermann, Felix. "Shakespeare als Bearbeiter des *King John.*" *Archiv für das Studium der neueren Sprachen und Literaturen.* 142. Band (December, 1921), pp. 177–202; 143. Band (April, 1922), pp. 17–46; 143. Band (August, 1922), pp. 190–203.

Lilly, William Samuel. "What Was Shakespeare's Religion?" Studies in Religion and Literature. London: Chapman & Hall, 1904, pp. 1–30.

Littlehales, Henry, ed. The Prymer, or Lay Folks' Prayer Book. Part I, Text. Part II, Introduction (Section I, The Origin of the Prymer, contributed by Edmund Bishop.) London: Early English Text Society, 1895 and 1897.

Malone, Edmond. An Inquiry into the Authenticity of Certain Miscellaneous Papers and Legal Instruments, Published Dec. 24, MDCCXCV. and Attributed to Shakespeare, Queen Elizabeth, and Henry, Earl of Southampton. . . . London: H. Baldwin, 1796.

———. The Plays and Poems of William Shakspeare, in Ten Volumes. Vol. I. London, 1790.

———. The Plays and Poems of William Shakspeare . . . edited by James Boswell. Vol. II. Third Variorum edition, 1821.

Maskell, William. Monumenta Ritualia Ecclesiae Anglicanae, or Occasional Offices of the Church of England according to the Ancient Use of Salisbury, the Prymer in English and other Prayers and Forms, with Dissertations and Notes. London: William Pickering, 1846, 1847. 3 vols.

Mathew, David. Catholicism in England: 1539–1935. London: Longmans, Green & Co., 1936.

Mathew, Frank. An Image of Shakespeare. London: Jonathan Cape, 1922.

Medina, José Toribio. La Imprenta en México (1539–1821), Tomo II. Santiago de Chile, Impreso en Case del Autor, 1909.

Morton, Richard K. "The Faith of Shakespeare." *Bibliotheca Sacra,* LXXXIX (July, 1932), 295–308.

Myrc, John. Instructions for Parish Priests. Edited by Edward Peacock for the Early English Text Society. London: Trübner & Co., 1868.

Nicolas, Sir Nicholas Harris. Testamenta Vetusta: Being Illustrations from Wills, of Manners, Customs, &c. . . . From the Reign of Henry the Second to the Accession of Queen Elizabeth. London: Nichols and Sons, 1826. 2 vols.

Noble, Richmond. Shakespeare's Biblical Knowledge and Use of the Book of Common Prayer, as exemplified in the plays of the first Folio. London: Society for Promoting Christian Knowledge, 1935.

Pfander, Homer Garrison. *"Dives et Pauper."* *The Library,* 4th Series, XIV (December, 1933), 299–312.

Plimpton, George A. The Education of Shakespeare, Illustrated from the Schoolbooks in Use in his Time. London: Oxford University Press, 1933.

Pollard, Alfred W. Records of the English Bible. London: Oxford University Press, 1911.

Pollen, John Hungerford. "Edmund Campion, Jesuit. Tyburn, December 1, 1581." Lives of the English Martyrs, Declared Blessed by Pope Leo XIII, in 1886 and 1895. Vol. II. Ed. by Dom Bede Camm. London: Longmans, Green and Co., 1914, pp. 266–358.

———. The English Catholics in the Reign of Queen Elizabeth. London: Longmans, Green and Co., 1920.

———, ed. "The First Entrance of the Fathers of the Society into England." The Memoirs of Father Robert Persons. Memoir III. Catholic Record Society, London, Miscellanea, II (London, 1906), 186–201.

———. "The Journey of Blessed Edmund Campion from Rome to England." *The Month* (September, 1897), pp. 243–64.

———. "A Shakespeare Discovery: His School-Master afterwards a Jesuit." *The Month,* CXXX (October, 1917), 317–23; (November, 1917), 401–9.

Pope, Hugh. "A Brief History of the English Version of the New Testament First Published at Rheims in 1582, Continued down to the Present Day." *The Library,* 4th Series, XX (March, 1940), 351–76; XXI (June, 1940), 44–77.

Prayer-Book of Queen Elizabeth, 1559, The. London: Griffith Farran & Co., n. d. (The Ancient and Modern Library of Theological Literature.)

Procter, Francis, and Walter Howard Frere. A New History of the Book of Common Prayer with a Rationale of Its Offices. London: Macmillan and Co., 1902.

Raich, Johann M. Shakespeare's Stellung zur Katholischen Religion. Mainz, 1884.

Raleigh, Walter. Shakespeare. London: Macmillan and Company, 1907. (English Men of Letters.)

Reed, Isaac, ed. The Plays of William Shakspeare in Fifteen Volumes. . . . Notes by Samuel Johnson and George Steevens. The Fourth Edition. . . . Vol. II. London, 1793.

Rolfe, William James. Shakespeare the Boy. New York: Harper & Brothers, 1896.

Rose, Edward. "Shakespeare as an Adapter." *Macmillan's Magazine,* XXXIX (November, 1878), 69–77.

Rowe, Nicholas, ed. The Works of Mr. William Shakespear in Eight Volumes. . . . Vol. I. London, 1714.

Salzman, L. F. English Life in the Middle Ages. London: Oxford University Press, 1927.

Sandys, Sir John Edwin. "Education." Shakespeare's England. Vol. I. Oxford: The Clarendon Press, 1916, pp. 224–50.

Sermons or Homilies Appointed to Be Read in Churches in the Time of Queen Elizabeth of Famous Memory. In Two Parts. The First American, from the last Oxford Edition. New York: T. and J. Swords, 1815.

Shakespeare's England: An Account of the Life & Manners of his Age. Oxford: The Clarendon Press, 1916. 2 vols.

Simmons, Thomas Frederick, ed. The Lay Folks Mass Book. London: Early English Text Society, 1879.

———, and Henry Edward Nolloth, eds. The Lay Folks' Catechism. London: Early English Text Society, 1901.

Simpson, Richard. Edmund Campion: A Biography. London: Williams and Norgate, 1867.

Smart, John Semple. Shakespeare, Truth and Tradition. London: E. Arnold & Co., 1928.

Smith, H. Maynard, Pre-Reformation England. London: Macmillan and Co., 1938.

Stopes, Charlotte C. Shakespeare's Environment. London: G. Bell and Sons, 1914.

———. Shakespeare's Family, Being a Record of the Ancestors and Descendants of William Shakespeare, with Some Account of the Ardens. London: Elliot Stock, 1901.

———. Shakespeare's Warwickshire Contemporaries. Stratford-upon-Avon: Stratford Head Press, 1907.

Stowe, Ancel Roy Monroe. English Grammar Schools in the Reign of Elizabeth. New York: Columbia University, 1908.

Strype, John. Annals of the Reformation and Establishment of Religion. . . . Vol. IV. 3rd edition, 1824.

Tannenbaum, Samuel A. The Shakspere Coat-of-Arms. New York: The Tenny Press, 1908.

Taunton, Ethelred L. The History of the Jesuits in England, 1580–1773. Philadelphia: J. B. Lippincott Company, 1901.

Thurston, Herbert. "A Controverted Shakespeare Document." *The Dublin Review*, CLXXIII (October-December, 1923), 161–76.

———. "The Religion of Shakspere." *The Month* (May, 1882), pp. 1–19.

———. "The Spiritual Testament of John Shakespeare." *The Month* (November, 1911), pp. 487–502.

Tucker, Stephen I. The Assignment of Arms to Shakespere and Arden, 1596–99. London: Mitchell and Hughes, 1884.

Vascila, J. Leo J. "John Shakespeare's Will." *The Commonweal*, XIX (January 12, 1934), 299–300.

The Victoria History of the County of Warwick. London: Archibald Constable and Company, 1908. 2 vols.

Villien, A. The History & Liturgy of the Sacraments. New York: Benziger Brothers, 1932.

Walsh, James J. "Was Shakespeare a Catholic?" *The Catholic Mind*, XIII (April 22, 1915), 191–210.

Walter, James. Shakespeare's True Life. London: Longmans, Green & Co., 1890.

"Was Shakespeare a Roman Catholic?" *The Edinburgh Review*, CXXIII (January, 1866), 146–85.

Watson, Foster. English Grammar Schools to 1660: their Curriculum and Practice. Cambridge University Press, 1908.

———. The Old Grammar Schools. Cambridge, England, 1916 (The Cambridge Manuals of Science and Literature.)

West, William. The First Part of Simboleography. Which May Be Termed the Art, or Description, of Instruments and Presidents . . . now newly augmented with diuers Presidents touching Merchants affaires. . . . London, 1615.

Wheler, R. B. A Guide to Stratford-upon-Avon. Stratford-upon-Avon: J. Ward, 1814.

———. An Historical Account of the Birth-Place of Shakespeare. Stratford-on-Avon, 1863.

———. History and Antiquities of Stratford-upon-Avon. . . . Stratford-upon-Avon: J. Ward, n. d. [1806].

Wilkes, George. Shakespeare, From an American Point of View; Including an Inquiry as to His Religious Faith, and His Knowledge of Law: with the Baconian Theory Considered. New York: D. Appleton and Company, 1877.

Wilson, John Dover, ed. King John. Cambridge University Press, 1936. (The Works of Shakespeare.)

——. The Manuscript of Shakespeare's Hamlet and the Problems of its Transmission. Vol. I. Cambridge University Press, 1934.

Wordsworth, Bishop Charles. Shakspeare's Knowledge and Use of the Bible. 3rd edition. London: Smith, Elder, & Co., 1880.

Wordsworth, Christopher, and Henry Littlehales. The Old Service-Books of the English Church. London: Methuen & Co., 1904. (The Antiquary's Books.)

Yeatman, John Pym. The Gentle Shakspere—A Vindication. London: The Roxburgh Press, n. d.

Yeo, Mrs. Margaret. Reformer: Saint Charles Borromeo. Milwaukee: The Bruce Publishing Co., 1938. (Science and Culture Series, Joseph Husslein, General Editor.)

APPENDIX I

An excerpt from the First Certificate of the
Warwickshire Commission returned at Easter, 1592

Stretford super Auonam

Wee present Mris Fraunces Jeffrys wife of Mr John Jefferies to bee a recusant and suspected to releeue Semynaries

Wee suspect on Mris Willoughbee which soiorneth with the saide Mris Fraunces Jeffreys, and also a daughter of one Mris Joane Cawdreys, which is with her, to be recusantes because they come not to the Church.

Wee present Mris Joane Cawdrie for the lyke and for harboringe Seminaries.

Wee suspect her sonne George to be a Semynarie preeste or Jesuite.

Wee present Alyce her Daughter for not comminge Moonthly to the Church

Wee present of Suspicion Rychard Dibdale of Shottry to bee a recusant because hee hath not beene at Church for this yeare.

Wee present for not comminge to the Church all the ͜e whoose names are subscribed monthly—

> William Clapton Esquier and his wife
> Mr Tho: Reynoldes and his wife
> Steephen Burmans wife of Shottry
>
> | | |
> |---|---|
> | Henry Rogers | John Lane senior |
> | John White | Als Carter |
> | Edwarde Greene and his wife | |
> | John Russell | William Slatter Junior |
> | Will: Hickox | Ann Cowrt |

Wee suspect theese nyne personns next ensuinge absent themselues for feare of processes—

> Mr John Wheeler
> John his sonne
> Mr John Shackspeare
> Mr Nycholas Barnehurste
> Tho: James alias Giles
> William Baynton
> Rychard Harington
> William Fluellen
> George Bardell

Wee present theese for not comminge monthly to the Church but deeme the cause to bee there impotencye

Mris Jefferys Widdowe
Mris Barber
Julian Cowrte
Griffin ap Robertes
Mris Wheeler and Jane Welch.

Wee present theese for not comminge to the Church for that they have been **excommunicated** neare a yeare sence and yett seeke not to bee restored

Edward Bromley
Rychard Heath *alias* Swann
Ryc: Johnes
Robert Griffin[1]

APPENDIX II

An excerpt from the Second Certificate of the
Warwickshire Commission returned at Michaelmas, 1592

The seconde Certificat of the Commissioners for the Countie of Warwicke, Touching all sutch persons As either haue bene presented to them Or haue bene otherwise fownde owt by the Endevoire of the sayd commissioners To be Jhesuites, Seminarye preestes, fugitiues Or Recusantes within the sayd Countie of Warwicke, Or vehementelye suspected to be sutche, Together with a true note of so manye of them as are allreadye Indicted for thear obstinate & willfull persisting in their Recusancy. sett Downe At Warwicke the XXVth day of September in the XXXIIIJ[th] yere of hir Ma[ties] most happie Raigne And sent vpp to the 11[e] of hir Ma[tie] most honorable prevye cowncell.

And first of sutch As doe yet wilfullye persiste in thear Recusancye, And are either allreddye Indicted for the sayd offence, with a remembrance also of sutch of them As haue beene by authoritie from the Lordes of hir Ma[ties] most honorable pryvye cowncell by theare Letters of the 13th of Auguste 1592 either committed to thear frendes vpon good bandes, Or els committed to the Gaole of Warwicke, And with the cawtions sett downe by the Lordes in theare sayd Letters to the Commissioners.

. . .
    In the parrisshe of Idlycote

. . .
Indicted. William Vnderhill gent. Lord of Idlycote, presented before our last Certificat to yo[r] LL[pps] in Stretforde vpon Avon in this Countie for a Recusante, continews sutche But the presenters here saye That he was not att Idlycote sins the xvijth day of November 1590, on wch daye they say he buryed his wife ther (p. 4[b]).

. . .
    In the Parrishe of Stratforde vpon Avon.
Indicted. Francis Jeffreyes, the Wyfe of John Jeffreyes gent., continueth still a Willfull recusant.

1. *Warwick Castle MSS*, transcribed in Fripp, *Minutes and Accounts*, IV, 148–49.

Indicted. Richard Dibdale presented also for a Willfull Recusant before o[r] laste certificate to yo[r] Ll[pps] continueth still obstinate in his recusancie Richard Joanes presented theare for a Recusante (p.5[b]).

. . .

The names of sutch daungerous and seditious Papistes and Recusantes As haue bene presented to vs or founde out by our endevoire to haue bene att any tyme heretofore of, or in this cowntye of Warwick And now either beyonde the Seas or vagrante within this Realme (p.6[b]).

. . .

In the parrisshe of Stratforde vppon Avon

Indicted. One George Coocke alias Cawdrey presented theare & indicted for a Recusant, is, as suspected by the presenters theare to be, a Seminarye Preeste or a Jhesuite, But where he now is they knowe not.

In the parrisshe of Henley in Arden

Indicted. One S[r] Robert Whateley presented theare for a Recusant, an old massinge preeste, resorting often thither, but hardly to be founde (p.8).

. . .

The Names of all sutche Recusantes As have beene hearetofore preasented within this Countye of Warwicke, And are now either Dwelling in other Counties, or gone oute of this Countye vppon their iuste occasions, or to lurke vnknowen in other Contryes (p.9).

. . .

In the Parrisshe of Kingesbury

Indicted. Mistris Fraunces Willughbye presented firste at Kingesbury, and after at Stratford vpon Avon, And indicted at Warwick for a Willfull Recusant, And now (as it is sayd) is in Leicester shere (p.9[a]).

. . .

In the Parrishe of Stratford vpon Avon.

Indicted. John Buswell presented theare for a Willfull Recusant, and Indicted Is, as the presenters says, fledd now out of Stratford, But whether they knowe not.

The wyfe of one Philippe Moore, a Phisicion, was theare presented for a Willfull Recusant & nowe departed from thence to Evesham in the Countye of Worcester (p.10).

. . .

The Names of all sutch Recusantes As haue bene hearetofore presented for not comminge Monethlie to the Churche, according to hir Ma[ties] Lawes. And yet are thoughte to forbeare the Church for debtte and for feare of processe, Or for soom other worse faultes, Or for Age, sicknes, or impotency of bodie (p.10).

. . .

In the parrishe of Stratford vpon Avon

Mr John Wheeler	
John Wheeler his Soon	
Mr John Shackespere	
Mr Nicholas Barneshurste	It is sayd that these laste nine
Thomas James alias Gyles	coom not to Churche for feare of
William Bainton	processe for Debtte.
Richard Harrington	
William Fluellen	
George Bardolfe	

Mris Geffreyes vidua	weare all here presented for Re-
Mris Barber	cusantes, And Doo all so continewe
Julian Coorte	saving Mris Wheeler who is con-
Griffen ap Robertes	formed, Griffen ap Robertes now
Joane Welche	Deade; But the presenters say y^t
Mris wheeler	all or the most of theese cannot
	coom to the Church for age and
	other infirmities (p.10).

. . .

The Names of all sutch persons hearetofore presented for Recusantes in this Countie, As have either Alreddy conformed themselues, Or els have promised theare conformitye, Together With the names of sutch of the said recusantes As are contented to have conference with men learned & well affected in religion, And appointed by the Commissioners, With Desyre to be resolued of sutch doubtes As doo yet make them forbeare to coome to the churche (p.11).

. . .

In the parrishe of Alston

The Wiefe of Richard Lane of the bridge towne, presented heartofore for a Wilfull Recusant, Hath now Dutifully conformed hirself and goeth to the Churche

In the Parrishe of Stretford vpon Avon

Mris Clapton the Wyfe of William Clapton Esquier now Deade, presented thear for a Recusant before o^r first certificat to yor ll^{pps} was mistaken & goeth now to the Churche (p.13^b).

The Wyfe of Stephan Bordman	William Hickcockes
Joane Cooke alias Cawdrey	Edward Grene
Alice Cooke hir Daughter	John Wyght alas Carter
Ann Courte	John Russell
Thomas Reynoldes gent. and	John lane the elder
his wiefe	Rowland Heath alias swan
Henry Rogers	Edward Bromleye
Robert Griffen	

Theese 16 weare all presented for Recusantes, But haue now all ether conformed themselues, And goe to the Churche, Or else haue promysed to conforme themselues And to goe to the Churche (p.14) . . .

Thomas Lucy	John Haryngton
Fowlke Grevyle H Goodere	Thomas Leigh
Clem. Fissher	Edw. Holte
Tho: Dabrygecourt	Robert Burgoyn (p.14).[1]

1. *S. P. Dom. Eliz. Vol. ccxliii. 76*, transcribed in Fripp, *Minutes and Accounts*, IV, 159–62.

INDEX

ABC book, Catholic editions, 124-125; in home, 124-125, 132; in school, 131, 132, 149

Acton, John, 24, 134

Allen, Dr. William, 87, 88

Angels, mediation of, 175

Arden, Edward, 45, 49

Arden, Mary, married to John Shakespeare, 7, 14-15; religion, 14-15, 120

Arden, Robert, Catholic, 9, 14; landlord of Richard Shakespeare, 9, 14

Arden, Simon, 14, 62

Asbies, mortgaged by Shakespeares, 35-38; willed to Mary Arden, 14-15

Ascension Day prophecy, Shakespeare's treatment of, 217-218

Aspinall, Alexander, 139-140

Bale's *Kynge Johan*, 184

Baptism, sacrament of, 176

Barton, the Rev. Richard, 156

Bastard, Faulconbridge, Shakespeare's characterization of, 209-212

Bible, Catholic version, Shakespeare's use of, 158-160; Genevan version, Shakespeare's use of, 160-163; in Catholic home, 126; in church, 155-156; in school, 149-150; Shakespeare's Catholic sympathies shown in use of, 167-169; Shakespeare's knowledge of, 163-167; Shakespeare's use of, 158-169

Bifield, the Rev. Richard, 156

"Books of Nurture," 125-126

Borromeo, St. Charles, 80, 81, 85, 86, 89, 98, 99

Bramhall, the Rev. John, 156

Bretchgirdle, John, 19, 20, 21, 150

Brownsword, John, 19

Campion, Edmund, 49, 85, 86, 87, 89

Carols, for religious instruction, 119-120

Cartwright, Thomas, 42, 49

Catechism, in church, 154-155; in school, 143-146; Nowell's, 144-146

Catholicism, criteria for, 4; in Snitterfield, 9-10; in Stratford, 7, 11; in Warwickshire, 6, 23; positive indications of Shakespeare's esteem for, 169-180; Shakespeare's attitude toward properties of, 172-173; Shakespeare's feeling for, 157; Shakespeare's precise knowledge of terminology, 170

Catholic officialdom, Shakespeare's treatment of, in *King John*, 212-216

Catholic piety, reminiscences in Shakespeare, 174

Ceremonial services, for religious instruction, 114-115

Church, religious influence upon William Shakespeare, 111, 150-157

Clergy, Shakespeare's treatment of, 169-170

Coat-of-arms, Arden, relation to John Shakespeare's religion, 61-63; Shakespeare, relation to John Shakespeare's religion, 60

Confession, Catholic, 179

Confirmation, sacrament of, 177

Cottam, John, 141, 142

Davenport, the Rev. James, 65, 70, 71, 74, 90, 91, 93, 102

Dives et Pauper, 117-118

Dudley, Ambrose, Earl of Warwick, 13, 42, 49

Dudley, Guildford, 13

Dudley, John, Earl of Warwick, 13